W9-BKJ-722

Cyberbullying in Social Media within Educational Institutions

Cyberbullying in Social Media within Educational Institutions

Featuring Student, Employee, and Parent Information

Merle Horowitz and Dorothy M. Bollinger

Published in partnership with the
American Association of School Administrators

ROWMAN & LITTLEFIELD
Lanham • Boulder • New York • London

Published in partnership with the
American Association of School Administrators

Published by Rowman & Littlefield
A wholly owned subsidiary of The Rowman & Littlefield Publishing Group, Inc.
4501 Forbes Boulevard, Suite 200, Lanham, Maryland 20706
www.rowman.com

16 Carlisle Street, London W1D 3BT, United Kingdom

British Library Cataloguing in Publication Information Available

Library of Congress Cataloging-in-Publication Data
Horowitz, Merle, 1952–
Cyberbullying in social media within educational institutions : featuring student, employee, and parent information / Merle Horowitz and Dorothy M. Bollinger.
pages cm
"Published in partnership with the American Association of School Administrators."
Includes bibliographical references.
ISBN 978-1-4758-0009-8 (cloth : alk. paper) — ISBN 978-1-4758-0011-1 (electronic)
1. Bullying in schools—Prevention. 2. Cyberbullying—Prevention. I. Bollinger, Dorothy M. II. American Association of School Administrators, issuing body. III. Title.
LB3013.3.H67 2014
371.7'82—dc23 2014014166

™ The paper used in this publication meets the minimum requirements of American National Standard for Information Sciences—Permanence of Paper for Printed Library Materials, ANSI/NISO Z39.48-1992.

Printed in the United States of America

Contents

Foreword by Lynn M. Cromley xi

Preface xiii

Acknowledgments xv

Introduction 1

1. CYBERBULLYING IN SOCIAL MEDIA: STUDENTS 7
Educational Aspects 7
Educators Defining Cyberbullying and Social Media 7
Examining the Behaviors of Cyberbullies against Their Victims 8
The Emotional Responses of Victims to Cyberbullying 9
The Peculiarity of Cyberbullying in Social Media 11
The Impact of Cyberbullying in Social Media on Educational Institutions 12
School Districts: Kindergarten through Twelfth Grade 12
• Safe Learning Environment 12
Students' Mental and Physical Health 13
Students' Privacy 14
Higher Education 15
Legal Aspects 16
Cyberbullying and Social Media Defined 16
Cyberbullying 16
• State Statutes, Regulations, and Policies 16
Social Media 20
• Louisiana 20
• Indiana 22
• Nebraska 23
• Definitions and Types of Social Media 24
Cyberbullying in Social Media: It Really, Really Hurts 25
Nafeesa Onque 26
Ryan Halligan 27
Jamey Rodemeyer 28
Phoebe Prince 28
Amanda Todd 29
Conclusion 30

Examination of Cyberbullying in Social Media Criminal Statutes and Proposed Federal Civil Legislation 32
State Statutes 32
Federal Statutes 33
Proposed Federal Civil Legislation 34
Examination of Adjudicated State and Federal Cyberbullying in Social Media Cases 35
First Amendment: School District Speech Cases 35
- Material and Substantial Disruption Standards 36
  - *Student-to-Student Speech* 36
  - *Student-to-Teacher and Student-to-Administrator Speech* 41
- Forecast of Substantial Disruption Standard 46
  - *Student-to-Student Speech* 46
  - *Student-to-Teacher and Student-to-Administrator Speech* 47
- Other Standards 50
  - *True Threat Standard* 50
  - *Fraser Standard* 51
  - *Hazelwood Standard* 52
  - *Morse Standard* 52

First Amendment: Higher-Education Speech Cases 53
Qualified Immunity 55
Defamation Cases 56
Harassment Cases, Statutes, and Regulations 58
- Title IX 59
- Sexting Cases and Statutes 60
- Title VI 63
- Civil Rights and Other Statutes, Educational Institutions' Policies 64
- Substantive Due Process 65
- Equal Protection 65
- The United States Department of Education Office of Civil Rights (OCR) Dear Colleague Letter 71

Invasion of Privacy Cases 73
Examination of Cyberbullying in Social Media Cases Filed, But Not Adjudicated 76
Conclusion 77

2. CYBERBULLYING IN SOCIAL MEDIA: EMPLOYEES **81**
Educational Aspects 81
Cyberbullying 81
Email Usage: Friend or Foe 82

Social Media 84
Disciplinary Actions 85
Privacy Issues 87
Use in Higher Education 87
Legal Aspects 88
Students Allegedly Cyberbullying Educators and Educators Allegedly Cyberbullying Students 88
Statutes: Students Cyberbullying Educators 88
- Arkansas 89
- California 89
- Colorado 89
- Florida 89
- Hawaii 90
- Mississippi 90
- North Carolina 91
- Oklahoma 93
- Utah 93

Cases: Students Allegedly Cyberbullying Educators 93
- Cases Where the Employees and Educational Entities Were Successful 94
- Cases Where the Students Were Successful 94
- Cases Filed, But Not Adjudicated 95

Cases: Educators Allegedly Cyberbullying Students 95
- Case Where Employee Was Disciplined, But Not Terminated 96
- Case Where the Employee Was Terminated 98
- Case Filed, But Not Adjudicated 100

Conclusion 101

3. CYBERBULLYING IN SOCIAL MEDIA: PARENTS 105
Educational Aspects 105
Cyberbullying 106
U.S. Concerns 106
International Concerns 108
Social Media 109
Health Benefits and Concerns 110
Public Health Approach 111
Responses to Parent Cyberbullying or Harassment 111
Legal Aspects 117
Civil and Criminal Statutes and Regulations 118
Parent/Student as Victims versus Educational Institutions 119
Educational Institution Victim versus Parent(s) and/or Student(s) 120

Contract Terms 121
Parent/Student Victim, Parent of Another Student, and Social Media Website 121
Parent/Student Victim, Other Students, and Social Media Website 122
Court Decisions Involving Parents and Educational Institutions 123
Civil Rights Cases 123
- Parent/Student Victims versus Educational Institutions 123
- Parent/Student Victims and Employee Victim 126
Social Media Privacy Case 129
Conclusion 130

CONCLUSION **131**

APPENDICES
A Table of State Bullying and Cyberbullying Laws 135
B Cyberbullying in Social Media Cases 155
C References 161
D Centers and Resources 169
E Questions and Ideas for Staff Development 173

Notes 175

About the Authors 195

Foreword

Nexus. Merriam-Webster defines it as a relationship or connection between people or things. In *Cyberbullying in Social Media within Educational Institutions*, Merle Horowitz and Dorothy M. Bollinger examine the nexus of current legal and educational perspectives and the complex issues of cyberbullying in social media in an effort to help those of us with a vested interest in creating and maintaining safe and orderly schools to navigate the myriad of issues these phenomena create in school settings.

Through an in-depth review of current literature and recent court decisions, Bollinger, an attorney specializing in technology issues and the Internet as well as a former school administrator, and Horowitz, a superintendent and lifelong educator, combine their impressive legal and educational expertise to provide an invaluable resource on issues encountered daily by virtually every educational institution in this country. In an easy-to-understand format, *Cyberbullying in Social Media within Educational Institutions* provides an up-to-date review of current research on cyberbullying and social media, an examination of legal and ethical issues, and a discussion of recent court cases and information on how the courts have addressed the many facets of cyberbullying.

As the director of a statewide school safety center, I believe that everyone has a vested interest in understanding and addressing cyberbullying in school settings. While the obvious actors include K–12 and college administrators, boards, teachers, student support staff, attorneys, law enforcement, mental and medical health professionals, and parents and students, this issue is significant enough to merit the attention and interest of policymakers and the public in general for three compelling reasons. First, cyberbullying in social media is creating potentially serious and adverse effects on our children and youth. While research on cyberbullying is still in its infancy, we do know, according to the U.S. Department of Health and Human Services website, stopbullying.gov, that kids who are cyberbullied are more likely to:

- use alcohol and drugs
- skip school
- experience in-person bullying
- be unwilling to attend school
- receive poor grades
- have lower self-esteem
- have more health problems

These consequences for our children are simply not acceptable.

Second, cyberbullying disruptions during the school day (which frequently begin outside the school day but are carried inside) cut into valuable instructional time, add complexity to maintaining school operations and safety, and can create costly legal issues for schools.

Third, how we understand and deal with this phenomenon now is establishing new practices, policies, and legal precedents, not to mention laying the groundwork for the future, as technology and accompanying issues continue to change at a rapid pace.

At its best, *Cyberbullying in Social Media within Educational Institutions* is an excellent tool for understanding this relatively new form of adolescent aggression and the unique ethical and legal challenges that it brings to schools. Until recently, a limited number of landmark court cases provided guidance in addressing a broad spectrum of school problems. Over the past several years, the number of technology-related cases has grown exponentially, making it difficult to keep abreast of relevant decisions. This book helps to navigate the complexities of school-related technology court decisions by outlining recent cases in an effort to aid in the development of a better understanding and application of these decisions. A current knowledge and understanding of how the courts have addressed cyberbullying can have a significant impact on treating students with equity and consistency when confronted with these challenges.

Kudos to Horowitz and Bollinger on the addition of an excellent resource to support the educational and societal shared goals of protecting students, preventing and responding to inappropriate behavior that uses technology, and helping students to become good digital citizens.

Lynn M. Cromley
Director
Pennsylvania Center for Safe Schools

Preface

Cyberbullying within social media is one of the most complicated and difficult topics affecting both K–12 and higher education educators. As technology continues to change and expand, it provides new and different ways for incidents to occur with students, employees, and parents. Merle Horowitz, EdD, and Dorothy M. Bollinger, Esquire, met several years ago when they served on a panel for a documentary about cyberbullying for CBS television in Philadelphia. Recognizing the necessity of providing resources about cyberbullying, Horowitz and Bollinger have presented this topic both independently and together at workshops throughout the United States. This book is the collaborative effort of Horowitz and Bollinger to provide as many resources that are as current as possible for educators and those who work with educators. The law is still evolving and will continue to evolve. The statutes are continually changing, and the courts are deciding cases more frequently. It is incumbent upon school district administrators to keep abreast of the law and to provide appropriate staff development for educators. It is also important to share this information with school board directors, students, and parents.

Acknowledgments

MERLE HOROWITZ

I want to thank my husband, Dr. Allan Horowitz, for his encouragement and support as I pursued my dissertation research and the writing of this book.

I want to thank my daughter, Dr. Allison Horowitz, for sharing her pediatric research and knowledge of patients who have experienced the pain and anguish of cyberbullying.

I want to thank my daughter, Jennifer Horowitz, for contributing her creative talents and graphic artwork for the cover and each section of the book.

DOROTHY M. BOLLINGER, ESQUIRE

I am deeply grateful . . .

To my family, who has been supportive and encouraging:
My husband, Barry, for his boundless love and encouragement;
My daughters, Brenda and Beth, for teaching my grandchildren kindness and concern for others;
My sons-in-law, Mike and Jeff, for their flexibility and support;
My granddaughters, Eliza and Madeline, for their drawings that are included in this book, and their brilliant creativity; and
My grandson, Trevor, for his enthusiasm and stories.

To Lynn M. Cromley, director, Pennsylvania Center for Safe Schools, who wrote the foreword for this book.

To my special friends, who have shared their legal knowledge and editing skills:
Ellen and Benjamin Enters, both attorneys, who read, edited, and improved the book; and
Tristram R. Fall, Esquire, who is mentioned last, but definitely is not least. He has been my brilliant mentor for many years, and has read, edited, and improved the book.

Introduction

For a victim of cyberbullying in social media, the agony can be a long and lonely journey that is difficult to escape—it can be continuous, all day and night, for weeks, months, and (in some confrontations) years. Then again, the shock of the cyberbullying can be a calamitous one-time event that traumatizes the victim for the rest of her life, or it can occur at any point along a continuum between these two extremes.

Anyone who uses social media can be a victim of cyberbullying. However, the focus of this book is cyberbullying that occurs within the setting of educational institutions. In that context, the victim or perpetrator of cyberbullying may be a student, an employee of the educational institution (teacher, coach, principal, or others), or a parent. Some examples of the kinds of cyberbullying that may occur are as follows: a student composes, sings, records, and publishes a song with vulgar verses insulting and criticizing two coaches, and then places it on YouTube; a teacher posts inappropriate statements about a student on Facebook; a parent assumes the identity of a student and befriends another student, after which the parent-imposter posts hurtful statements to the befriended student on MySpace; a student posts a sexual video of another student on YouTube; a student impersonates a principal and posts untrue statements on Facebook; or a principal claims a parent engaged in an action that is disputed by others. What is important to remember is that the victim or perpetrator of cyberbullying may be a student, an employee of an educational institution, a parent, or anyone even marginally connected to these people or the educational institution.

The pervasiveness of cyberbullying in social media can be found in numerous studies and research articles, but cyberbullying is more than just statistics. Cyberbullying is felt by real human beings who are embarrassed, humiliated, and harmed, so that their life is negatively altered, their talents and potential accomplishments are minimalized, and they are mentally and emotionally harmed. All of that harm is caused by the intentional and unintended actions of other human beings. More often than not, social media is a tool for people to connect with one another in a positive way. But social media, just like the Internet itself, is merely a tool that can be used in both good and harmful ways. Cyberbullying may arise in cyberspace, but at its core it is about real people harming real people in the real world. What can be done to stop or reduce cyberbullying, or at least minimize its negative impact within the educational setting? What are the educational and legal aspects of cyberbullying in social media?

Some cyberbullies need counseling; others need psychological, psychiatric, and/or medical help. Some need to be disciplined by the educational institution and/or reported to law enforcement. Some victims need a legal remedy through criminal punishment or civil liability. This book is useful to help learn about the education, prevention, intervention, and legal aspects of cyberbullying in social media.

We wrote the book because we needed to pull together and organize information to help us answer the questions: What are the educational and legal aspects of cyberbullying in social media, and what do you do? We felt inspired to help others with the problem of cyberbullying in social media and want to encourage others to lend a hand in preventing the injuries that result from cyberbullying in social media.

The educational and legal aspects of cyberbullying in educational institutions, whether in public school districts or higher education, are different from bullying. Unlike bullying, in which a person is physically assaulted and/or battered by being punched, thrown against a locker, hit with items, stabbed, sexually assaulted, or verbally abused face to face, cyberbullying involves a person being emotionally or mentally threatened, attacked, or harassed by an anonymous or a known bully (or bullies) through some type of electronic or digital means. Bullying has been around for centuries, but cyberbullying issues are fresh each day—shifting, kaleidoscopic, psychedelic, unstable, unpredictable, and mutable.

Resources are sorely needed. Informal conversations among educators and administrators reflect their growing concern. An examination of how educational institutions are coping with these issues is crucial, particularly as they relate to students, employees, and parents.

Each chapter of this book is divided into two parts: the educational aspects and the legal aspects of cyberbullying in social media. Chapter 1 tackles the subject relevant to students, chapter 2 the realm of employees, and chapter 3 the realm of parents.

Dr. Merle Horowitz, a school district superintendent, presents the educational aspects, and Dorothy M. Bollinger, Esquire, presents the legal aspects. In the educational strand, Dr. Horowitz presents her dissertation research and findings about cyberbullying and social media and the impact on the emotional, health, and safe learning environment for educational institutions. In the legal strand, Bollinger provides publicly reported examples of cyberbullying in social media; current examples of relevant state and federal criminal, civil, and education code statutes; and proposed federal legislation relevant to cyberbullying in social media. Furthermore, she examines and discusses interesting and relevant adjudicated state and federal cyberbullying in social media cases, and cases that have been filed in court but have not yet been adjudicated, all applicable to students, employees, and parents. The cases address First Amendment standards, defamation, harassment, civil rights, invasion of privacy, and contract actions.

Extensive appendices provide resource materials for use by educators, administrators, parents, policymakers, the public, and attorneys. For example, appendix A presents a table of the states' and the District of Columbia's bullying and cyberbullying laws, appendix B furnishes a list of cases used in the book that pertain to cyberbullying in social media, appendix C gives a list of educational references, and appendix D gives a list of centers and resources. Appendix E offers discussion scenarios, projects to create day-to-day practical items to use in educational institutions, and questions for staff development workshops.

Now, on to chapter 1 and the rest of the book for information that will benefit students', employees', and parents' lives, and hundreds and thousands of lives that touch educational institutions.

STUDENTS

1

Cyberbullying in Social Media: Students

Cyberbullying differs from traditional bullying in that cyberbullying can attack anonymously, it can instantly go viral globally, it allows many people to harass the same target all at once, it hides and guards the cyberbully from the emotional toll his/her bullying creates, and it allows the culprit to push further than he or she might in a face-to-face relationship where the adverse effects are clearly perceived. Furthermore, many parents and employees of educational institutions do not have the technological know-how to monitor these actions.[1]

EDUCATIONAL ASPECTS

Cyberbullying has become one of the major issues school districts must contend with today and one of this generation's greatest social problems. As we look at cyberbullying in social media from the educational perspective, we not only need to know what it is but also need to examine the behaviors of cyberbullies against their victims, the emotional responses of victims to the cyberbullying, the peculiarity of cyberbullying in social media, and the impact of all of this on educational institutions.

Cyberbullying and social media are defined differently by educators and by state and federal law. This section, "Educational Aspects," frames cyberbullying of students in social media from the educational research and education practice perspective. The next section of this chapter will address cyberbullying in social media from a legal perspective.

Educators Defining Cyberbullying and Social Media

A common general definition of *cyberbullying* is "willful and repeated harm, inflicted through computers, cell phones, and other electronic devices" (Hinduja & Patchin, 2011, 1). Shariff and Gouin (2005) explain that "cyberbullying consists of covert, psychological bullying, conveyed through electronic mediums, such as cell phones, web-logs and websites and online chat rooms" (3). They assert that cyberbullying is actually easier to accomplish than traditional bullying for the following reasons: increased accessibility, increased risk of exploiting others, anonymity, disinhibition, lack of supervision, its viral nature, and limitless victimization.

Social media, too, is defined in different ways and has different meanings for different people. As we examine social media from an educational perspective, it includes Internet and mobile-based technologies that allow the creation and exchange of user-generated content. Social media involves communication and collaborative sharing (Marple Newtown School District, 2012). Social media differs from traditional media in that it is dynamic and is constantly being altered by users.

Examining the Behaviors of Cyberbullies against Their Victims

Cyberbullies are malicious aggressors (Hinduja & Patchin, 2006) who seek implicit or explicit pleasure or profit through the mistreatment of another individual. Cyberbullying also involves harmful behavior that may be of a repetitive nature. Due to the very nature of the behavior, cyberbullies have some perceived or actual power over their victims. Online power may simply stem from proficiency. Individuals who are able to navigate the electronic world and use technology in a way that allows them to harass others are in a position of power relative to a victim (Hinduja & Patchin, 2006). Many different terms have been used to refer to online behavior that is harmful, untrue, or cruel and may be considered a form of harassment.

As more individuals are using online communication in ways that are inappropriate and potentially criminal, researchers (Willard, 2006; Shariff & Gouin, 2005; Bocij, 2004; Ogilvie, 2000) have begun to define these types of cyberbullying behaviors. Nancy Willard (2006), from the Center for Safe and Responsible Internet Use, used the phrase *online social cruelty* to describe various forms of cyberbullying. Willard's conceptual typology of these definitions in increasing order of seriousness follows:

Exclusion	Intentional exclusion in an online environment; individual is an outcast
Impersonation	Impersonation of a target posted online; can involve a threat; reflects badly on target
Denigration	Speech that is harmful, untrue, or cruel posted online or sent to others; gossip or rumors designed to damage relationships
Outing	Disseminating intimate, private information that is embarrassing, sexually suggestive, or explicit
Trickery	Tricking someone into disclosing private, embarrassing information that is disseminated online

Flaming	Deliberate, hostile, short-lived argument; generally includes offensive, rude, and vulgar language, insults, and threats; long series called a flame war that involves more than one individual
Harassment	Repeated, ongoing offensive messages sent online; unsolicited words or actions intended to annoy, harm, or abuse another individual; mostly one-sided
Cyberthreat	Direct threats or distressing material that raises concerns that the creator may intend to inflict harm or violence to self or others
Cyberstalking	Repeated sending of unwanted messages that include threats of harm; persistent behaviors instill apprehension and fear; highly intimidating and extremely offensive; may be criminal behavior

These forms of online social cruelty are frequently exhibited during online communication in social media and may be considered a form of harassment.

The anonymous nature of transmissions and postings make it difficult to identify one's aggressors. It frees the bully of societal norms, morals, and conscience. Less courage is required to express hurtful thoughts. Disinhibition makes it more difficult to control impulsive behavior given a lack of clear consequences. A victim's reaction is masked by technology. There is a lack of face-to-face emotion, as well as a loss of the feedback loop through body language. The viral nature of the Internet enables a rapid spread of information to large numbers of people in a very short period of time: texting takes seconds; posting photos on websites/email increases the audience dramatically from bathroom-stall comments. Content is spread from one person to another, making it impossible to control the rapid dissemination. Cyberbullying is not confined to the school day.

The Emotional Responses of Victims to Cyberbullying

As a school district superintendent for nine years, I have witnessed, discussed with colleagues, and can substantiate the emotional impact of cyberbullying on different types of student victims. The effects include declining grades, multiple absences from school, increasing depressive symptoms, suicidal ideation, and even suicide. Adolescents who experience cyberbullying may be sad, anxious, have low self-esteem, experience anger, frustration, embarrassment, or fear. Some students are smart, popular, and have "it all put together." Jealous classmates target them. Other students have a low self-esteem and/or a low commitment to school, avoid school totally, and become truant. Engagement in alcohol, tobacco, and/or drug use is common among victims. Delinquent tendencies may be exhibited, such as bringing weapons to school or demonstrating aggressive and rule-breaking behavior. Students feeling cyberbullied may unexpectedly stop using their computer and/or cell phone, as well as avoid their use of social media for a period of time or completely. They may get jumpy when a text or instant message is received, or appear angry, frustrated, or depressed after using the computer or cell phone. Students who experience cyberbullying may avoid discussing what they are doing online. These emotional responses have caused educators, psychologists, and researchers to study their impact on students in the school setting.

A Pew Internet Research Study (2007) reported that:

- 32 percent of online teens say they have been targets of a range of annoying or potentially menacing online activities
- 15 percent of teens overall say someone has forwarded or posted a private message they've written
- 13 percent say someone has spread a rumor about them online
- 13 percent say someone has sent them a threatening or aggressive message
- 6 percent say someone has posted embarrassing pictures of them online
- 38 percent of online girls report being bullied
- 26 percent of online boys report being bullied
- 41 percent of older girls (fifteen to seventeen) report being bullied more than any other age or gender group

Cyber Bully Alert (2012) reports:

- 20 percent of teens have been bullied through cell phone or over the Internet
- nearly 20 percent of teens have cyberbullied in their lifetimes
- 17 percent of boys have cyberbullied others
- 21 percent of girls have cyberbullied others
- 16.6 percent of boys have been cyberbullied
- 25 percent of girls have been cyberbullied
- the percentage of victims being cyberbullied is not much different from the percentage of people bullying
- although cyberbullying happens every day, it is rarely reported
- only one in ten teens who have been cyberbullied tell a parent or adult
- only one in five cyberbullying incidents are reported to law enforcement

There are many similarities between the studies in 2007 and those in 2012. Although the percentages may vary slightly, adolescents are still experiencing cyberbullying or are aware of others who have been affected by it.

Although cyberbullying offers the perpetrators anonymity, several studies have shown that many victims know who bullied them (Mishna et al., 2010). Often, the individual doing the bullying was considered a friend. Gender differences in cyberbullying remain unclear. An earlier study of cyberbullying found that, unlike traditional bullying, in which boys are more likely to be perpetrators, girls are more likely to be perpetrators and victims of cyberbullying (Agatston, Kowalski, & Limber, 2007). However, another study found no significant gender differences (Mishna et al., 2010). Studies indicate that those most likely to be involved in traditional bullying, both victims and perpetrators, are the same individuals that are most likely to be involved in cyberbullying.

The Peculiarity of Cyberbullying in Social Media

Using social media sites is among the most common activities of today's preadolescents and adolescents. Websites that allow social interaction are considered social media sites, including social networking sites/services such as Facebook, Twitter, and Instagram, and video sites such as YouTube and blogs. These sites offer today's youth a portal for entertainment and communication and have grown exponentially in recent years.

Engaging in various forms of social media is a routine activity that research has shown to benefit preadolescents and adolescents by enhancing communication, social connection, and even technical skills. Social media sites such as Facebook and YouTube offer multiple daily opportunities for connecting with friends, classmates, and people with shared interests. During the last five years, the number of preadolescents and adolescents using such sites has increased dramatically.

According to the Pew Research Center (Lenhart, 2012), 36 percent of teenagers exchange messages though social networking sites like MySpace or Facebook. Some 77 percent of teenagers now own cell phones: 25 percent use them for social media, 63 percent use them for texting, 23 percent use them for instant messaging, and 8 percent use them for email. Smartphones are gaining teenage users. Some 23 percent of those ages twelve to seventeen have a smartphone, and ownership is highest among older teens, ages fourteen to seventeen, at 31 percent. Smartphone-owning teens are avid users of a number of social media applications: 91 percent of teen smartphone owners use social networking sites and 25 percent are Twitter users.

Students today have access to the world at their fingertips through their computers, cell phones, social media sites, the Internet, email, and instant messaging. Thus, a large part of this generation's social and emotional development is occurring while on the Internet and on cell phones.

Due to their limited capacity for self-regulation and susceptibility to peer pressure, some preadolescents and adolescents are at some risk as they navigate and experiment with social media. Educators realize that there are frequent online expressions of offline behaviors, such as bullying, clique forming, and sexual experimentation (sexting) that have introduced cyberbullying problems into the school environment.

As an example, sexting, defined by the National Center for Missing and Exploited Children (2012) as the practice of youth writing sexually explicit messages, taking sexually explicit photos of themselves or others in their peer group, and then transmitting these photos and/or messages to their peers, has become an offline behavior that schools must deal with frequently. Children use various tools to take and distribute sexually explicit images, including cell phones, computers, web cameras, digital cameras, and video game systems. These images can be produced, transmitted, reproduced, and retransmitted with ease, without the subject's approval or even knowledge, and they can quickly reach a wide audience.

Research studies about sexting vary in the percentages of teenagers acknowledging having sent or received sexting messages. A 2011–2012 survey from the Massachusetts Aggression Reduction Center revealed that 30 percent of subjects reported that they had sent nude pictures at some point during their four years of high school and 45 percent reported that they had received such pictures on their cell phones. A 2011 survey (Rice et al., 2012) of more than 1,800 Los Angeles students ages twelve to eighteen found that 15 percent with cell phones acknowledged sexting and 54 percent knew someone who had sent a sext. A 2009 Pew Research Center Study revealed three main scenarios in which sexting tends to occur: 1) exchanges of images solely between two romantic partners; 2) exchanges between romantic partners that are then shared with others outside the relationship; and 3) exchanges in which at least one person would like to start a romantic relationship. Pew's data suggests that sexting has become a form of "relationship currency," with girls in particular sometimes feeling pressure to send images.

These offline behaviors can affect a safe learning environment, the students' mental and physical health (social media/Internet addiction and concurrent sleep deprivation), and the students' privacy, among other things.

The Impact of Cyberbullying in Social Media on Educational Institutions

Students who attend any type of educational institution could be a cyberbully or a victim. School districts and higher education have both been affected.

School Districts: Kindergarten through Twelfth Grade

Safe Learning Environment The mission of public schools in America is to prepare students to be engaged, ethical citizens in a democratic society. This infers creating a safe learning environment that teaches respect for the rights of students guaranteed under the U.S. Constitution. This also ensures that student speech does not disrupt the learning environment or degenerate into cyberbullying, bullying, discrimination, and/or harassment in their many forms.

Educating citizens requires teaching students about the value of free speech in light of the Internet and cyberactivities. Students will sometimes hear offensive, even hateful, speech. The fact that some speech upsets, offends, or angers students is not a justification for banning or limiting that speech. The skill of listening to speech with which one disagrees nevertheless remains an essential element of preparation for democratic citizenship. Professional staff members and administrators need to exercise special care in responding to controversial speech so that they do not either coerce or silence protected expressions. At the same time, they cannot abdicate their responsibilities to protect students. They must establish a safe learning environment and convey the school district's mission and duties.

Schools must balance the need for safe and effective learning environments with the need for free expression. The balance between the two changes depending upon the specific circumstances and is affected by the age of the students involved. Analyses of the First Amendment speech rights of students, employees, and parents and educational institutions' legal rights and responsibilities are provided later in this book in the legal sections.

With students' social lives moving increasingly into cyberspace, what previously might have been a private bickering is reproduced, publicized, and documented for all to see. School officials find themselves on unfamiliar ground in dealing with emails, text messages, profile pages, videos, and the like that may result in hurt feelings or suicidal ideation.

Students' Mental and Physical Health

Educators are also concerned about the physical and mental health of all students.

As reported in *Pediatrics* (O'Keeffe & Clarke-Pearson, 2011), there are some benefits of students using social media. Social media sites allow teens to accomplish online many of the tasks that are important to them offline: staying connected with family and friends, sharing photographs, and exchanging ideas. Social media participation can also offer adolescents deeper benefits that extend into their view of self, community, and the world, including:

1. Opportunities for community engagement through fund-raising for charity and volunteering for local events, including philanthropic events.
2. The enhancement of individual and collective creativity through developing and sharing of artistic and musical endeavors.
3. The growth of ideas from the creation of blogs, podcasts, videos, and gaming sites.
4. The expansion of one's online connections through shared interests to include others from more diverse backgrounds (such communication is an important step for all adolescents and affords the opportunity for respect, tolerance, and increased discourse about personal and global issues).
5. Fostering one's individual identity and unique social skills (O'Keeffe & Clarke-Pearson, 2011).

Middle and high school students are using social media to connect with one another on homework and group projects. For example, Facebook and similar social media sites allow students to gather outside of class to collaborate and exchange ideas about assignments. Some schools successfully use blogs as teaching tools, which has the benefit of reinforcing English, written expression, and creativity.

Adolescents are finding that they can access online information about their health concerns easily and anonymously. Excellent health resources are increasingly available to youth on a variety of topics of interest to this population.

However, using social media becomes a risk to adolescents more often than adults realize. Most risks fall into the categories of peer-to-peer communication, inappropriate content, a lack of understanding of online privacy issues, and outside influences of advertising.

Indeed, researchers have proposed a new phenomenon called "Facebook Depression." This is defined as depression that develops when adolescents spend a great deal of time on social media sites, such as Facebook, and then begin to exhibit classic symptoms of depression. Acceptance by and contact with peers is an important element of adolescent life. The intensity of the online world is thought to be a factor that may trigger depression in some adolescents. As with offline depression, adolescents who suffer from Facebook Depression are at risk for social isolation and sometimes turn to risky Internet sites and blogs for help that may promote substance abuse, unsafe sexual practices, or aggressive or self-destructive behaviors (O'Keeffe & Clarke-Pearson, 2011).

Students' Privacy

Important risks of social media to adolescents are risks from one adolescent to another, risks of improper use of technology, lack of privacy, sharing too much information, or posting false information about themselves or others. These types of behaviors put their privacy at risk.

When Internet users visit various websites, they can leave behind evidence of which sites they have visited. This collective, ongoing record of one's web activity is called the digital footprint. One of the biggest threats to adolescents on social media sites is to their digital footprint and future reputations. Adolescents who lack awareness of privacy issues often post inappropriate messages, photographs, and videos without understanding that "what goes online stays online." As a result, future jobs and college acceptances may be put into jeopardy by inexperienced and rash clicks of the mouse. Indiscriminate Internet activity also can make teenagers easier for marketers and fraudsters to target (I Keep Safe, 2012).

Many social media sites display multiple advertisements such as banner ads that target individuals on the basis of their web-browsing behavior. There are also demographic-based ads that target individuals on the basis of a specific factor such as age, gender, education, or marital status. These advertisements influence not only the buying tendencies of adolescents but also their views of what is normal. Adolescents are particularly vulnerable, being unaware of how advertisements can easily manipulate them.

Higher Education

The use of social media, particularly social networking sites, is on the increase at U.S. colleges and universities, as those institutions have recognized the important role of social media in today's world. A 2010–2011 study (Barnes & Lescault, 2011) analyzed the trending of social media among four-year higher-educational institutions in the United States. Colleges and universities are using social media to recruit and research prospective students. This new online marketing tool has enabled institutions to garner information to see which students would be a good match for their school. The study demonstrated that online behavior can have important consequences for prospective students, especially by college admissions officers.

According to Barnes and Lescault (2011), the most common form of social networking use at colleges and universities is Facebook, followed by Twitter and YouTube. They also state that it is important for higher-educational institutions to develop a social media policy for staff and students who engage in online communications. Almost all college students use some form of social networking. A study by Sponcil and Gitimu (2012) indicated that Facebook and email are the social networking websites of choice, with 99 percent of college students using Facebook and 90 percent using email. The participants in the study reported communicating with friends and family on social media websites several times a week.

College students need to make good decisions when using social networking sites. They should be informed and properly educated about social networking etiquette. Improper or negative etiquette can reflect negatively on that student. The dean of students at the University of Louisville (2012) developed a list of considerations for smarter social media use:

- Are you revealing too much?
- If it gives you pause, pause.
- Do I have the okay of my peers to post their information and pictures?
- Are you adding value?
- Perception is reality.
- What is a "meat puppet," and why should I care?

Stephanie Buck (2012) suggested twelve things students should never do on social media:

1. post illegal activities
2. bullying
3. trash your teachers
4. post objectionable content from computers or networks
5. post confidential information
6. overly specific location check-ins
7. lie/cheat/plagiarize
8. threaten violence
9. ignore school-specific policies
10. unprofessional public profiles
11. rely on privacy settings 100 percent
12. post emotionally

These recommendations are valuable for all ages of individuals engaged in the use of social media.

LEGAL ASPECTS

The legal aspects of cyberbullying in social media involve a mixture of federal, state, and local statutes, case law, administrative agency regulations, school district policies, regulations, rules, and procedures, and social media contract terms, among others. This area of the law is dynamic because technology is dynamic—new laws are enacted frequently, old laws are occasionally repealed, and existing laws are altered. Consequently, cyberbullying laws relevant to social media today may be different day to day, month to month, year to year, and in the future. Nevertheless, school districts and higher educational institutions must deal with students' cyberbullying acts now. When a student has been inflicted with some harm or injury recognized by society as a wrongful act, the educational institution must enforce a right or satisfy a court decision. Some cyberbullying requires legal recourse through criminal punishment, civil liability, or discipline from educational institutions; other incidents of cyberbullying require counseling, psychological, psychiatric, or medical help. But overall, education, prevention, and intervention are essential.

What is cyberbullying and social media? What are the rights and relevant court decisions?

Cyberbullying and Social Media Defined

Cyberbullying

State Statutes, Regulations, and Policies Cyberbullying is defined by many sources, and the definitions vary greatly. Definitions of cyberbullying in laws—

statutes, state boards of education regulations, and school district boards of education policies and other legal sources—are distinguishable from the definitions of cyberbullying in educational research and the general commercial media. Beyond these discrepancies, the definition of cyberbullying varies from state to state and at the federal level. For example, as noted above, in educational research, *cyberbullying* is defined as "willful and repeated harm, inflicted through computers, cell phones, and other electronic devices,"[2] and "consists of covert, psychological bullying, conveyed through electronic mediums, such as cell phones, web-logs [*sic*] and websites and online chat rooms."[3]

The legal definition of cyberbullying is governed by the jurisdiction (for example, state and/or school district) and type of action (for example, discipline, civil, or criminal), as well as the facts and circumstances of the particular case or situation. All of the fifty states and the District of Columbia have a state law that addresses bullying. Forty-nine of the states have a statute, one state (Montana) has a state regulation, and the District of Columbia has a municipal regulation. As to cyberbullying, of the fifty states, forty-seven include a definition of cyberbullying in the states' statutes. The other states delegate the defining of cyberbullying. Wisconsin delegates the definition of bullying to the State Department of Education (cyberbullying is included in the department's model policy).[4] Montana delegates the definition of bullying to the local school board. The Montana Office of Public Instruction has developed a model policy for local school districts that includes electronic communications.[5] Alaska defines bullying, but it does not explicitly include cyberbullying.[6] The District of Columbia's Municipal Code includes a definition of cyberbullying (electronic communications). Therefore, fifty of the fifty-one jurisdictions[7] define cyberbullying, and most include reference to electronic acts and/or electronic communications ("cyberbullying").

For example, the definition of cyberbullying in one state is "any act of bullying through the use of the Internet, interactive and digital technologies, cellular mobile telephone or other mobile electronic devices or any electronic communications," with electronic communications defined as "any transfer of signs, signals, writing, images, sounds, data or intelligence of any nature transmitted in whole or in part by a wire, radio, electromagnetic, photo electronic or photo-optical system."[8] Five of the states also expressly include forms of social media in their definition of cyberbullying; in so doing, they specifically notify individuals of the law's applicability to social media instead of relying on broad and/or vague statutes.[9] For the definitions of cyberbullying and bullying for all fifty-one jurisdictions, see appendix A, "Table of State Bullying and Cyberbullying Laws."

Of the fifty jurisdictions that target cyberbullying, approximately fifteen permit school districts to discipline students for their off-campus bullying acts. In general, for a student to be disciplined for his/her off-campus cyberbullying, he/she must (i) cause physical or emotional harm to a student or damage to the student's property; (ii) place a student in reasonable fear of harm to himself/herself or of damage to his/her property; (iii) create an intimidating, threatening, hostile, or abusive educational environment for the student; (iv) infringe on the rights of the student's education and right to participate in school activities; (v) materially and substantially disrupt the education process or the orderly operation of a school; or (vi) engage in an expression, physical act, or gesture that may include, but is not limited to, an incident or incidents that may be reasonably perceived as being motivated by characteristics such as race, color, religion, ancestry, national origin, gender, sexual orientation, gender identity and expression, or mental, physical, or sensory disability, intellectual ability, or by any other distinguishing characteristic.[10]

In addition to the above fifteen jurisdictions, Pennsylvania requires that school districts discipline students for their on-campus cyberbullying acts but permits its school districts to decide whether they want to define cyberbullying "in such a way as to encompass acts that occur outside a school setting"[11] when the acts (1) are directed at another student or students; (2) are severe, persistent, or pervasive; and (3) have the effect of doing any of the following: (i) substantially interfering with a student's education; (ii) creating a threatening environment; or (iii) substantially disrupting the orderly operation of the school.[12] Also, effective July 1, 2013, New York ended its on-campus-only position and permits discipline for both on-campus and off-campus cyberbullying acts, if the act "occurs off school property and creates or would foreseeably create a risk of substantial disruption within the school."[13] Finally, ten states specifically prohibit students from using the school district's computers, computer networks, or computer systems to cyberbully others whether they use the school district resources on or off school district property, and they permit school districts to discipline students for cyberbullying that is conducted off campus when the students use the school district's computers, computer networks, or computer systems. Therefore, twenty-seven jurisdictions permit school districts to discipline students for off-campus cyberbullying in some form. Three states delegate authority to the local school districts.[14]

Twenty jurisdictions permit school districts to discipline students for on-campus cyberbullying acts only. Typical on-campus language states that the school district may discipline "[b]ehavior that takes place on school property, on a school bus, or at a school-sponsored function."[15]

Other provisions of the cyberbullying laws include requirements such as:

- prohibiting cyberbullying, adopting a school district bullying/cyberbullying policy
- establishing the location to which the policy applies
- incorporating the policy into the code of student conduct

- establishing a range of consequences and appropriate remedial actions for those who commit an act of cyberbullying (including harassment, intimidation, and bullying)
- establishing a uniform reporting procedure (including anonymous reporting)
- establishing disciplinary actions for students who knowingly make false accusations
- providing protection from retaliation of a person for having reported an incident or provided reliable information during an investigation
- establishing procedures for notifying parents of victims and perpetrators
- training students, employees, and parents about bullying and cyberbullying prevention, including immunity for reporting
- providing requirements for the publishing of the policy
- requiring that prevention, intervention, and education programs be established

The statutory sections for all fifty-one jurisdictions are listed in appendix A, "Table of State Bullying and Cyberbullying Laws."

In addition to state laws aimed at school districts, legislatures have enacted criminal laws that address cyberbullying that occurs off campus. For example, Idaho's criminal code[16] provides that "any student who commits or conspires to commit, an act of harassment, intimidation or bullying shall be guilty of a misdemeanor"; Kentucky's law requires the school's discipline code to prohibit harassment, intimidation, bullying, or cyberbullying against students and to define the term,[17] in addition to expanding the crime of harassment to include harassment, intimidation, bullying, or cyberbullying by students on school property and at school-sponsored events.[18] Other states with criminal laws that address cyberbullying include Florida (the Jeffrey Johnston Stand Up for All Students Act),[19] Arkansas, Illinois, Louisiana, Mississippi, Missouri, Montana, Nevada, North Carolina, North Dakota, Tennessee, Virginia, and Wisconsin. See appendix A, "Table of State Bullying and Cyberbullying Laws."

Although state and federal legislators have responded to cyberbullying situations by enacting legislation to target cyberbullying acts, schools are struggling with exceptionally complex and unsettled legal questions. First, when cyberbullying occurs off campus, do school districts have the authority to discipline students?[20] In other words, when is the matter for parents, for the school, for law enforcement, or for the courts? Educational institutions also need to be mindful, when investigating these matters, not to cross the line and invade the perpetrators' privacy, and/or to be mindful of balancing the investigation to the severity of allegations.

Second, what are the school districts' boundaries in disciplining students for their cyberbullying acts made off campus, especially in their personal social media? Parents, students, and others ask, demand, and expect the school district to take action and correct cyberbullying conducted in social media while at the same time other students and/or their parents claim that their speech rights have been violated.

State laws may permit discipline for off-campus cyberbullying, but their enforcement is tricky. Will the school district's discipline be upheld when challenged in court? How do courts interpret the "substantially disruptive standard," and do they uphold school administrators' enforcement actions as constitutional? Is the state law language constitutional? To examine the school districts' boundaries, we must look at the state and federal laws and the decisions of the courts concerning them. However, before we address these questions, we must first examine what we mean by social media.

Social Media

Social media, too, is defined differently in laws, in educational research, and in the general public media. As with cyberbullying, the use of the definition depends on the jurisdiction, the type of action, and the facts and circumstances of the particular case. Use of the term *social media* is also complicated because some sources refer to social networking, but actually mean social media; some sources include different Internet platforms, websites, and services in their definition of social media; and some definitions are considered too broad, vague, or unconstitutional.

Five states include some type of social media in their statutory definition of cyberbullying intended for school districts. For example, California includes "social network Internet website," Kansas and Rhode Island include "blogs," Massachusetts includes "blogs and web pages," and Mississippi includes "social networking."[21] However, none define them or define social media.

In its postsecondary education Social Media Privacy statute, California has defined *social media* to mean "an electronic service or account, or electronic content, including, but not limited to, videos or still photographs, blogs, video blogs, podcasts, instant and text messages, e-mail, online services or accounts, or Internet Website profiles or locations."[22]

In order to protect minors from sexual predators in social media websites, many states have enacted criminal statutes aimed at registered sex offenders. Louisiana, Indiana, and Nebraska are examples of states that have a legitimate interest in protecting minors and juveniles as they use social media; therefore, the states enacted statutes that regulate unlawful access and/or use of social media by registered sex offenders—including chat rooms, instant messaging, peer-to-peer networks, and social networking in social media.

Louisiana Louisiana enacted the Unlawful Use or Access of Social Media Act,[23] which created the crime of unlawful use or access of social media by registered sex offenders who were previously convicted of a crime involving a sex offense against a minor or juvenile, unless the offender is granted permission by his/her probation or parole officer or the court.[24] The types of social media that registered sex offenders are prohibited from accessing are social networking websites, chat rooms, and peer-to-peer networks.[25] The Act embraced, but did not define, *social media*:[26]

> (1) "Chat room" means any Internet website through which users have the ability to communicate via text and which allows messages to be visible to all other users or to a designated segment of all other users.
>
> (3) "Peer-to-peer network" means a connection of computer systems whereby files are shared directly between the systems on a network without the need of a central server.
>
> (4) "Social networking website" means an Internet website that has any of the following capabilities:
>
> (a) Allows users to create web pages or profiles about themselves that are available to the general public or to any other users.
>
> (b) Offers a mechanism for communication among users, such as a forum, chat room, electronic mail, or instant messaging.

Two registered sex offenders challenged the Act, claiming it was facially overbroad and unconstitutional in that it significantly infringed on their First Amendment rights because the Act would not only ban them from accessing Facebook and MySpace, but also make it a felony for them to browse the rest of the Internet, including, among others, CNN.com, ESPN.com, NYTimes.com, Getagameplan.org (Louisiana's official hurricane preparedness website), Gmail, Yahoo!, Hotmail, AOL, and USAJOBS.gov (the federal government's employment database), because these websites "offer a mechanism for communication among users" in the form of comments and content forwarding.[27] The sex offenders asserted that they were afraid to access and use their web-based email accounts and Internet-based information services to obtain professional information relevant to safety and technical information for their work and work websites that would fall within the definition of a social networking website because they contain bulletin-board features and other social networking features against the law. They also claimed the Act violated the due process clause of the Fourteenth Amendment of the U.S. Constitution, which protects the public from vague criminal statutes.[28]

Louisiana responded that the sex offenders do not know whether the Act would pose any First Amendment problems because they never attempted to claim an exemption from the Act that permits them to use or access the social media when granted by their probation or parole officer or the court, and that the court should consider the Department of Correction's regulation that provides additional guidance about how the Act is intended to operate.[29]

The court concluded that the Act's prohibition from accessing and using social media was unconstitutionally overbroad and void for vagueness, thereby entering a judgment in favor of the sex offenders and prohibiting enforcement of the Act.[30] Moreover, the court stated, "The definitions are insufficiently defined, considering the criminal sanctions imposed in the legislation."[31]

Indiana Indiana enacted a law that established the sex offender Internet offense, which bans certain registered sex or violent offenders from knowingly or intentionally using or accessing social networking sites, instant messaging programs, and chat room programs that allow access by persons under the age of eighteen.[32] The law defines each type of social media as follows:

> (c) . . . "[I]nstant messaging or chat room program" means a software program that requires a person to register or create an account, a username, or a password to become a member or registered user of the program and allows two (2) or more members or authorized users to communicate over the Internet in real time using typed text. The term does not include an electronic mail program or message board program.
>
> (d) . . . "[S]ocial networking web site" means an Internet web site that:
>
> (1) facilitates the social introduction between two (2) or more persons;
>
> (2) requires a person to register or create an account, a username, or a password to become a member of the web site and to communicate with other members;
>
> (3) allows a member to create a web page or a personal profile; and
>
> (4) provides a member with the opportunity to communicate with another person.
>
> The term does not include an electronic mail program or message board program.[33]

John Doe challenged the statute claiming it violated his and similar registered sex offenders' First Amendment rights by prohibiting certain registered sex offenders from accessing and using social networking websites, instant messaging programs, or chat room programs that allow access by persons under the age of eighteen.[34] Specifically, Mr. Doe challenged the language that made it a misdemeanor to knowingly or intentionally use the platforms if the offender knows that minors are allowed access or use of the site.[35] He did not challenge the definitions of the platforms.

Mr. Doe had physical custody of his teenage son and wanted to "(1) use Facebook to monitor his teenage son's social networking activity; (2) participate in certain political speech online that requires social networking accounts; (3) advertise for his small business using social networking; (4) view photographs and videos of family members who are scattered throughout the United States; and (5) participate in certain communications and petitions relevant to pilots (Mr. Doe is also a pilot)." The state responded that the statute is narrowly directed to those found most likely to commit repeated offenses and victimize children.[36]

The court found that the statute was narrowly tailored to bar the targeted registered sexual offenders from using some platforms that could enable communication between sexual predators and their prey, leave open ample alternative channels of communication for Mr. Doe, and is not overly broad. Therefore, the statute did not violate Mr. Doe's First Amendment rights. The court stated that *Jindal*, the Louisiana case, was distinguishable because *Jindal* banned an extreme array of websites and potentially imposed "a sweeping ban on many commonly read news and information websites, whereas Indiana's statute did not prevent Mr. Doe from surfing all basic news and information sites, and Mr. Doe still had alternative forms of communications at his disposal."[37] Also, in Mr. Doe's case, the parties agreed that the statute was content neutral, and therefore the content of the statute was not analyzed; instead, the time, place, and manner of the statute was analyzed to determine whether the statute was narrowly tailored to serve the state's interest of protecting minors from sex predators and whether it left ample alternate channels for Mr. Doe to communicate information. The *Jindal* court did not use this framework; instead, the *Jindal* court relied heavily on the framework that regulated expression based on content that required the statute to be tailored precisely toward the conduct the state desired and proscribed.[38]

Nebraska Nebraska enacted a law that created the crime of unlawful use of the Internet by a prohibited registered sex offender[39] who knowingly and intentionally uses a social networking website, instant messaging service, or chat room service that allows a person who is less than eighteen years of age to access or use its social networking website, instant messaging service, or chat room service.[40] Each of the platforms was defined as follows:[41]

> (3) Chat room means a web site or server space on the Internet or communication network primarily designated for the virtually instantaneous exchange of text or voice transmissions or computer file attachments amongst two or more computers or electronic communication device users;
>
> (10) Instant messaging means a direct, dedicated, and private communication service, accessed with a computer or electronic communication device, that enables a user of the service to send and receive virtually instantaneous text transmissions or computer file attachments to other selected users of the service through the Internet or a computer communications network;
>
> (13) Social networking web site means a web page or collection of web sites contained on the Internet (a) that enables users or subscribers to create,

> display, and maintain a profile or Internet domain containing biographical data, personal information, photos, or other types of media, (b) that can be searched, viewed, or accessed by other users or visitors to the web site, with or without the creator's permission, consent, invitation, or authorization, and (c) that may permit some form of communication, such as direct comment on the profile page, instant messaging, or email, between the creator of the profile and users who have viewed or accessed the creator's profile.

Several registered sex offenders challenged the constitutionality of the statutes that criminalized their use of social networking websites, instant messaging, and chat room services accessible by minors on First Amendment grounds,[42] and they challenged the definitions of social networking websites, instant messaging, and chat room[43] on free speech grounds. The Nebraska court used the same content-neutral analysis that the Indiana court had used in the above *Doe* case, but found the Nebraska statute unconstitutional because it was not narrowly tailored to the state's interest in protecting children from sexual predators on the Internet and because the statute did not leave open ample alternate channels for communication of information.[44] As in the decision by the Louisiana court, the Nebraska court found that the sweeping restrictions on the use of the Internet imposed severe unwarranted restrictions on protected speech of the sex offenders that did not relate to the state's interest, even without applying the content analysis used by the Louisiana court. In addition, the court found that the definitions of the platforms were unconstitutional because they were expansive and vague and did not leave the sex offenders comparable alternatives of communication. For example, the definitions restricted the exchange of text between adults, restricted the exchange of oral and video communication between adults, and potentially restricted the targeted offenders from communicating with hundreds of millions and perhaps billions of adults and their companies despite the communication not having anything to do with minors.[45] The court also found the statutes overbroad.

Definitions and Types of Social Media As illustrated above, social media has been defined in many ways and has different meanings for different people and different uses. Social media uses websites and mobile technology to electronically and widely share and disseminate information in real time. It uses an interactive, user-generated dynamic and constantly altered content dialogue that is created and exchanged between publishers and users.

The many types of social media, platforms, and features vary, but they typically have profiles containing personal information, privacy settings to restrict or widen public access, preferences, lists of friends, interaction with friends, comments, and some kind of content such as videos, photographs, or text. Social media includes:

- Social networking sites, such as Facebook or MySpace, that allow users to interact by adding friends, having discussions, and commenting on activities.
- Social bookmarking sites, such as Delicious or BlinkList, that allow users to tag websites and search those tagged by other people.
- Social news sites, like Digg or Reddit, that allow users to vote for and comment on articles.
- Social photo and video sharing sites, such as YouTube and Flickr, that allows users to interact by sharing videos or photos.
- Wikis, such as Wikipedia, that allow users to add articles and edit existing articles.
- Blogging or microblogging sites, such as Twitter, that allow users to share information and comment on other users' information.
- Virtual worlds, such as Second Life, that allow users to use web- or software-based platforms to create avatars or representations of themselves, and through these avatars to meet, socialize, and interact with other users for social purposes and ecommerce, nonprofit fund-raising, and videoconferencing.[46]

In addition to social media for personal use, schools create their own social media for educational use. Examples include Google Docs, Ning, Flat Classroom, TeacherTube, and Moodle.

Defining social media is intricate. Enforcing the social media statute, regulation, or policy is complex. As illustrated above, reference to social media is easy, but crafting language to protect students' privacy in using social media, the rights of children to safely use social media, and students' rights to not be cyberbullied in social media, whether by sexual predators or other students, is difficult when weighed against the First Amendment and other laws important to the rights of many different individuals. As educators face cyberbullying in social media, they enforce policies and statutory requirements, report incidents to proper authorities, and guard the rights of many different individuals. Examining the language of the law for its broad or narrow interpretation of social media is important.

Students, employees, parents, and others who use their personal social media to cyberbully risk unintended and unauthorized consequences.

Cyberbullying in Social Media: It Really, Really Hurts

Cyberbullying in social media is mean, despicable, callous, cruel, uncaring, and appalling—it really, really hurts. It is a serious and growing problem in educational institutions whether at the elementary school, middle school, high school, and college or university level. Most cyberbullying confrontations do not make it to court. Some do.

Nafeesa Onque[47]

Nafeesa Onque's Facebook page included her cell phone number, favorite movies, relationship status, photographs of herself, and photo albums. She was a popular teen cheerleader who was working toward a Rutgers University scholarship. But someone else had built a profile and stolen Nafeesa's online identity and was using it to destroy her real-life identity.

Nafeesa had created her own Facebook page signed "Nafeesa McPomPoms Onque," in reference to her cheerleading. The bully created the fake page under the slightly different name "NaFeesa McPomPoms Onque Onque." Over the years, the bully followed Nafeesa and hounded her and her friends on MySpace, Facebook, and ooVoo. The bully started impersonating Nafeesa, using several fake profiles to hold her online personality hostage until police tracked down the impostor. Her mother, Karima, worked to end the bullying, pleading with Internet providers, school officials, and the police, but every time the mother managed to get a page deleted, a new one would spring up within days.

The imposter sent friend requests to dozens of city teens, as well as family members on Facebook. Shortly after accepting an invitation from the imposter, friends found their inboxes and Facebook walls flooded with threats, sexually explicit comments, and profanity-laced tirades. One girl became so angry she attacked the real Nafeesa, striking her in the face outside a city school.

Nafeesa was terrified. Friends, even people she didn't know, would approach her and ask why she was sending nasty messages to them. Nafeesa began to withdraw from the social world of her school. She didn't know whom to trust. The imposter could have been anybody pretending to be her friend.

As time passed, the cyberbullying became more personal, and far more disturbing.

The impostor started posting Facebook status updates saying Nafeesa "just had sex." Reportedly, the fake Nafeesa would sometimes flirt with random men on Facebook and proposition them for sex. The imposter posed naked from the neck down in a video on ooVoo, and someone tagged it as the real Nafeesa in the web clip on Facebook, making it visible to hundreds of relatives and classmates. During an online conversation, the imposter started cursing at the real Nafeesa's mother, telling her things no parent would want to hear.

Nafeesa did not take her own Facebook profile down because others would have believed that the fake page was the real one.

Nafeesa's mother filed reports with the local and state police and provided them with records detailing "several months" of abuse on Facebook. Detectives poured through the records of the attacks, and dozens of MySpace, Facebook, and ooVoo profiles. They were searching for the imposter's Internet protocol address, which would reveal the predator's online identity. Eventually, they discovered the name and hometown of their suspect. The IP address led law enforcement to a home near the townhouse complex where the Onques had lived for years. Authorities confirmed Nafeesa's tormentor was the fifteen-year-old girl she had suspected. She was arrested and charged with wrongful impersonation.

The case was referred to Essex Vicinage Family Court, Superior Court of New Jersey–Family Division, where juvenile matters are held confidential.

Ryan Halligan[48]

Ryan Halligan attended Hiawatha Elementary School and Albert D. Lawton Middle School in Essex Junction, Vermont. During his elementary school days, Ryan experienced some developmental delays affecting his speech and physical coordination, but he overcame them by the fourth grade. Ryan suffered bullying at the hands of a group of students at his school because of his learning disability. He ignored the bullying and received counseling. The bullying continued on and off for the next two years in middle school.

Ryan decided to learn how to box so that he could defend himself. He had a fight with a bully, after which the bully stopped bothering him. After the fight Ryan and the boy became acquaintances, and Ryan told the boy about an embarrassing examination required after he had stomach pains. He later learned that the bully misused the story to spread a rumor that he was gay.

Ryan began to spend more time online, where he was cyberbullied by schoolmates who thought he was gay. He was also bullied at school. One online exchange involved Ashley, a popular girl that Ryan had a crush on. She pretended to like him to gain personal information about him, and then she would copy and paste their private exchanges into other instant messages, sending them to his schoolmates to embarrass and humiliate him. After he discovered what she was doing, he told her that "it's girls like you who make me want to kill myself."

He began communicating online with a pen pal about suicide and death, and he told him he was thinking about suicide. They had been exchanging information they had found on sites relating to death and suicide, including sites that taught them how to painlessly kill themselves. The pen pal answered, "Phew. It's about [___] time," shortly after Ryan told him he was thinking about suicide. This was the last conversation he had with the pen pal. At thirteen, Ryan Halligan committed suicide by hanging himself. His body was found later by his older sister. Ryan's pen pal was a boy Ryan knew up until third grade, when the boy and his parents moved away.

Ryan's father wanted to file charges against the bully, but the police reportedly said there was not a criminal law that covered the circumstances. He began to lobby for legislation in Vermont to improve how schools address bullying and suicide prevention. Vermont enacted a Bullying Prevention Policy Law in May 2004 and later adopted a Suicide Prevention Law (Act 114) in 2005, closely following a draft submitted by Mr. Halligan. See appendix A, "Table of State Bullying and Cyberbullying Laws."

Other students "really, really hurt," too. Some experience cyberbullying that involves lesbian, gay, bisexual, and transgender (LGBT); others involve sex, sexting, and cyberstalking.

Jamey Rodemeyer[49]

Jamey Rodemeyer was a fourteen-year-old student who attended Williamsville North High School (New York) and blogged often about the bullying he endured for being bisexual. Anonymous posts on Jamey's social media pages included "JAMIE IS STUPID, GAY, FAT ANND [*sic*] UGLY. HE MUST DIE!" and "I wouldn't care if you died. No one would. So just do it :) It would make everyone WAY more happier!" Jamey's parents were aware of the bullying, but they did not believe it bothered Jamey. Jamey posted inspirational, anti-suicide messages on his YouTube and social media pages, telling other victims of bullying to be strong. Jamey hanged himself on September 18, 2011, after years of bullying and cyberbullying for his sexual orientation.[50]

Within a year, in July 2012, New York passed the Dignity for All Students law,[51] a cyberbullying law that includes requiring teachers to report incidents of online stalking to an official within twenty-four hours. See appendix A, "Table of State Bullying and Cyberbullying Laws."

Phoebe Prince[52]

Phoebe Prince was a fifteen-year-old student at South Hadley School District (Massachusetts). She was the brunt of verbal harassment and threatened physical abuse, reportedly because some students did not believe a new student should date a popular football player, referring to her as an "Irish slut."

Reportedly, the crux of the cyberbullying came after a November 21, 2009, event at Phoebe's house. She had asked a friend to stay with her overnight when her mother was gone for the night. The other girl texted some boys, and soon Phoebe's home had many high school students. The students brought many kinds of drugs. The group was so rowdy that a neighbor reportedly called the police, who allegedly sent the students home. Phoebe was left alone without the police calling her mother. The police said they do not have a log of their involvement. After the students left, she took an overdose of medication and was taken to the hospital. Phoebe continued to be harassed by her peers at school and online, referring to her as an "Irish whore."

Phoebe lived in almost constant terror at school during the last week of her life. One student assailed her in class in front of other students, and another student's threats shook her up so much that Phoebe skipped classes and went to the school nurse. A third girl made disparaging remarks about Phoebe outside the school auditorium and threw a can at her while she was walking home on the day of her suicide.[53] She hung herself with her scarf on January 14, 2010.

The school district had to defend itself for its handling of the matter. Several of her classmates were charged with crimes, ranging from disturbing a school assembly to civil rights violations. Six of her classmates were charged with criminal harassment, statutory rape, and other related crimes. Five of the six either pleaded guilty or admitted sufficient facts for a guilty finding. Three defendants' cases were closed in Hadley Juvenile Court. Two other cases were resolved a day earlier in Hampshire Superior Court. None were sentenced to jail time.

Amanda Todd[54]

On September 7, 2012, Amanda Todd posted a video on YouTube titled "Amanda Todd's Story: Struggling, Bullying, Suicide, Self-Harm," which showed her using a series of flash cards to tell of her experiences of being bullied. The video post went viral. During the video, Amanda wrote that, when she was in seventh grade, she used video chat to meet new people over the Internet, and she received compliments on her looks. A stranger convinced her to bare her breasts on camera. The individual later blackmailed her with threats to expose the topless photo to her friends unless she gave a "show."

Amanda wrote that police informed her that the photo was circulating the Internet. She wrote that she experienced anxiety, depression, and panic disorder because of this. Her family moved to a new home, where Amanda stated that she began using drugs and alcohol.

Later, the individual reappeared, creating a Facebook profile that used the topless photograph as the profile image. The individual began contacting classmates at her new school. Again, Amanda was teased, eventually changing schools for a second time. She wrote that she began chatting to "an old guy friend" who appeared to her. The friend asked her to come to his house, where they had sex while his girlfriend was on holiday. The following week, the girlfriend and a group of others attacked Amanda at school while shouting insults and punching her to the ground. Following the attack, Amanda attempted suicide by drinking bleach, but she was rushed to the hospital, where her stomach was pumped.

After returning home, Amanda discovered abusive messages about her failed suicide attempt posted to Facebook. Her family moved to another city to start afresh, but Amanda was unable to escape the past. Six months later, further messages and abuse were still being posted to the social networking sites. Her mental state worsening, she began to engage in self-mutilation. Despite taking antidepressants and receiving counseling, she overdosed and spent two days in the hospital.

She was teased by other students at her school for her low grades, a consequence of a language-based learning disability and the time she spent in the hospital to treat her severe depression. On October 10, 2012, Amanda was found hanged at her home.

Conclusion

Suicides may be a rare consequence for the enormous number of cyberbullying confrontations that occur. However, we cannot express the torment, pain, and suffering victims of cyberbullying and parents of cyberbullied students who commit suicide (or attempt to commit suicide) experience and the hurt they bear as they work through the confrontations. The parents of Ryan Halligan, Jamey Rodemeyer, and Tyler Clementi (see "Invasion of Privacy" section below) are only a few of the parents who had a mission to help others so that cyberbullying does not happen to other children. The Clementi family has helped Rutgers University establish the Clementi Center to promote accepting social environments at school, at home, in church, and online, to turn bystanders into upstanders to prevent bullying, and to build an infrastructure of support for LGBT and vulnerable youth and their families.[55] Jamey Rodemeyer's family persisted in helping New York pass the Dignity for All Students Act, and Ryan Halligan's family helped Vermont enact the Bullying Prevention Policy Law and Suicide Prevention Law, all to help prevent cyberbullying of other students.

The victims of cyberbullying are difficult to read. They have conflicted "inside and outside feelings." Parents, friends, and educators need to recognize that the victims of bullying and cyberbullying are prone to having conflicted "inside and outside feelings" that may be difficult to read. Many victims try hard to appear normal and put on a brave face on the outside even while they "really, really hurt" on the inside. Every person is unique in how they might respond to being bullied and cyberbullied. Every case of bullying and cyberbullying is as unique as its victim.

Nafeesa did not want to take her real Facebook presence out of social media even though she was being tormented because she didn't want people to think the fake website was really her. On the outside, Ryan tried to ignore the bullies and fought back, but inside he was planning his suicide. On the outside, Jamey posted inspirational, anti-suicide messages on YouTube telling others to be strong, but inside he was so hurt he hung himself. In each of these cases, the outside face did not match the inside face. And because parents, friends, and educators cannot readily tell from outward appearances who may or may not be able to handle being bullied, every case must be handled with caution, care, and concern.

Cyberbullying in social media can be a one-time event, or it can be continuous, all day and night, for weeks, months, and in some situations, years. For the victim of a cyberbully, it can be a painful, long, and lonely journey that is difficult to escape. Cyberbullies can say whatever they want because they can be anonymous. The victim may not know whether the cyberbully is a friend, an acquaintance, or an unknown student from his/her school, his/her neighbor, a jealous enemy, or an adult from another state.

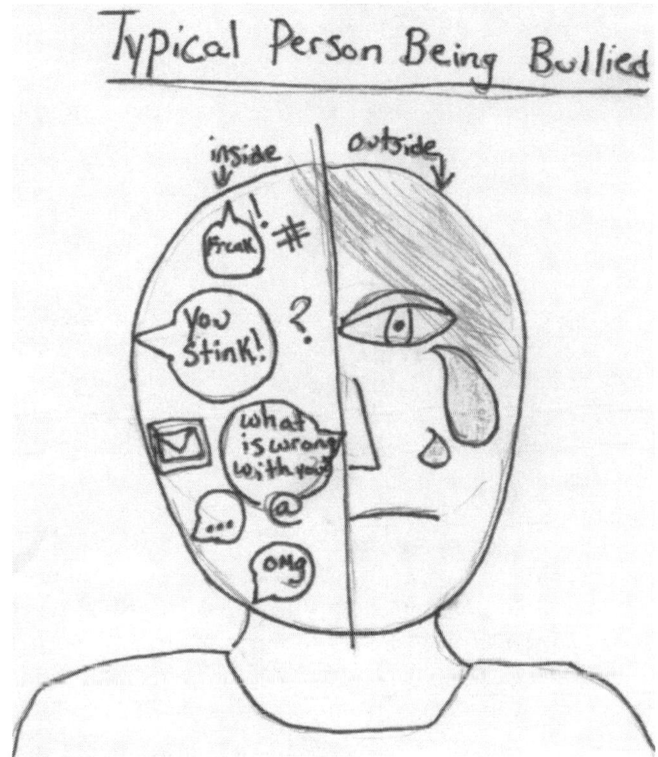

Cyberbullying in social media is a critical and expanding problem in educational institutions. It ranges from primary schools through college, and from off campus to on campus. While the ages of victims may vary, the variety of mechanisms for legal redress and punishment have some similarities. Specifically, liability or culpability may be imposed by courts under common law tort actions, state criminal actions, and various federal laws. In addition, educational institutions may enforce their bullying/cyberbullying and disciplinary policies against students.

The next three sections address the legal foundations for cyberbullying culpability. In the first section, we examine cyberbullying in social media criminal statutes and proposed federal civil legislation. In the second section, we examine adjudicated state and federal cyberbullying in social media cases, and in the third section, we examine cyberbullying in social media cases filed, but not adjudicated.

Examination of Cyberbullying in Social Media Criminal Statutes and Proposed Federal Civil Legislation

Civil and criminal statutes can be used as the basis for an action against a cyberbully. Examples of some current state and federal statutes are provided below.

State Statutes

State terroristic threat statutes can be used against a person who posts online based on the facts, circumstances, and evidence, among other legal considerations. If found liable, the cyberbully could be criminally liable.

Various statutes criminalize the deliberate posting of defamatory or threatening information directed at another on a social media website. See North Carolina's Protect Our Kids/Cyber Bullying Misdemeanor statute.[56]

Under California law, a person can be charged with a misdemeanor, punished up to one year in jail, and/or fined up to $1,000 if that person posted or distributed a message or photo with the purpose of harassing someone or making that person fear for his/her safety.[57]

Under Pennsylvania's Sexting Cyberbullying law,[58] which only applies to photos transmitted among teens and which became effective on December 24, 2012, there are three levels of culpability that depend on the severity of the transmission of sexually explicit images of teens. In order to punish teens for sexting, but not ruin their lives, the law reduces the penalties for teens engaged in conduct that before would have constituted sexual abuse of children, a felony according to the Pennsylvania Crimes Code. A teen who knowingly transmits, distributes, publishes, or disseminates a sexually explicit image of himself/herself or knowingly possesses or views a sexually explicit image of a minor who is twelve years of age or older commits a summary offense.[59] A teen who knowingly transmits, distributes, publishes, or disseminates a sexually explicit image of another minor who is twelve years of age or older commits a misdemeanor of the third degree.[60] A teen who intends to coerce, intimidate, torment, harass, or otherwise cause emotional distress to another minor, makes a visual depiction of any minor in a state of nudity without the knowledge and consent of the depicted minor, or transmits, distributes, publishes, or disseminates a visual depiction of any minor in a state of nudity without the knowledge and consent of the depicted minor could be charged with a second-degree misdemeanor.[61] With all three classifications, the special status cannot occur if the minor subject/victim is sexually abused.[62]

Pennsylvania may confiscate any communication devices used in violation of the law, and a judge may assign a teen violator to a diversionary program that may include an educational program. If the program is successfully completed, the teen's record may be able to be expunged. An adult committing these acts could be prosecuted under felony child pornography charges.[63]

In addition, many states have enacted cyberstalking laws or include proscriptions against cyberstalking in their harassment or stalking statutes to protect children and adults from being victims.[64] A few states have both stalking and harassment statutes that criminalize threatening and unwanted electronic communications.

Federal Statutes

Congress has enacted criminal and civil statutes that can be used as the basis for an action against a cyberbully. Charges could be brought under the Computer Fraud and Abuse Act[65] if the person is involved in hacking, exceeding one's authorization, and/or accessing another person's email account and/or computer without authorization. The charge could be a misdemeanor or felony.

Also, if a person obtained information that (s)he posted by intercepting someone's email or using someone's password without his/her consent, that person may be subject to prosecution under the Electronic Communications Privacy Act,[66] which carries a possible penalty of jail time and/or a fine. Civil actions may also be brought under the Electronic Communications Privacy Act.

The deliberate posting of threatening information directed at another person on a social media website is prohibited under 18 U.S.C. § 875(c), which makes it a federal crime, punishable by up to five years in prison and a fine of up to $250,000, to transmit any communication in interstate commerce, including by the Internet, which contains a threat to injure the person or another.

The federal law criminalizing stalking was amended in 2006 to expressly include cyberstalking (e.g., stalking through the mail or any interactive computer service).[67] Additionally, the requisite intent has been expanded from an intent to "kill or injure" to include the intent to "harass or place under surveillance with the intent to . . . harass or intimidate or cause substantial emotional distress." When the Internet is involved, the cases refer to this as a cyberstalking statute.[68] Here, stalking means:

> (A) traveling with the intent to kill, injure, harass, or intimidate another person and, in the course of, or as a result of, such travel, placing the person in reasonable fear of death or serious bodily injury to that person or an immediate family member of that person; or (B) using the mail or any facility of interstate or foreign commerce to engage in a course of conduct that places that person in reasonable fear of the death of, or serious bodily injury to, that person or an immediate family member of that person.[69]

However, in 2011, a court determined that the statute was unconstitutional because the language criminalizes acts that are constitutional.[70] Numerous bills have been proposed in the 2013 Congress to modify the language of the statute, but as of the preparation of this book, a bill has not been passed. Congress also enacted the Anti-Cyberstalking law.[71]

Most stalking laws require that the perpetrator make a credible threat of violence against the victim; others include threats against the victim's immediate family; and still others require that the alleged stalker's course of conduct constitutes an implied threat, an intent to annoy (absent a threat), abuse, harassment, or encouragement of others to harass. When analyzing the facts and circumstances of the cyberbullying incidents with the statutes, one needs to determine whether the perpetrator is anonymous; whether the stalking was conducted through interstate or foreign activity; whether the cyberstalking was conducted by telephone, email, the Internet, a bulletin board, or a chat room; and whether a state or federal statute is applicable. For example, some statutes may only be applicable to teens, while others may only apply to higher-education students; still others may apply to both. Additionally, some statutes may only be enforced by law enforcement, while others permit individuals to bring suit. Stalking and cyberstalking may also be referred to as criminal harassment.

Proposed Federal Civil Legislation

The Safe Schools Improvement Act introduced into Congress on March 8, 2011, included language connecting anti-bullying policies to federal funding, requiring schools to have a code that prohibited bullying conduct, and set new reporting standards. The Act died in committee. The bill was reintroduced as S.403 on February 28, 2013, to amend the Elementary and Secondary Education Act (ESEA) (20 U.S.C. § 7101 et seq.) to include cyberbullying and harassment of students in public elementary and secondary education.

In 2013, the Student Non-Discrimination Act (SNDA) also was introduced as H.B. 1652 and S.1088. The Act was introduced as an amendment to the ESEA and as a separate, stand-alone bill. The SNDA establishes LGBT students as a protected class and prohibits schools from discriminating against any student based on actual or perceived sexual orientation or gender identity. The discrimination includes cyberbullying against them. The bill also contains sections that advocate for a positive school climate and requires reporting of incidents of bullying, including on the basis of sexual orientation and gender identity.

The Internet affords today's youth more opportunities to interact with many different people and supplies countless avenues for reckless behavior and callousness. Sometimes students do not understand the consequences of their actions until it is too late. What students do in the online world affects who they are in the real world. There appear to be an endless supply of platforms for students to denigrate their classmates. Next, we examine cases that have been adjudicated by the courts that directly and indirectly address cyberbullying in social media.

Examination of Adjudicated State and Federal Cyberbullying in Social Media Cases

Lawsuits that examine students' cyberbullying in social media and that concern educational institutions involve issues from many different legal bases for relief and defenses and do not always appear to be adjudicated consistently. First Amendment speech rights, defamation (libel and slander), impersonation, intimidation (including online threats, violence, threats of violence by electronic acts, and hate violence), harassment, invasion of privacy, cyberstalking, hazing, sexting, and violations of a school's policy are examples of actions filed in courts, argued and adjudicated. Some of these actions are discussed below.[72]

First Amendment: School District Speech Cases

The First Amendment of the U.S. Constitution provides for the right of "freedom of speech."[73] The U.S. Supreme Court has clearly stated and it has been accepted that students do not "shed their constitutional rights to freedom of speech or expression at the schoolhouse gate."[74] The Court also stated that "the constitutional rights of students are not automatically coextensive with the rights of adults in other settings,"[75] and that student's rights must be "applied in the special characteristics of the school environment."[76] The U.S. Constitution and state constitutions protect students' speech in public schools, but they are not without exceptions. Educational institutions may regulate student speech that is not protected.

But what standard will a court use to determine whether students' speech is protected or not protected in social media? Students' expressions can be posted on blogs, in instant/email/text messages, in chat rooms, through avatars, and in videos, photographs, and written or spoken messages on websites (to name a few) when the students are at school, beyond the school, or both. Expressions posted in social media are accessible by many people even when the students think that the posts are accessed only by their "friend(s)."

To date, the U.S. Supreme Court has not accepted and adjudicated a First Amendment speech case that involves issues relevant to cyberbullying in social media within educational institutions. On January 17, 2012, the Supreme Court decided to not accept three cases that did involve cyberbullying in social media: *Layshock v. Hermitage School District*,[77] *J.S. v. Blue Mountain School District*,[78] and *Kowalski v. Berkeley County Schools*.[79] Therefore, courts rely on various standards established by the U.S. Supreme Court in the past that they believe are most applicable. Educational personnel need to know what the standards are so that they can respect the rights of students and at the same time maintain a safe and orderly environment for students to learn and for teachers to teach. Below is a sampling of cases; this is not an exhaustive compilation.

Material and Substantial Disruption Standards School officials may restrict student expression if the officials can show "that the students' activities would materially and substantially disrupt the work and discipline of the school."[80] The Supreme Court in *Tinker v. Des Moines Independent School District* (1969)[81] stated, "[C]onduct by the student, in class or out of it, which for any reason—whether it stems from time, place, or type of behavior—materially disrupts classwork or involves substantial disorder or invasion of the rights of others is, of course, not immunized by the constitutional guarantee of freedom of speech."[82] What is a school administrator to understand is considered "materially or substantially disruptive"?

In *Tinker*, the wearing of black armbands by students to school in protest of the Vietnam War was held not to satisfy this standard, even though it was in violation of the district policy forbidding such displays. Here, the Court stated that there were no interrupted school activities, no intrusion into school affairs, no intrusion into the rights of others, and no disorder. Therefore, school officials had no reason to anticipate that the wearing of the armbands would substantially and materially interfere with the work of the school or impinge on the rights of other students.[83]

Student-to-Student Speech Courts have applied the *Tinker* material and substantial disruption standard when they have analyzed student-to-student expression on and off campus.

In *Kowalski v. Berkeley County Schools* (2012), the Fourth Circuit Court of Appeals upheld a school's discipline of a student for engaging in off-campus cyberbullying of another student.[84] A student (Kowalski) created a MySpace profile called "S.A.S.H.," which she said was short for "Students Against Sluts Herpes." Another student, however, claimed it really stood for "Students Against Shay's Herpes," referring to a particular student. The student invited about one hundred people to join the page, and about twenty-four people joined. Students posted comments and images making fun of Shay N. One student posted a picture of her and put "red dots on Shay N.'s face to simulate herpes and added a sign near her pelvic region, that read, 'Warning: Enter at your own risk.' In the second photograph, he captioned Shay N.'s face with a sign that read, 'portrait of a whore.'"[85]

Shay N. complained and school officials determined that Kowalski created a "hate website" that violated school policy. Kowalski was suspended for five days and received a "social suspension" for ninety days, making her ineligible to participate in various social events at school. Kowalski sued, claiming that the discipline violated her First Amendment free speech rights. The court concluded that the school was justified in imposing discipline under the material and substantial disruption test. A quote from the court's opinion helps to clarify their conclusion:

According to a federal government initiative, student-on-student bullying is a "major concern" in schools across the country and can cause victims to become depressed and anxious, to be afraid to go to school, and to have thoughts of suicide. Just as schools have a responsibility to provide a safe environment for students free from messages advocating illegal drug use, schools have a duty to protect their students from harassment and bullying in the school environment. Far from being a situation where school authorities "suppress speech on political and social issues based on disagreement with the viewpoint expressed," school administrators must be able to prevent and punish harassment and bullying in order to provide a safe school environment conducive to learning.

We are confident that Kowalski's speech caused the interference and disruption described in Tinker as being immune from First Amendment protection. The "S.A.S.H." webpage functioned as a platform for Kowalski and her friends to direct verbal attacks towards classmate Shay N. The webpage contained comments accusing Shay N. of having herpes and being a "slut," as well as photographs reinforcing those defamatory accusations by depicting a sign across her pelvic area, which stated, "Warning: Enter at your own risk" and labeling her portrait as that of a "whore." One student's posting dismissed any concern for Shay N.'s reaction with a comment that said, "screw her." This is not the conduct and speech that our educational system is required to tolerate, as schools attempt to educate students about "habits and manners of civility" or the "fundamental values necessary to the maintenance of a democratic political system."[86]

Kowalski argued that the speech took place at her home and should be outside the school's power to regulate, but the court concluded:

Kowalski indeed pushed her computer's keys in her home, but she knew that the electronic response would be, as it in fact was, published beyond her home and could reasonably be expected to reach the school or impact the school environment. She also knew that the dialogue would and did take place among Musselman High School students whom she invited to join the "S.A.S.H." group and that the fallout from her conduct and the speech within the group would be felt in the school itself. Indeed, the group's name was "Students Against Sluts Herpes" and a vast majority of its members were Musselman students. As one commentator on the webpage observed, "wait til [Shay N.] sees the page lol." Moreover, as Kowalski could anticipate, Shay N. and her parents took the attack as having been made in the school context, as they went to the high school to lodge their complaint.

There is surely a limit to the scope of a high school's interest in the order, safety, and well-being of its students when the speech at issue originates outside the schoolhouse gate. But we need not fully define that limit here, as we are satisfied that the nexus of Kowalski's speech to Musselman High School's pedagogical interests was sufficiently strong to justify the action taken by school officials in carrying out their role as the trustees of the student body's well-being. . . .

> Given the targeted, defamatory nature of Kowalski's speech, aimed at a fellow classmate, it created "actual or nascent" substantial disorder and disruption in the school. See *Tinker*, 393 U.S. at 508, 513; *Sypniewski v. Warren Hills Reg'l Bd. of Educ.*, 307 F.3d 243, 257 (3d Cir. 2002) (indicating that administrators may regulate student speech any time they have a "particular and concrete basis" for forecasting future substantial disruption). First, the creation of the "S.A.S.H." group forced Shay N. to miss school in order to avoid further abuse. Moreover, had the school not intervened, the potential for continuing and more serious harassment of Shay N. as well as other students was real. Experience suggests that unpunished misbehavior can have a snowballing effect, in some cases resulting in "copycat" efforts by other students or in retaliation for the initial harassment.
>
> Other courts have similarly concluded that school administrators' authority to regulate student speech extends, in the appropriate circumstances, to speech that does not originate at the school itself, so long as the speech eventually makes its way to the school in a meaningful way. . . .
>
> Thus, even though Kowalski was not physically at the school when she operated her computer to create the webpage and form the "S.A.S.H." MySpace group and to post comments there, other circuits have applied *Tinker* to such circumstances. To be sure, it was foreseeable in this case that Kowalski's conduct would reach the school via computers, smartphones, and other electronic devices, given that most of the "S.A.S.H." group's members and the target of the group's harassment were Musselman High School students. Indeed, the "S.A.S.H." webpage did make its way into the school and was accessed first by Musselman student Ray Parsons at 3:40 p.m., from a school computer during an after-hours class. Furthermore, as we have noted, it created a reasonably foreseeable substantial disruption there.[87]

The U.S. Supreme Court decided not to hear the appeal of the decision, leaving the Fourth Circuit's opinion standing. Here, the court upheld the school district's discipline based on the reasonably foreseeable standard. The Fourth Circuit upheld the school district's discipline because the nexus of the student's speech to the school district's pedagogical interests was sufficiently strong to carry out its role as the trustees of the student body's well-being. The school had documented the nexus between the speech and the school and how it created a disruption.

In *J.C. v. Beverly Hills School District* (2010), the U.S. District Court for the Central District of California found that the fact that a student's conduct took place off campus did not preclude the school district from disciplining the student, but, considering the facts involved, there was no substantial and material disruption of the school. Therefore, the school district violated the student's First Amendment rights by disciplining her.[88]

According to the *J.C.* court, after school was dismissed one day, a student video recorded the student and some of her friends as they sat in an off-campus restaurant talking about a classmate and making vulgar and derogatory remarks about her. That evening, the student posted the video on YouTube, and then contacted some other students, suggesting that they watch the video. Next, the student called the classmate and told her about the video and asked her if she wanted the video to stay posted. The classmate, on the advice of her mother, said to leave the video up. The classmate and her mother informed the school about the video the next morning. The reason for keeping the video posted was so they could show it to the administration when they made the complaint. The school district investigated the matter, demanded that the student delete the video from YouTube and her home computer, required that the student and her friends write a statement about the incident, and then suspended the student for two days. Subsequently, the student claimed that the school had violated her First Amendment rights because it did not have authority to suspend her for out-of-school activities in which there was no consequent disruption to the educational environment.[89]

The Court considered three principles applicable to U.S. Supreme Court precedents involving off-campus speech. It found that (1) there was no substantial and material disruption of the school, (2) that it was reasonably foreseeable that the video would make its way to the school campus because it was posted on a website accessible by the general public, and (3) that the vulgar, derogatory nature of the video increased the foreseeability that it would come to the school. The Court found that even though the posted video upset the classmate, no substantial and material disruption had occurred, and that there was not a sufficient nexus between the off-campus conduct and the school district to justify discipline by the school district. According to the Court, only a small number of students discussed the video at the school, and school officials' "fear that students would gossip or pass notes in class did not rise to the level of a substantial disruption."

In addition, the Court stated that, because the school blocked YouTube, only those with cell phones who had access to YouTube through their cellular service could access the video. Because students were not permitted to access their cell phones during the school day, the Court believed that "only administrators had accessed the video during the investigation." The Court rejected the school district's position "that it should be accorded some deference to decide how best to protect the emotional well-being of its young students."[90] The Court stated:

> The Court in large part agrees. Indeed, no one could seriously challenge that thirteen-year-olds often say mean-spirited things about one another, or that a teenager likely will weather a verbal attack less ably than an adult. The Court accepts that C.C. was upset, even hysterical, about the YouTube video, and that the School's only goal was to console C.C. and to resolve the situation as quickly as possible.

> Unfortunately for the School, good intentions do not suffice here. Defendants have failed to present sufficient evidence that the YouTube video caused a substantial disruption to school activity on May 28, 2008. Further, Defendants' fear that a substantial disruption was likely to occur simply is not supported by the facts. The Court cannot uphold school discipline of student speech simply because young persons are unpredictable or immature, or because, in general, teenagers are emotionally fragile and may often fight over hurtful comments. To create a genuine issue for trial, Defendants must tie those conclusions to the situation presented to them on May 28, 2008. On this record, they have failed to do so.[91]

The court held that the administrators were entitled to qualified immunity, which is discussed below.

In *S.J.W. v. Lee's Summit R-7 School District* (2012), the Eighth Circuit Court of Appeals found that both the material and substantial disruption standard and the forecast of substantial disruption standard were met.[92]

Twin brothers created NorthPress, a website that included a blog that was a place "to discuss, satirize, and 'vent' about events at Lee's Summit North." The website was registered with a Dutch domain name registrar to prevent users from finding the website with a Google search; however, with the website address, anyone could reach the website because it was not password protected. The posts on the blog "contained a variety of offensive and racist comments as well as sexually explicit and degrading comments about particular female classmates, whom they identified by name. The racist posts discussed fights at Lee's Summit North and mocked black students."[93]

School district records showed that on one day the website was accessed by one of the twin brothers to upload files and accessed by some unknown school users, and that on two other days the records showed that the website was accessed but the school could not determine how it was used. The administration learned of NorthPress, investigated, and suspended the twins, who were permitted to enroll in another school. Nonetheless, they claimed that the new school was not academically challenging enough and, because they wanted to pursue a career in music or theater, their chances for scholarships would be injured if they could not participate in Lee Summit North's band.[94]

The twins and their parents sued, claiming that the school district violated their First Amendment rights because the posts were intended to be satirical rather than serious. The school district responded that the website caused substantial disruption at the school because school district computers were used, teachers testified that they were having difficulty managing their classes because students were distracted and upset by the website, local media arrived on campus, and parents were contacting the school with concerns about safety, bullying, and discrimination.

The District Court granted the twins a preliminary injunction, but the school district appealed to the Eighth Circuit, which reversed the District Court's decision.[95] The Eighth Circuit held that, because NorthPress was "targeted at" Lee's Summit North and the posts caused a considerable disturbance and substantial disruption, the twins were not likely to succeed on the merits of the case. Whether the off-campus expressions caused on-campus disruption, the court stated the twins "speech was 'off campus,' but the location from which the [twins] spoke may be less important . . . the NorthPress posts could reasonably be expected to reach the school or impact the environment."[96] The court also stated:

> The specter of cyber-bullying hangs over this case. The repercussions of cyber-bullying are serious and sometimes tragic. The parties focus their arguments on the disruption caused by the racist comments, but possibly even more significant is the distress the Wilsons' return to Lee's Summit North could have caused the female students whom the Wilsons have targeted.[97]

Reportedly, the parties reached a settlement on January 3, 2013.[98]

In these student-to-student cases involving cyberbullying in social media, the courts were faced with situations in which the students' verbal attacks in social media were extremely hurtful, derogatory, vulgar, racist, and offensive, and where the school district disciplined students for their off-campus expressions. All three of the courts recognized that school districts can discipline students for their off-campus speech, but the school district must meet certain requirements and must produce sufficient evidence to support the basis of their decision to discipline. The three courts agreed that material and substantial disruption at the school is sufficient to discipline off-campus speech, that there must be a strong-enough nexus between the student's off-campus conduct and the school for the school district to carry out the school district's discipline, and that it is foreseeable that the speech would make its way to the school campus or impact its environment. As illustrated above, two of the cases found off-campus requirements were present for the students' off-campus speech to foreseeably make its way to the school campus or impact the school environment and that there were material and substantial disruptions at the school. Yet one court found that the off-campus speech did not preclude the school district from disciplining the students, but in the end the court found that the school district did not present sufficient evidence to support its position that there was a material and substantial disruption at the school in order to have disciplined the student.

Student-to-Teacher and Student-to-Administrator Speech Courts have applied the *Tinker* material and substantial disruption standard when they have analyzed student-to-teacher or student-to-administrator expression on and off campus, too.

In *Requa v. Kent School District No. 415* (2007), the U.S. District Court for the Western District of Washington denied a student's request for a temporary restraining order, holding that the student was not likely to succeed on the merits of his allegations—namely, that he was suspended because of his speech, not his conduct, and that the video he made was protected speech.[99] The court found that the student surreptitiously took video footage of a teacher in her classroom at least twice. The raw footage and audio were edited, and graphics and a musical soundtrack were added, then posted on YouTube from the student's home. The resulting video "included commentary on the teacher's hygiene and organizational habits," with the "student standing behind the teacher making faces, putting two fingers up at the back of her head and making pelvic thrusts in her general direction. Additionally, in a section preceded by a graphic announcing 'Caution Booty Ahead' there were several shots of the teacher's buttocks as she walked away from the videographer, and as she bends over, the music accompanying this segment is a song titled 'Ms. New Booty.'"[100]

The student claimed that all he did was create a link from his MySpace account to the video on YouTube, but once the information about the video was aired on local TV, he removed the link. According to the court, statements obtained by the administration from other students involved in making the video proved his involvement. The student also claimed that, even if the school could prove that he was involved in the production of the video, it was protected speech. The court upheld the Board of Education's decision to discipline the student because his conduct violated the school district's sexual harassment policy (for the two episodes dealing with the pelvic thrusts and close-up recording of the teacher's buttocks and bending over with the accompanied music). The school district's personal electronic device policy also prohibited the use of video recorders, cameras, and other personal electronic devices. The court found that the school district was not punishing the student for off-campus speech, but rather for the student's on-campus conduct. The court stated:

> The Court has no difficulty in concluding that one student filming another student standing behind a teacher making "rabbit ears" and pelvic thrusts in her direction, or a student filming the buttocks of a teacher as she bends over in the classroom, constitutes a material and substantial disruption to the work and discipline of the school. . . . The "work and discipline of the school includes the maintenance of a civil and respectful atmosphere toward teachers and students alike—demeaning, derogatory, sexually suggestive behavior toward an unsuspecting teacher in a classroom poses a disruption of that mission whenever it occurs."[101]

In *J.S. v. Bethlehem Area School District* (2002), the Pennsylvania Supreme Court found that off-campus speech can be considered on-campus speech by a student when it is viewed or accessed on school district property, or is aimed at a specific school district, school personnel, and/or student audience and others connected with the particular school district (i.e., not a random audience), or is brought onto the school district's property and there is a sufficient nexus between the website and the school campus.[102] Further, the court found that the "web site caused actual and substantial disruption of the work of the school."[103]

J.S., a middle school student, created a website called "Teacher Sux" at home with his home computer that contained a number of derogatory, profane, offensive, and threatening comments and images directed at his algebra teacher and principal. The website included a drawing of the teacher's head cut off with blood dripping from her neck, and it was titled "Why Should She Die?" It also offered to pay a hit man $20 to kill the teacher. After viewing the website, the teacher became physically and emotionally distraught, and she could not finish the year teaching. Substitute teachers were hired to teach her class. Student morale was "comparable to [that of] the death of a student or staff member."[104] Parents voiced their concerns to the school about their children's safety and the quality of instruction from the substitutes.[105] Consequently, the school district suspended and later expelled the student.

The parents of the student filed an action alleging that the district infringed upon his First Amendment speech rights. The Pennsylvania Supreme Court stated that discipline must be based on an "approach that considers and balances both the constitutional rights of the student with the preservation of order and a proper educational environment."[106] The court held that the website did not contain "true threats" but reasoned "there is a sufficient nexus between the website and the school campus to consider the speech as occurring 'on-campus.'"[107] Further, the subsequent disruption caused by the website within the school caused a disturbance sufficient to merit disciplinary action by the school district, and that the speech "undermined the basic function of a public school."[108] Accordingly, the court held that the actions of the school district did not infringe the student's First Amendment rights.[109]

In *Evans v. Bayer* (2010),[110] the U.S. District Court for the Southern District of Florida found that the student's speech "was made off-campus, never accessed on-campus, and was no longer accessible when the [teacher] learned of it."[111] The student had created a Facebook group at home after school hours with her own computer that focused on one teacher, claiming that the teacher was "the worst teacher she ever met." Other students were invited to voice their dislike of the teacher—"Here is the place to express your feelings of hatred." Three postings were made to the page, all of them in support of the teacher. The student was suspended for three days, transferred from an advanced placement class to a lesser weighted honors class, and received a notice of suspension for "bullying/cyberbullying/harassment toward a staff member" and "disruptive behavior." No threats of violence were posted, the posting was removed after two days, and the teacher did not see the messages while they were posted.

The court concluded that the school district's actions did not satisfy any First Amendment standard that would permit the school district to discipline the student for speech: no disruption occurred at school; no reasonably foreseeable disruption could be found; the student expressed an opinion about the teacher, which in this case was not a libelous statement; and no lewd, vulgar, threatening, or advocating of illegal or dangerous behavior occurred.[112] Therefore, the student's speech was protected by the First Amendment; the school district's desire to avoid discomfort or unpleasantness was not sufficient.

In *Layshock v. Hermitage School District* (2011),[113] the Third Circuit Court of Appeals held that taking a photograph of the principal off the school district's website and posting what the school district considered a profile containing vulgar, lewd, and offensive expressions about the principal were not sufficient to establish a nexus between the school and the profile that the student posted on MySpace. Therefore, the school district did not have authority to discipline the student for his expressive conduct outside the school. The U.S. District Court for the Western District of Pennsylvania found that the school district "could not establish a sufficient nexus between Justin's [the student's] speech and a substantial disruption of the school environment, and the School District does not challenge that finding on appeal."[114]

The student had used his grandmother's computer at her house to access and create a fake MySpace "profile" of his high school principal that insulted and mocked him. The school district suspended the student for violating its disciplinary code that forbade "disruption of school processes" and "disrespect," and it forbade him to attend graduation and assigned him to an alternative education program. The student claimed "he made the profile to be funny, and did not intend to hurt anyone."[115] The principal and administration did not think the profile was a funny parody.

The court found that the student's speech was off-campus speech that did not reach the school, stating, ". . . because the School District concedes that [the student's] profile did not cause disruption in the school, we do not think the First Amendment can tolerate the School District stretching its authority into [the student's] grandmother's home and reaching [the student] while he was sitting at her computer after school in order to punish him for his expressive conduct that he engaged in." In applying the *Fraser* standard (explained and illustrated below), the court stated that *Fraser* "was careful to note that had Fraser delivered the same speech in a public forum outside of the school context, it would have been protected."[116] Finally, the court dismissed the school district's claim that the student's "speech can be treated as 'on-campus' speech because it was aimed at the School District community and the Principal and was accessed on campus by [the student] and it was reasonably foreseeable that the profile would come to the attention of the School District and the Principal." The Third Circuit stated that there was no evidence that lewd or profane speech reached the school, and the school district did not establish a nexus between the student's speech and a substantial disruption at school. The Third Circuit held that the punishment violated the student's First Amendment rights. The U.S. Supreme Court denied certiorari.

In contrast to *Layshock*, in *Barnett v. Tipton County Board of Education* (2006), the U.S. District Court for the Western District of Tennessee found that two high school students' profiles prepared about their assistant principal and coach were not protected speech.[117] One student (Student 1) created a fake profile of his assistant principal on MySpace that contained his photograph and information from the Board of Education's website, as well as sexually suggestive comments about female students. Another student (Student 2) created a similar profile of a high school coach. Both profiles were prepared at the students' homes with home computers, but they were accessed at school during at least one class. A parent and local reporter believed the profiles were prepared and posted by the assistant principal and coach, so they called the school to complain about the sexually suggestive comments about the high school girls. After the school investigated the matter, the two students were identified and suspended. After the suspension, Student 1 created a website containing a "Wanted" poster that included a photograph of a high school student whom he thought had told school officials that he had created the assistant principal's profile. Hearings were held, and the board determined that Student 1 should be sent to an alternative school for the remainder of the year and Student 2 should be placed on a zero-tolerance policy for the remainder of the year. The students and their parents sued the school district, claiming that the students were deprived of their First Amendment rights because the profiles were parodies, which are protected by the First Amendment.[118]

The court found no evidence to support the students' claims that visitors to the website would find the profiles to be parodies. Instead, the court found that visitors believed they were authentic and that the assistant principal and coach had engaged in the inappropriate behavior. Both a news reporter and a parent had called the school believing the website was true. Therefore, the court found that the parodies and websites were not protected speech under the First Amendment, and the school district's discipline was upheld.[119]

In these student-to-teacher and student-to-administrator cases involving cyberbullying in social media, the courts were faced with situations in which the students' verbal attacks in social media were extremely hurtful, demeaning, derogatory, sexually suggestive, vulgar, lewd, and/or offensive, and where the school district disciplined students for their off-campus expressions or conduct. As illustrated above, three of the courts recognized that school districts can discipline students for their off-campus speech, but the school district must meet requirements as discussed above and must produce sufficient evidence to support the basis of their decision to discipline (*J.S. v. Bethlehem*, *Layshock*, and

Evans), although two of the courts ruled that the students' speech did not reach the school district, that there was not a nexus between the students' speech, and that there was not a material and substantial disruption at school. One court recognized that the student's discipline was based on his conduct, not his speech, thereby upholding the school district's discipline, and one case upheld the school district's discipline based on the court's determination that the student's speech was not a parody.

Forecast of Substantial Disruption Standard *Tinker* also states that "facts which might reasonably have led school authorities to forecast substantial disruption of, or material interference with, school activities"[120] may be the basis to punish students. However, "undifferentiated fear or apprehension of disturbance is not enough to overcome the right to freedom of expression."[121] "The burden is on school authorities to meet *Tinker*'s requirements to abridge student First Amendment rights, [but] the School District need not prove with absolute certainty that substantial disruption will occur."[122] In short, "a school district is not required to wait until disruption actually occurs before they may act."[123] As stated above, the *Tinker* Court did not believe that wearing a black armband to peacefully protest the Vietnam War would be a sufficient basis to impose discipline on the student.[124] What is a school administrator to understand is considered sufficient to forecast substantial disruption of, or material interference with, school activities?

Student-to-Student Speech Courts have applied the *Tinker* forecast of substantial disruption standard when they analyzed student-to-student expression on and off campus.

In *D.J.M. v. Hannibal Public School District* (2011), the U.S. Court of Appeals for the Eighth Circuit held that the student's speech was not protected by either the *Watts/Doe* "true threat" standard[125] or the *Tinker* "reasonably foreseeable substantial and material disruption standard."[126] The student had sent instant messages to his friends when they were at home using their home computers. One of his friends became concerned about D.J.M.'s statements and sent them to an adult and later to the principal. At first, D.J.M. discussed his frustration with having been "spurned" by a girl he liked, and then discussions followed about using a "357 magnum" to kill specifically named students he would have to "get rid of" (but not the girl who had spurned him because he still liked her), and individuals in specific groups he did not like. D.J.M. and the friend expressed amusement at the prospect of shooting particular individuals or groups—for example, by exclaiming "lol" and "haha." They also discussed other topics, such as music preferences and TV shows. The friend reported that, among other things, D.J.M. had been "talking about taking a gun to school to shoot everyone he hates [and] then shoot himself," that he "want[ed] [the school district] to be known for something," that his friend was "kinda scared," and that D.J.M. had "talked to a friend . . . [who] said he would give him a gun." The adult asked the friend to determine whether D.J.M. was serious, which the student did and then sent excerpts of the conversation to the adult and the principal.[127]

The police were contacted, D.J.M. was placed in juvenile detention and sent for a psychiatric examination, and was suspended by the school district for the remainder of the year. The principal received numerous telephone calls from parents asking what the school was doing about D.J.M.'s threats and whether their children were on the hit list. School officials spent considerable time dealing with the students' parents' concerns and increasing security. The court relied on *Doe v. Pulaski County Special School District*, a school district "true threat" case derived from *Watts* (see the "true threat standard" section below), and the *Tinker* "reasonably foreseeable substantial and material disruption standard" discussed above. Accordingly, the student's speech was not to be protected by the First Amendment and could be disciplined by the school district when true threats make their way to school and cause substantial disruption to the school environment.[128]

Student-to-Teacher and Student-to-Administrator Speech Courts have applied the *Tinker* forecast of substantial disruption standard when they have analyzed student-to-teacher or student-to-administrator expression on and off campus.

In *J.S. v. Blue Mountain School District* (2011), the Third Circuit Court of Appeals, sitting *en banc*, did not find the facts of the case were sufficient to support the forecast of substantial disruption standard. Two students had posted a fake MySpace profile of the principal of a middle school from a home computer, portraying him as a pedophile and insulting and disparaging him. The students were suspended by the school district. The parents of the students brought an action alleging violations of the First Amendment.

The court found that the students' vulgar and offensive profile of the principal on MySpace would be considered a joke, unbelievable and nonsensical, that the profile could not be viewed on school computers because MySpace was blocked, and the only copy of the profile on school property was one brought at the principal's request. In addition, the court stated that only "general rumblings, a few minutes of talking in class, and some officials rearranging their schedule" to assist the principal in dealing with the profile occurred—"no disruptions."[129] The court quoted the Supreme Court in *Tinker*, stating that an "undifferentiated fear or apprehension of disturbance is not enough to overcome the right of freedom of speech."[130] Accordingly, the Court held that the punishment violated the student's First Amendment rights. The U.S. Supreme Court denied certiorari.

In *Wisniewski v. Board of Education of Weedsport Central School District* (2007), the Second Circuit Court of Appeals applied the forecast of substantial disruption standard and held that the "student's actions in creating and transmitting [a] drawing depicting [the] shooting of a teacher posed [the] reasonable foreseeable risk [that the] drawing would come to [the] attention of school authorities and would materially and substantially disrupt [the] work and discipline of [the] school."[131] The student had used instant messaging software on his home computer to communicate with other students. When he sent instant messages, for three weeks they included an icon depicting a pistol firing a bullet at the head of one of his teachers, with dots representing splattered blood above the head and text below the head stating "Kill Mr. VanderMolen" (his English teacher). The icon was brought to the attention of the teacher and administrators by another student weeks after it was used.

The incident required the administrators to focus special attention on the matter, to arrange for a criminal investigation to be conducted, to replace the student's teacher (at the teacher's request), and to conduct student investigations during class time. The court stated that "[t]he fact that [the] creation and transmission of the IM icon occurred away from school property does not necessarily insulate [the student] from school discipline," where the icon's off-campus display "pose[d] a reasonably foreseeable risk that [it] would come to the attention of school authorities" and "materially and substantially disrupt the work and discipline of the school." Therefore, suspension of the student did not violate his First Amendment speech rights.[132]

The student claimed that the icon was a joke, but the hearing officer found that the icon was threatening, not understood as a joke. It violated school rules and disrupted school operations. The court did not analyze whether this was a true threat that met the *Watts* standard. Instead, the court stated that school officials have "broader authority to sanction student speech than the true threat standard allows."[133]

In *Doninger v. Niehoff* (2011), the Second Circuit Court of Appeals found that school officials could reasonably forecast that a substantial disruption or material interference would occur.[134] The fear or apprehension of a disturbance was sufficient for school administrators to discipline the student for her off-campus speech posted in a publicly accessible blog hosted by livejournal.com when she called administrators "douchbags" and asked people to contact the superintendent "to piss her off more."[135]

After posting the blog message, the student was denied the opportunity to run for senior class secretary because the blog post failed to demonstrate good citizenship in compliance with a written school policy for an extracurricular council of which she was a member, and the blog message included information that was not accurate. High school students began wearing a T-shirt in support of the student. Candidate speeches before an assembly of six hundred students were held the next day, but the student was not permitted to give a speech. Based on rumors heard by the principal, the principal stood outside the auditorium addressing the T-shirt issue by preventing the wearing "of any shirt that [she] felt would cause disruption" at the assembly. During the assembly students were shouting, "Vote for Avery." The principal warned the students to be respectful. After tallying the ballots, the student received the most votes, but the principal awarded the position to the person receiving the next highest number of votes. The student and her parents sued the school district. The court granted qualified immunity to all school district parties.

The court examined the "blog incident" as an off-campus matter and the T-shirt matter as an on-campus matter. As to the blog incident, the court stated, "We have determined . . . that a student may be disciplined for expressive conduct, even conduct occurring off school grounds when the conduct 'would foreseeably create a risk of substantial disruption within the school environment,' at least when it was similarly foreseeable that the off-campus expression might also reach campus."[136]

Further, "territoriality is not necessarily a useful concept in determining the limit of [school administrators'] authority . . . when students both on and off campus routinely participate in school affairs, as well as in other expressive activity unrelated to the school community, via blog postings, instant messaging, and other forms of electronic communications."[137] As to the on-campus T-shirt matter, the court determined that the school administrators were entitled to qualified immunity.[138]

In *Bell v. Itawamba County School Board* (2012),[139] the U.S. District Court for the Northern District of Mississippi found that a student's song "caused a material and/or substantial disruption and it was reasonably foreseeable that such a disruption would occur," thereby meeting two standards.[140] A student while off campus had composed, sang, and recorded a rap song and then published it on Facebook to more than 1,300 friends. The video of the song was also seen by an unknown number of viewers on YouTube. The song had included many vulgar verses insulting and criticizing two coaches and one of their wives, specific allegations of improper contact with female students, and two threatening lyrics. At the school board disciplinary hearing, the student was found to have "threatened, harassed and intimidated school employees with the publication of his song."

The court agreed that the lyrics caused a material and substantial disruption at school because both coaches testified that their teaching style had been adversely affected after knowing of the song. One coach perceived that the students were wary of him, and the other coach feared that the students suspected him of inappropriate behavior. Furthermore, one coach felt threatened by the references to killing him. In addition, the court concluded that it was reasonably foreseeable to school officials that the song would cause such a disruption because of the charges of sexual misconduct using vulgar and threatening language and because of the extent of the publication of the song. Therefore, the school district's suspension and placement of the student in alternative education for five weeks was upheld, and the student's speech was held to not be protected by the First Amendment.

In these student-to-teacher and student-to-administrator cases involving cyberbullying in social media, the courts were faced with situations in which the students' verbal attacks in social media were extremely hurtful, threatening, intimidating, demeaning, derogatory, vulgar, offensive, and inaccurate, and where the school district disciplined students for their off-campus expressions or conduct. As illustrated above, three of the courts recognized that school districts can discipline students for their off-campus speech, but the school district must meet certain requirements and must produce sufficient evidence to support the basis of its decision to discipline, although one of the courts ruled that the student's speech was considered a joke, unbelievable, and nonsensical, and that neither the forecast of substantial disruption standard nor the material and substantial disruption standard was supported by the evidence. Two of the courts found that it was reasonably foreseeable that the students' off-campus speech would reach the school and that it was reasonably foreseeable that the speech would create a risk of substantial disruption to the school. One of the courts ruled that the students' off-campus speech was sufficient to meet both the forecast of substantial disruption and the material and substantial disruption standard based on the song's threatening and vulgar language and the extent of the publication.

Other Standards Other standards that have been applied to student speech cases, depending on the circumstances and the law, include the true threat standard, the *Fraser* standard, the *Hazelwood* standard, the *Morse* standard, and some higher-education standards. They are described below.

True Threat Standard The U.S. Supreme Court established the meaning of "true threat" in *Watts v. United States* (1969).[141] The case involved a criminal prosecution for violating a federal statute that provides for punishment for "knowing and willfully . . . mak[ing][a] threat against the President." At a public rally on the grounds of the Washington Monument, the defendant said, "If they ever make me carry a rifle the first man I want to get in my sights is L.B.J." Because this statute made a form of speech a crime, the First Amendment must be clearly considered. "What is a threat must be distinguished from what is constitutionally protected speech. The statute initially requires the Government to prove a 'true threat.'"[142] The *Watts* "true threat" standard has been applied in cases in which students have threatened to kill a school official.[143]

In *Doe v. Pulaski County Special School District* (2002), a school district "true threat" case derived from *Watts* established the definition of "true threat" to be a "statement that a reasonable recipient would have interpreted as a serious expression of an intent to harm or cause injury to another." The speaker must have intended to communicate his statement to another, and the element of a true threat is satisfied if the "speaker communicates the statement to the object of the purported threat or to a third party."[144] The *Doe* "true threat" definition was applied by the Eighth Circuit Court of Appeals in *D.J.M.*, in which a student intended that his instant message be received by another student, who was a third party and who interpreted the message as a serious expression to harm or cause injury to another person, thereby qualifying as a "true threat."[145] (See above summary of the case.)

Fraser Standard Vulgar or offensive speech may legitimately be the basis of disciplinary action by a school district because the school has a "responsibility in teaching students the boundaries of socially appropriate behavior."[146]

Schools generally argue that the expression at issue is not entitled to First Amendment protection because it is lewd, vulgar, and/or plainly offensive. In *Bethel School District No. 403 v. Fraser* (1986), the U.S. Supreme Court held that the First Amendment does not prevent school officials from punishing "vulgar and lewd . . . speech [that] would undermine the school's basic mission."[147] In *Fraser*, a student made a speech that included sexual references in a school assembly. The school administration suspended Fraser for several days. His speech did not cause a substantial and material disruption, but the Supreme Court held that the First Amendment does not prevent a school from punishing a student's lewd, vulgar, offensive, and/or inappropriate speech.[148]

The *Fraser* standard does not apply to off-campus speech. The Court asserted that the same type of expression would not be punished if spoken outside the schoolhouse gates.[149]

The *Fraser* standard was addressed in *T.V. v. Smith-Green.* Here, the U.S. District Court for the Northern District of Indiana stated that "the First Amendment protects entertainment as well as treatises on politics and public administration . . . [that] ridiculousness and inappropriateness are often the very foundation of humor."[150] In this case, teenage girls took raunchy photos at a slumber party, and then posted them online. The court concluded that the acts depicted in the photos, the taking or existence of the images, and the posting of the photographs to the Internet all qualify as speech within the meaning of the First Amendment, and that the students' conduct in the photographs was intended to be humorous.[151] The court further found that the sexual poses, objects, and activities were not considered obscene, child pornography, or deviate sexual conduct. In the final analysis, the court found that the school district violated the student's First Amendment rights.[152]

The *Fraser* standard was not met because it does not apply to off-campus speech, the substantial or material disruption standard was not met because the students cannot be punished for "nondisruptive speech," and the reasonably foreseeable standard was not met because a specific and significant fear of disruption did not exist. Administrators' reliance on a parent's complaint that the photographs had caused divisiveness on school extracurricular teams was found to be confusing. During their depositions, the superintendent stated that discipline was based on causing a disruption in the extracurricular teams, but in the principal's deposition, he stated that he did not rely on any actual disruption as a basis for the action he took.[153]

Hazelwood Standard As long as school officials' actions are "reasonably related to legitimate pedagogical concerns," educators are entitled to exercise editorial control over school-sponsored expressive activities such as school publications and theatrical productions. These controls "assure that participants learn whatever lessons the activity is designed to teach, that readers or listeners are not exposed to material that may be inappropriate for their level of maturity, and that the views of the individual speaker are not erroneously attributed to the school."[154]

In *Hazelwood School District v. Kuhlmeier* (1988), the U.S. Supreme Court recognized that "[a] school need not tolerate student speech that is inconsistent with its 'basic educational mission,' even though the government could not censor similar speech outside the school."[155] The Court created a distinction between school-sponsored speech and incidental expression when it held that school administrators could censor student writings from school-sponsored publications and activities as long as the restriction is based on "legitimate pedagogical concerns."[156] In *Hazelwood*, the principal ordered that two articles about teen pregnancy and the impact of divorce on teenagers be removed from the school newspaper that was published by the journalism class.[157]

Morse Standard Schools may also "take steps to safeguard those entrusted to their care from speech that can reasonably be regarded as encouraging illegal drug use."[158] The U.S. Supreme Court considered the special nature of the school environment and the serious and palpable dangers possessed by student drug use when it established this standard.[159]

In *Morse v. Frederick* (2007), a student was suspended from school for refusing to take down a fourteen-foot banner reading "BONG HiTS 4 JESUS" that he unfurled when students were permitted to line the public streets while the Olympic torch was passing in front of the school. The student's speech occurred off campus, but the U.S. Supreme Court considered it to be "on-campus speech" because it occurred during a school-sponsored and supervised event, during the school day, and while the student was standing among his fellow students, teachers, and administrators.[160]

The Court recognized that there is uncertainty about when courts should apply school speech precedents; however, the Court did not delineate a clear on-campus/off-campus distinction to apply to students' speech. The Supreme Court concluded that the substantial disruption rule of *Tinker* is not the only basis for restricting student speech, noting the special nature of the school environment and the governmental interest in preventing illegal drug use. "Schools may regulate some speech . . . even though the government could not censor similar speech outside the school."[161] The Court carved out another exception to *Tinker* by restricting student speech that advocates illegal drug use.[162] The location of where the speech is published is not the only focus in determining whether the school should consider the speech to be on campus or off campus.[163]

First Amendment: Higher-Education Speech Cases

Higher-education students are different from K–12 students in many ways. Some are adults, others are minors; some attend two-year programs, others attend four-year or longer programs; some attend undergraduate schools, others attend graduate or professional schools. Some attend private colleges, and others attend public universities. But all of the students have speech rights and responsibilities, whether granted by the First Amendment, college or university policies, rules, contracts, or other sources. Two social media cases involving speech rights of higher-education students illustrate how courts have dealt with higher-educational institutions' discipline of students' speech. Whether these principles would be applied in a cyberbullying case remains an open question.

In *Tatro v. University of Minnesota* (2012), the Supreme Court of Minnesota held that a private university did not violate the free speech rights of a student when the university disciplined her for her posts to a social networking website that violated the academic program rules.[164] The student, a Mortuary Science Program student, posted statements on Facebook that she thought only "friends" and "friends of friends" could see. The university's discipline focused on four of her posts about "Bernie," the name the student gave to the human cadaver that she and her anatomy laboratory classmates were using for training. One post referred to dissecting Bernie with her scalpel, one about releasing aggression with her trocar, one about updating her "Death List #5," and one about saying good-bye to Bernie.[165]

The university staff met to discuss the student's Facebook posts. Fears were expressed about the student stabbing someone with a trocar, other items posted on the student's Facebook page, and other episodes of school violence outside of Minnesota. University police were called, and they met with the student, who was directed to stay away from the Mortuary Science Department and staff members while they were investigating the matter. The student began sharing her punishments on Facebook and in other media. After this activity, the Anatomy Bequest Program that provides human cadavers for the Mortuary Science Program received letters and calls from donors' families and the general public expressing their concerns about the student's professionalism, poor judgment, and immaturity. At the end of the course, the student was notified that her Facebook postings violated the anatomy lab rules and policies of the Anatomy Bequest Program, and she was given an "F" for the course.[166]

The court considered various standards to apply to the case, but based on U.S. Supreme Court guidance that "the mode of analysis in *Tinker* is not absolute and that courts must consider the special characteristics of the school environment,"[167] it applied a standard that took into account the fact that the course was a professional program in which ethics are a fundamental part of the program. Accordingly, the court found that, considering curricular, professional, and ethics requirements, the university may regulate the student's speech on Facebook that violated established professional conduct standards, and that the university did not violate the student's First Amendment rights by disciplining her for her Facebook posts.[168]

In *Barnes v. Zaccari* (2012), the U.S. District Court for the Northern District of Georgia heard a civil rights claim brought by a student at Valdosta State University against the then president of the university for retaliation against the student for exercising his rights under the free speech clause of the First Amendment, and a claim that individuals at the university conspired to retaliate against his constitutionally protected speech when they had him administratively withdrawn (i.e., expelled) from the university.[169] The district court found that a counselor was not part of a conspiracy and that the president was not entitled to qualified immunity.[170] The president appealed the denial of qualified immunity and the district court's finding that the student's due process rights were violated to the Eleventh Circuit Court of Appeals. The Eleventh Circuit upheld the district court's finding that the president was not entitled to qualified immunity.[171]

The student, who was passionate about the environment, opposed a proposed campus parking structure and, in doing so, raised the ire of the university president. The student had passed out flyers, emailed members of the Board of Regents and other students, and electronically posted information and responses about the construction project on his Facebook page. After discovering that the president was inquiring about his activities, the student removed the flyers and postings on Facebook and wrote a letter to the president saying that this was not a personal attack on him and asked that it not result in an adverse response to his activities. However, he remained focused on his interest and created and posted a satirical collage on Facebook protesting the garage, and he contacted board members prior to their scheduled vote on the garage project.[172] The student did not intend to harm anyone.

The president met with the student, informing him that the student had personally embarrassed him and was making life difficult for him. The student continued to oppose the project by sending email messages and communicating with the editor of the student newspaper, among other means. After additional meetings with the student and university administrators, counselors, a psychologist, and faculty members to discuss the student, all of whom did not see the student as a threat to himself or to others, the president administratively removed the student from the university, claiming that the student presented a clear and present danger to the campus. The president claimed the student's Facebook collage, with satirical images of the president, constituted an emergency threat, which permitted the president to dismiss the student without any formal hearings.[173]

As to the student's claim of conspiracy to violate his First Amendment rights, the court stated that the student must show, among other things, that there was an understanding to violate the student's rights, that there must be more than a scintilla of evidence, and that one cannot just string together adverse acts of individuals to establish a conspiracy. The court found that because no evidence had been presented to support any of these requirements and the president alone made the decision to administratively withdraw the student, the conspiracy claim could not survive summary judgment. As to the due process claim, the court ruled that the student was deprived of his due process rights.[174] The U.S. Supreme Court had clearly established that a notice and a hearing are required before a student is terminated. The court remanded the case to the lower court.

Qualified Immunity

Qualified immunity is a complete protection for a school official sued in his/her individual capacity as long as his/her conduct violates no clearly established statutory or constitutional rights of which a reasonable person would have known. To claim qualified immunity, a defendant must first show that (s)he was performing a discretionary function. The burden then shifts to the plaintiff to show that (1) the defendant violated a constitutional right; and (2) the right was clearly established at the time of the violation.[175]

It remains unclear what First Amendment speech standards public officials should follow in the area of cyberbullying in social media. In *T.V. ex rel. B.V. v. Smith-Green School District* (2011), the court stated that many courts have granted qualified immunity to school personnel when they are sued individually because the second inquiry of the immunity standard—whether the constitutional right has been clearly established at the time of the alleged violation—cannot be met since the constitutional right at issue is not clearly established.[176] The *T.V.* court illustrated its conclusion by stating that, in *J.S. v. Blue Mountain School District* (2011), the majority, concurrence, and dissent each used a different standard, and in *J.C. v. Beverly Hills Unified School District*, the judge recognized five different approaches taken in "this murky area of the law" by the U.S. Supreme Court in *Morse v. Frederick*.[177]

In conclusion, there are many standards that the courts have chosen to apply in school speech cases. Cases involve students' First Amendment speech rights when cyberbullying and access in social media is unsettled and confusing.

School officials are placed in a position in which they must determine when "undifferentiated fear or apprehension of disturbance is sufficient to transform into a reasonable forecast that a substantial disruption or material interference will occur" and when the court will uphold their decisions.[178]

School districts are subject to the U.S. Supreme Court's decisions and the decisions of the courts of its jurisdiction. Generally, school districts must first determine whether the student's speech occurred on campus or off campus. But just because the speech occurred off campus does not mean that the court will consider the expression to have occurred off campus, thereby denying the school district the right to discipline the student—that is, the off-campus speech can be determined to be on-campus speech. After the on-campus or off-campus determination is made (i.e., whether it actually occurred on campus or is deemed to have occurred as on-campus speech), the school district must next determine whether the speech substantially and materially disrupted the school, whether a reasonable forecast of substantial disruption can be made, or whether the circumstances meet one of the additional above discussed standards, or whether the matter is actually conduct (i.e., not speech) that can be disciplined. So, too, criminal actions may be viable actions brought by law enforcement against students for their cyberbullying in social media.[179]

Defamation Cases

Beyond speech, there are additional claims that can be made by victims of cyberbullying in social media, one of which is defamation. Often a student will believe that what was posted or communicated was not true and "really, really hurts," prompting him/her to believe that he/she was defamed through either libel or slander. Libel is written defamation; slander is spoken defamation. This claim is, like many others, not as simple as "he said something untrue about me and it hurts."

In a defamation action, the plaintiff (the student who believed (s)he was cyberbullied by having something untrue and hurtful communicated about him or her) must prove the defamatory character of the communication, its publication by the defendant (cyberbully), its application to the plaintiff, the understanding by the recipient (the person who viewed, read, or heard the communication, typically a third person or persons) of its defamatory meaning, the understanding by the recipient that it was intended to be applied to the plaintiff, that special harm resulted to the plaintiff because of its publication, and that no privilege applied.[180]

The defendant must prove the truth of the defamatory communication, that a privilege applied to what was published, or that the character of the subject matter of the defamatory comment was of public concern.[181] For example, an opinion cannot be defamatory, but simply saying it was your opinion will not make it so. The court will look to determine whether a reasonable reader or listener would understand the statement to be an opinion or statement of verifiable fact.[182] Also, if a plaintiff is a public figure then (s)he must also prove "actual malice."[183]

For example, in *Finkel v. Daubert* (2010), the Supreme Court of Nassau County, New York, decided a case involving an adolescent who sued a Facebook group of adolescents and their parents for defamation.[184] The group, "90 Cents Short of a Dollar," had members who were referred to as "cents." Membership was by invitation only. The information page listed six "cents" as members, while the group's newsletter listed ten "cents" in their news. The adolescent-plaintiff claimed to be the eleventh "cent" referred to in some explicit posts that the court described as "adolescent insecurities and indulgences, and vulgar attempts at humor." The purpose of the group was listed as "just for fun" and "inside jokes." Allegedly, this was a secret group with no public content, and no reference to the group appeared in member Facebook profiles.

In addressing the defamation requirement that "the statement is false," the court reasoned that "only facts are capable of being proven false," and in this case, given that the statements made by the group could not meet the court's guidelines for finding that the posts were believable, they could not be considered facts. "The statements can only be read as puerile attempts by adolescents to outdo each other." The court denied the plaintiff-adolescent's motion. The attorney for the plaintiff-adolescent stated that the posts constituted cyberbullying. The court responded as follows in this 2010 case: "The Courts of New York do not recognize cyber or internet bullying as a cognizable tort action." After this case was decided, the New York legislature revised its definition of bullying to include cyberbullying, effective as of July 1, 2013.[185]

In another case, *D.C. v. R.R.* (2010),[186] a high school student and his parents brought, among others, a defamation action against other students and their parents for the students' posting of derogatory comments about D.C. and threatening him with bodily harm. In response, one of the student-defendants (R.R.) and his parents claimed that his comments were "jocular humor" entitled to First Amendment protection under the "strategic lawsuit against public participation" (SLAPP) statute (the purpose of an anti-SLAPP statute is to protect defendants from interference with the valid exercise of their constitutional rights, particularly the right of freedom of speech and the right to petition the government for the redress of grievances[187]).[188] The student-defendant had posted a message stating, in part, "I want to rip out your f**king heart and feed it to you. . . . I've . . . wanted to kill you. If I ever see you I'm . . . going to pound your head in with an ice pick. F**k you, you dick-riding penis lover. I hope you burn in hell." The trial court denied the anti-SLAPP motion on the ground that the lawsuit did not arise out of a statement made in connection with a "public issue."[189] Other students had posted additional false statements identifying him as a homosexual.[190]

The California Court of Appeals, Second District, Division 1, disagreed with the student-defendant, finding that he did not make the requisite showing that the posted message was protected speech, was intended as "jocular humor," and that assuming the message was a "joke"—played by one teenager on another—it did not concern a "public issue" under the statute. Therefore, D.C. was not subject to the anti-SLAPP statute.[191]

The court denied the defendant's petition, stating, "Under either a subjective or objective standard, defendants failed to show that the post, which they claimed was intended as jocular humor, was not a 'true threat.'" The court stated:

> Even assuming that R.R. believed that his message was humorous, he may still have intended it as a threat. Self-amusement and wrongful conduct are not mutually exclusive. . . . When teens were asked why they think others cyberbully, 81 percent said that cyberbullies think it is funny. The particular sense of humor attributable to this defendant does not lessen the seriousness of the legal consequences of his acts. Individuals of a completely distorted sense of humor or pranksters with juvenile minds have . . . induced fear by their acts. We reject R.R.'s argument that his statements were not "true threats" because they were merely "jests to show toughness and to establish a position among other students." (Citations omitted.)[192]

Accordingly, the court allowed the action to proceed to trial to determine whether R.R.'s message was a true threat.

Criminal defamation has also been used as a claim; however, whether it will be successful depends on, among other factors, the statute's constitutionality. In *In Re I.M.L.*, UT 110 (2002),[193] a sixteen-year-old student was charged under a one-hundred-year-old state criminal liable statute after he created a website listing various students and their purported sexual histories, and displaying disparaging statements about his teachers, classmates, and principal. In this specific action, the court made a determination that the Utah statute in question was unconstitutional and overbroad on its face, as it did not require "actual malice" and allowed prosecution for true statements. Accordingly, the court dismissed the charges filed against the student.[194]

A cybermessage that is believed to be false may be found to be defamatory and therefore not protected by the First Amendment. Proving that the message is a joke or humorous may mean that the joke or humorous statement qualifies as protected speech, but, at the same time, just because the cybermessage is intended to be humorous does not mean that it was not also intended to be a threat.

Harassment Cases, Statutes, and Regulations

To address cyberbullying, in addition to speech, defamation, and numerous other types of actions, students and parents bring cases based on Title IX of the Education Amendments of 1972 (Title IX), which prohibits discrimination on the basis of sex;[195] Title VI of the Civil Rights Act of 1964 (Title VI), which prohibits discrimination on the basis of race, color, or national origin;[196] Section

504 of the Rehabilitation Act of 1973 (Section 504);[197] Title II of the Americans with Disabilities Act of 1990 (Title II);[198] and the Individuals with Disabilities Act (IDEA),[199] which prohibits discrimination on the basis of disability. They also bring cases claiming the school violated the students' substantive due process and equal protection rights and use the U.S. Code § 1983, which is part of the Civil Rights Act.[200] The plaintiff-students/parents claim that the peer-to-peer bullying constituted harassment of a characteristic that was protected under the federal civil rights statutes and that the educational institution was a recipient of federal funds.

To state a claim under Section 1983, a student and/or parent "must allege the violation of a right secured by the Constitution and laws of the United States, and must show that the alleged deprivation was committed by a person acting under color of state law"[201]—for example, a public educational institution. "The court must consider (1) whether the Plaintiff [has] asserted the deprivation of a constitutional right and (2) whether the Board is responsible for that deprivation. To establish the Board's liability, [the] Plaintiff must demonstrate that an officially executed policy, or the toleration of a custom within the school district led to, caused, or resulted in the deprivation of a constitutionally protected right."[202]

Title IX *Davis v. Monroe County Board of Education* (1999), decided by the U.S. Supreme Court, supports a Title IX claim for student-on student sexual harassment when the plaintiff can demonstrate "(1) that the sexual harassment was so severe, pervasive, and objectively offensive that it could be said to deprive the plaintiff of access to the educational opportunities or benefit provided by the school, (2) the funding recipient had actual knowledge of the sexual harassment, and (3) that the funding recipient was deliberately indifferent to the harassment."[203] A "damage remedy will not lie under Title IX unless an official who at a minimum has authority to address the alleged discrimination and to institute corrective measures on the recipient's behalf has actual knowledge of discrimination in the recipient's programs and fails adequately to respond."[204]

A Title IX claim was decided by the U.S. District Court for the District of New Jersey in *Tafuto v. New Jersey Institute of Technology* (2012).[205] The court applied the *Davis* standard when it addressed a sexual harassment claim by a student who alleged other students ridiculed and bullied him. The students allegedly called him names, posted edited photographs on Facebook, and posted large posters in the classroom studio. The professor became aware of the conduct, felt empathetic for the student, but did not report it to the administration or discipline the students. Another student overheard the bullied victim say that "he wanted to kill some of his classmates," and the student reported it to the professor, who then reported it to the dean of students. The victim-student was removed from class, met with the dean and a psychologist, was suspended, and was required to undergo a psychiatric evaluation or risk assessment to determine his propensity to "kill" other students before he could return to school. The student refused to undergo the evaluation and was prohibited from returning to campus but was permitted to finish his semester at home. The student filed a suit to compel the Institute to allow him to return to campus without submitting to the evaluation.[206] The court denied his request because the dean's decision was reasonable, since the student used the word *kill*.[207]

The student's complaint alleged that, during his meeting with the dean, the student showed the dean the photos and informed him of the offensive depictions about him, and the following day the student and his parents met with the dean and again told him about the bullying. The victim-student and his family also alleged that the dean and Institute attorneys never investigated the matter, that the students continued to post harassing depictions of the student on the Internet, and that the Institute violated federal law[208] by allowing the students to sexually harass him after he gave the dean notice of it.[209] The dean claimed that he told the victim-student that he would investigate the matter after he submitted to the evaluation.[210]

The court rejected the Institute's response that it did not have actual knowledge of the harassment because the professor was aware of the harassment, the harassing photos were placed in classroom windows and were visible from the outside, photos were posted on the Institute's projects web pages and on the student Facebook pages, and the dean and school attorneys were aware of the activities after the student told them.[211] After the victim-student was suspended, the harassment continued when he was off campus, but the Institute did not respond.[212] Consequently, the court, after reviewing whether the Institute's conduct was deliberately indifferent, stated, "There are questions of facts regarding the Institute's investigation, and/or actions that occurred after it had knowledge of the harassing activity which may constitute deliberate indifference."[213] Consequently, the court denied the Institute's motion to dismiss, thereby permitting the student's case to proceed against the Institute.

Sexting Cases and Statutes In another Title IX case involving sexting, *Logan v. Sycamore Community School Board* (2011), decided by the U.S. District Court for the Southern District of Ohio,[214] the parents of a deceased student brought suit against the school district (for failing to protect the student from harassment), individual students (who allegedly harassed her), a school resource officer (SRO) (who was an employee of the city but worked with school district students), and the city of Montgomery (which was the employer of the SRO).

The individual students settled their cases with the parents.[215] The SRO and city were dismissed from the case when the court granted qualified immunity to them. The victim-parents accused the SRO of being responsible for increasing the risk of harm to the victim-student when he allegedly encouraged her to appear on a television show about bullying. The SRO actually gave the victim-student the television reporter's telephone number, but the victim-student's parents agreed to her being interviewed, and the victim-student thought it would be a good thing to raise awareness about the pitfalls of bullying. The SRO was surprised when her parents consented to the television interview.[216]

The school district was not dismissed from the case.[217] The victim-student's parents' complaint alleged that the school district violated her civil rights under Title IX and her due process rights under the Fourteenth Amendment. Regrettably, the student committed suicide after suffering harassment from other high school students who were "sexting" a nude picture of the student, from the neck down. The parents alleged that the student sought help from a school guidance counselor, who referred her to the SRO, who allegedly told her that he could ask the students to delete the photo from their cell phones but that there was nothing else he could do.[218] Ostensibly, the SRO advised the student to submit to a television interview on the subject of "sexting." The parents alleged that after the interview the harassment became worse, including, among other actions, harassing her over the telephone and online.[219]

The school district "contend[ed] reasonable minds could not conclude that the Board or any of its employees possessed knowledge that Sycamore High School students had subjected the student to sexual harassment." It stated that no report was made to anyone, the SRO did not tell the administrators about the photo or harassment, and the statements about the harassment made by the student's mother to a teacher did not establish knowledge of sexual- or gender-related harassment.[220]

The U.S. District Court for the Southern District of Ohio found that material issues of fact existed as to whether school district's policies deprived the student of her rights. In addition, the court stated that the names ("porn queen," "slut," "whore," etc.) that the student was allegedly called after the photo began circulating supported the parents' contention that the student was being sexually harassed. "[The Principal and Assistant Principals] are all appropriate persons as they each had authority and responsibility under school district policies to investigate sexual harassment complaints and enforce sexual harassment and bullying policies."[221] The court agreed with the parents that these individuals either knew that the student's photograph was being circulated at the school or viewed the television interview in which she described the harassment she faced at school. The court stated that "appropriate persons do not need to be aware of the exact details of a [student's] experience to have notice, as long as they 'reasonably could have responded with remedial measures to address the kind of harassment' that was reported." "Applying this standard the court found that the parents demonstrated that sufficient facts were in dispute."[222] Therefore, the court did not dismiss the school district from the case, allowing the case to proceed on both the sexual harassment and the equal protection claims.[223]

In *Tyrrell v. Seaford Union Free School District* (2011),[224] the U.S. District Court for the Eastern District of New York heard a Title IX case involving student sexual harassment and a due process claim. A female high school student went drinking with friends and their acquaintances one night when she allegedly became drunk, was subjected to a sexual assault by another female student in a vehicle at a Dunkin' Donuts parking lot, and was videotaped by some of the boys in attendance, who then posted the video on the photo-sharing website Photobucket.com. Ostensibly, the student did not remember much of what happened and discovered her actions through the video recording.[225]

A social worker and counselor at the Seaford Union Free School District (SUFSD) was notified by a social worker employed by a neighboring school district about the posted video and the SUFSD student. A student at the neighboring school told his social worker about the incident. The SUFSD social worker called the victim-student to her office, interviewed her about the incident, asked if she was all right, and told her that she wanted to call the victim-student's parents. According to the social worker, the student seemed upbeat, was more angry than upset, and told her that a few students made snide remarks to her but that she was fine. The social worker worked with others to have the images removed from the Internet. The victim-student specifically said that she did not want her parents contacted. The social worker believed that she was subject to confidentiality obligations of the New York State Office of Mental Health and Drug Abuse; however, the superintendent believed that the parents should be contacted because the incident could present a danger to the health and safety of the student. After consultation with the school's attorney, the school notified the student's parents. The harassment and bullying increased, even after the parents removed the student from school and while she was being homeschooled.[226]

Reports arose that images of the student's incident were placed as "wallpaper" on school district library and computer lab computers by a student. School district policy prohibited such action, and after a technology department review of system activity, the purported wallpaper incident did not appear to have occurred. The school district reportedly complied with the Federal Children's Internet Protection Act (CIPA) requirements for creating and enforcing an Internet policy and implementing technology protection measures (i.e., e-Rate requirements).[227] CIPA and the Neighborhood Children's Internet Protection Act (NCIPA) require an acceptable use policy by school districts and that they block/filter school district web services who receive e-Rate funds.[228] Congress amended the Acts "to educate minors about appropriate online behavior, including interacting with other individuals on social networking websites and in chat rooms and cyberbullying awareness and response."[229]

The *Tyrrell* court granted the school district's motion to dismiss the case in its entirety. According to the court, the student could not establish a Title IX sexual harassment claim based on sexual orientation, the school district did not have actual notice of any alleged sexual harassment by her peers (here she asked the court to find the school district had constructive notice of the harassment, which the court held to be insufficient), and the school district could not be found to be deliberately indifferent where the school district did not have control over the alleged harassment and did not have the authority to take remedial action. The court found that the school district had "responded expeditiously and reasonably once being notified even though the assault occurred off of school grounds, during non-school hours, and by an individual who was not a student of the Seaford Union Free School District."[230]

In addition, the student's claims that the school district did not take any disciplinary action against the perpetrator and that it did not immediately alert the student's parents about the photos were unsuccessful. The perpetrator had never been identified, so the school would have had to discover the identity by contacting each student in the school district, which would have "been unfeasible, unnecessary and unsound because it would have further disseminated the information about the images that the student did not want disclosed and even after her mother was told about the images and the police were aware of the incident the student was still harassed."[231]

As to the due process claim, the court stated that the student may have a property interest to a free and appropriate public education (FAPE), but she did not demonstrate that she was deprived in any way of a FAPE by the school district's conduct.[232]

Title VI Courts have recognized a Title VI private right of action against public educational institutions that receive federal funds if the violations alleged involve intentional discrimination by the funding recipient on the basis of race, color, and/or national origin. Deliberate indifference is found if the school administrator "responds to known peer harassment in a manner that is . . . clearly unreasonable."[233] This standard is the same for both Title IX and Title VI.[234] Liability only arises if a plaintiff establishes (1) substantial control by the funding recipient over the harasser, (2) severe and discriminatory harassment, (3) actual knowledge, and (4) deliberate indifference.[235]

A Title VI claim was decided by the U.S. District Court for the Western District of Texas in *Fennell et al. v. Marion Independent School District* (2013).[236] Students claimed that the school district was aware of the racial harassment and bullying by teachers, coaches, administrators, and students. An eighteen-year-old African American student claimed that she was subjected to racial discrimination from the time she was in first grade. She alleged that racially based comments, taunts, and electronic images were sent by text messages and placed on social media websites. For example, white students sent the student a text message with an animation of a Klansman swinging a noose to the tune of a popular song. Also, she stated that the students tormented her when she tried out for the cheerleading team and then, when she made the team, excluded her from some cheerleading activities and ostracized her. Further, a white coach/teacher said in front of others that the student was a bad influence because she had had a child at the age of seventeen; the fiancé of the teacher who made the comment confronted the student's mother about her Facebook post (about the teacher's comments), and he was then escorted from a basketball game. The student was subjected to numerous additional alleged verbal attacks and discriminatory incidents.[237]

The student's mother, fearful for the student's safety, filed Title VI and Equal Protection claims against the school district and some of its employees. The court dismissed the claims against the individual employees as redundant and ruled that they were entitled to qualified immunity. The court dismissed the claims against the school district, stating that the student failed to allege sufficient facts for its § 1983 and Title VI claims, but they permitted the student to amend her complaint to include additional facts to support her claims by March 14, 2013. The student filed a Second Amended Complaint on March 14, 2013.[238] No ruling has been made at the time of this writing.

Civil Rights and Other Statutes, Educational Institutions' Policies Courts have applied the *Davis* standard when § 504 and ADA claims are filed against educational institutions. Other statutes could be applicable. Examples include when peer harassment is claimed to deny the student of a "free appropriate public education" under the IDEA 2004,[239] and state statues. For example, criminal harassment charges have been brought against cyberbullies.

In May 2011, prosecutors in King County, Washington, charged two eleven-year-old girls in juvenile court with first-degree computer trespass and cyberstalking under Washington state law.[240] This action stemmed from their online harassment of a classmate by illegally accessing and defacing her Facebook account. The Washington statute imposes criminal liability on an individual who "without authorization, intentionally gain(s) access to a computer system or electronic database of another; and (a) the access is made with the intent to commit another crime."[241]

Under Washington state law, cyberstalking occurs when an individual "with intent to harass, intimidate, torment, or embarrass any other person, and under circumstances not constituting telephone harassment, makes an electronic communication to such other person or a third party: (a) [u]sing any lewd, lascivious, indecent, or obscene words, images, or language, or suggesting the commission of any lewd or lascivious act; (b) [a]nonymously or repeatedly whether or not conversation occurs; or (c) [t]hreatening to inflict injury on the person or property of the person called or any member of his or her family or household."[242]

Because the names of juveniles and juvenile court actions are typically held confidential, further public information about this case is not available at this time.[243] Educational institutions' anti-harassment, discipline, and other policies can also form the basis of challenges and defenses.

Substantive Due Process The due process clause of the U.S. Constitution provides that a state shall not "deprive any person of life, liberty, or property without due process of law."[244] Generally, courts have ruled that educational institutions are not required to protect students from harm inflicted by private actors (i.e., classmates), except "(1) where a state or local government agency takes a person into custody and restrains his/her liberty, such that it renders the person unable to care for herself [also referred to as the 'special relationship' exception, or custody exception]; and (2) the 'state-created danger' exception when the state takes an affirmative act to increase the risk of harm to its citizens."[245] Courts have found that the first exception is not applicable to school districts.[246] For the state-created danger exception to apply, according to the Sixth Circuit Court of Appeals, the plaintiff must show: (1) school personnel either created or increased the risk that the student would be exposed to an act of violence by a third party; (2) the school's actions subjected the student to a special danger and placed her specifically at risk (as distinguished from a risk that affects the public at large); and (3) the school district knew or should have known that its actions specifically endangered the student.[247]

Equal Protection To succeed on an equal protection claim, the student and/or his/her parent(s) must show that the state actor (educational institution) intentionally discriminated against the student because of the student's membership in a protected class (for example, sex, race, or disability), and that school officials were deliberately indifferent to the allegations of student-on-student bullying and harassment. Deliberate indifference can be shown by the actions and/or inactions of the defendant-educational institution in light of the known circumstances.[248] Essentially, the plaintiff-student must show that he received adverse treatment compared to other similarly situated individuals and that the selective treatment was based on impermissible considerations (such as sex, race, or religion) to inhibit or punish the exercise of constitutional rights, or malicious or bad faith intent to injure a person.[249] In *Shively v. Green Local School District Board of Education et al.*[250] and *G.D.S. v. Northport-East Northport Union Free School District*,[251] courts addressed substantive due process and equal protection claims combined with many other claims.

In *Shively v. Green Local School District Board of Education* (2013),[252] the U.S. District Court for the Northern District of Ohio considered civil rights actions filed by parents of a minor student against the school district alleging that the school board and employees of the school district failed to prevent or respond to gender- and religion-based bullying (electronic, physical, and verbal) and harassment directed at their daughter, T.S. They claimed violations of her constitutional rights—substantive due process, equal protection, First Amendment, and free exercise of religion—and Title IX, Monell (action against the board), and negligence claims, and challenged the school district's statutory immunity claims. The court ruled on the school district's motion for judgment on the pleadings and dismissal for lack of subject-matter jurisdiction, denying dismissal of the substantive due process, equal protection, gender discrimination, Monell (inaction), and negligence claims, thereby permitting them to remain pending against the school district.

In this case, T.S. identified herself as Jewish. Several students created a Facebook page asking students to join if they believed she was a whore. The mother of one of the girls who created the page posted comments on the page. Examples of the bullying and harassment included: two students creating a "kill list," which included T.S. as a target; harassing her with numerous hateful and verbal assaults related to her religion;[253] kicking her into lockers while she was walking in the hallway; tripping, shoving, hitting, kicking, and knocking her books out of her hands on a regular basis; spitting on her in the bus; stabbing her in the leg with a pencil during class, resulting in her being transported to an urgent-care center; and being assaulted by a boy in the choir room, resulting in an injury that required her to be taken to the hospital and use crutches for several weeks.[254]

In April 2008, after months of bullying and harassment, T.S.'s mother informed school district administrators about the bullying and cyberbullying and told the superintendent that she would keep T.S. out of school until the situation was addressed. T.S. was kept out of school for a week, but her mother returned T.S. to school even though nothing was done to address the situation. After returning T.S. to school, the bullying and harassment continued. In January 2011, three weeks after the administrators had assured her mother that the perpetrators would never be able to set foot in the high school again, one of the perpetrators was seen in the cafeteria. Again, the bullying and harassment continued. Finally, in September 2011, T.S. was offered an alternative placement.[255]

The court, in responding to the many claims, found that the parents pled facts that "credibly supported a state created danger claim" (i.e., that "school district employees turned a blind eye to T.S. and her parents") and that the "employees allegedly made conscious choices and took the affirmative steps to disregard [the mother's] complaints and to permit gender- and religion-based bullying in violation of T.S.'s substantive due process rights."

Next, the court found that the parents stated a possible claim under the equal protection clause because the administrator told the mother that the perpetrators would never set foot in the high school again, but one of the perpetrators was seen by T.S. in the cafeteria just three weeks after the incident. The court stated that the administrators' actions and/or inactions would allow for the inference that the students were not expelled or disciplined in any meaningful way.[256] Additionally, the Court stated:

> Despite the defendants knowing that T.S. had withdrawn from school because of the pervasive bullying and due to the school district's failure to address it, and despite knowing that T.S. was out of school and being asked by Lisa Shively to find an alternative placement for T.S., the school district defendant and defendant Nutter took three weeks to place T.S. in a suitable alternative public school, while providing only two hours per day of tutoring for part of that three-week period, thus depriving T.S. of her educational opportunities for that period of time.
>
> According to Plaintiffs, T.S. had to withdraw from the Green Local School District in October 2011 because of the daily, day-long harassment which was driving her to depression. T.S. spent three weeks out of school, with minimal tutoring, before Defendants found another school for her to attend.[257]

Next, the court found that the parents provided sufficient facts for a plausible gender discrimination claim under Title IX of the Civil Rights Act, but not a claim for student-on-student harassment based on religion.[258] Also, the court found that the parents' claim against the board met the plausibility standard for violations of the Fourteenth Amendment in which the parents could state violations of the student's constitutional rights (substantive due process and equal protection), and where the board had constructive knowledge through the administrators but turned a blind eye toward the incidents brought to its attention by the parents ("by tacitly approving bullying, and not enforcing its anti-bullying policies") through inaction: "By their inaction, the Board actually created a policy tacitly approving bullying; thus violating [the parent's] rights."[259] Finally, the court let the negligence claims survive for possible use at a later stage in the proceedings.[260]

In *G.D.S. v. Northport-East Northport Union Free School District* (2012),[261] the U.S. District Court for the Eastern District of New York also addressed religion-based bullying (electronic and verbal), harassment, and civil rights claims, among others, filed by the parents against the school district and some administrators. The parents claimed that the administrators were deliberately indifferent to the student-on-student religious harassment of their minor son and that he was discriminated against based on his creed.[262]

At first, students called G.D.S. names and made various overt anti-Semitic comments and jokes about him in front of others. But the insults and jokes grew worse in severity, including disgusting and tormenting insults and actions based on the acts of Germans taken against Jews during the Holocaust. Then one student-perpetrator placed anti-Semitic slurs and photos with anti-Semitic captions on Facebook about G.D.S. for his classmates to read. For an English class essay assignment, G.D.S. wrote an essay titled "Anti-Semitism," in which he wrote "it gets lonely in school" and recounted specific incidents in which he was the subject of anti-Semitic slurs. The teacher read and edited the essay, but neither she nor the administration took any action in response to the incidents in the essay.[263]

Months later, the parents became aware of the extent of the harassment and bullying. They requested a meeting with administrators, at which they asked them to take steps to protect G.D.S. and provided the administrators with a list of slurs and copies of the Facebook messages. The administration told the parents that they would investigate and take remedial measures to protect G.D.S., such as meeting with social studies teachers to instruct them to discuss the issue of tolerance in class by the end of the school year; having a "tolerance week" at the start of the next school year; and modifying the curriculum to include religious tolerance. The court stated that "it appears that these offered measures were not done."[264] The principal and a school social worker met with G.D.S. and reportedly told G.D.S. "that he should consider what the bullies were going through at home."

There were only two meetings between the school, the parents, and G.D.S. The harassment continued and, according to the court, "no one from the school administration ever contacted the student or his parents about the incident and it appears that no action was ever taken to address the bullying."[265] Toward the end of the school year, G.D.S. resubmitted his essay, and his mother spoke with the social worker about the slurs, but, according to the court, "it appears no action was ever taken to address the slurs."[266] During the summer, additional anti-Semitic Facebook postings continued. "Due to the anti-Semitic harassment and the [school district's] 'deliberate indifference,' [G.D.S.] decided not to return to the Northport High School."[267] The court denied the school district's request to dismiss the equal protection and creed claims. Therefore, these claims were permitted to proceed against the school district.

In *Shively* and *G.D.S.*, students and their parents brought constitutional claims (e.g., equal protection and substantive due process) and Title IX claims against educational institutions. They won when they opposed the educational institutions' motions to dismiss because the educational institutions and/or administrators did not attend to the bullying and harassment in a meaningful way. Conversely, students and parents have been unsuccessful when the educational institutions enforced their policy(ies), complied with state and federal laws as they investigated bullying and harassment claims, provided students with their procedural rights and protections, and disciplined students by considering their legal rights and other relevant issues. *Zimmerman v. Board of Trustees of Ball State University* is illustrative.

In *Zimmerman v. Board of Trustees of Ball State University* (2013),[268] the U.S. District Court for the Southern District of Indiana denied the summary judgment motion of the students and granted the summary judgment motion of the university when students claimed harassment and privacy violations by the university, and the university defended its position by relying on a state statute, their school policy, and an agreement entered into by the students and the university.

Zimmerman and his roommate, Sumwalt, lived off campus with another student, whom the court named "Target." During a school vacation while Target was out of the apartment, the students placed a sandwich in his bedroom to rot and locked the door to prevent Target from entering his room. At the beginning of the new school year, the students moved out of the apartment with Target. But they continued to harass him by creating a fictitious Facebook page for a female high school sophomore named Ashley and initiating conversations with Target. The students also secured a fifteen-year-old student at a high school (Emily) to pose as Ashley in cell phone and text message communications with Target. Eventually, Target asked Ashley if they could meet and go to a movie together. Ashley agreed and continued to communicate with Target. When Target entered the theater lobby, the students videotaped him and told him that Ashley was fictitious and that Target was actually communicating with them. Then the students posted the video on YouTube with the title "[Target] is a pedophile." The devices used, the location of the events, and the computers, electronic services, and networks involved were not the property of the university.[269]

Target complained about the harassment to the university and detailed the events. He informed administrators that he was having trouble focusing on school because he was in the same program as the perpetrator-students, that he was a nervous wreck, that he was having trouble sleeping at night, that he was worried about what type of bullying he might be a victim of next, and that he had sought medical advice and was prescribed Zoloft, a drug used to treat depression, obsessive-compulsive disorder, and panic and anxiety disorders.[270]

The university notified the students that they had violated the university's conduct code harassment and privacy sections, after which the students met with a university official to discuss the allegations. The students admitted to their actions and their violation of the university policy. They signed a writing agreeing to the admissions and policy violations. After deliberation, the university disciplined the students by suspending them for one year, requiring them "to raise awareness of fellow students regarding the responsible use of social media," and placing them on "probation upon their return, continu[ing] the restrictions against making contact with [Target], and a meeting with [the disciplinary office] prior to their return."[271] The students appealed the sanctions, claiming the sanctions were too harsh (they thought the sanctions emphasized punishment instead of rehabilitation and/or academic growth), and they objected to the investigation process, the meeting, the evidence, and that their honesty and cooperation were not taken into consideration. The university upheld the disciplinary action.[272]

As a result of the university upholding its sanctions, the students filed § 1983 First Amendment, due process, and institutional liability actions in court, essentially claiming that the university did not have the legal authority to regulate their conduct because it took place off campus, and even if the university had the authority to regulate their off-campus conduct, the students' actions did not violate the code of conduct. The university responded by stating that its actions were within its authority and that the students waived their objections to the university applying the code of conduct when they provided a written statement agreeing that they violated the code. In addition, the university stated that the students received due process and that they did not engage in protected speech.[273]

The court found that the university had the authority to regulate the students' off-campus conduct under a state statute[274] because the conduct was "objectionable and it violated the Conduct Code's provisions which were designed to protect the academic community from conduct presenting a serious threat to members of the community."[275] The students' "catfishing"[276] mission was an attempt to involve Target in a criminal scheme. The court stated that "no reasonable jury could conclude that the students' entire scheme . . . was not objectionable."[277] In addition, the court stated that the students did not bring a viable due process claim.

Finally, the court heard the students' claim that their conduct was protected by the First Amendment because their conduct involved communications. In this claim, the students argued that the sandwich incident was "communication" to express their dissatisfaction and frustration with Target's behavior so he would change it, that the Facebook incident was "clearly communications," and that posting the video was a "communication" that would be seen by others at the university and embarrass him.[278] The university responded by asserting that intending to express an idea does not necessarily amount to speech, that this conduct was not protected speech, and that the communications were not protected because they were false.[279]

The court addressed the students' Facebook claim,[280] declaring that some false speech is protected and other false speech is not protected; for false speech to not be protected, it must be a knowing or reckless falsehood.[281] In this case, the court stated that the students knew the communications were false and that "they were made knowingly and in furtherance of a scheme to inflict emotional harm on the Target." In addition, the court stated, "It appeared . . . that these communications fall within the type [of false speech] which do not enjoy constitutional protection." However, the court concluded that falsity is "not irrelevant to [the Court's] analysis, but neither [is] it determinative."[282] Consequently, the court found that it did not need to make that determination because the administrators "enjoyed qualified immunity because the students' right to protection for the speech was not clearly established at the time of the alleged violation so that a reasonable public official would have known that his conduct was unlawful."[283]

In a nutshell, on the one hand, the students claimed that the educational institution did not have the legal authority to regulate their conduct. On the other hand, the educational institution claimed that it did have the legal authority. The court agreed with the educational institution that it did have the legal authority under its university policy, state statute, and agreement with the students. The students' speech (communication) was not protected by the First Amendment, and even if it was protected by the First Amendment, the administrators were granted qualified immunity because the student's right to protection was not clearly established.

The United States Department of Education Office of Civil Rights (OCR) Dear Colleague Letter The OCR sent a "Dear Colleague Letter" on October 26, 2010, to school districts issuing guidance that student behavior classified as bullying may violate not only relevant school policies but also federal civil rights laws.[284] OCR stated that school districts are responsible for tackling harassment based on federally protected classes that "is sufficiently severe, pervasive, *or* persistent" about which "it *knew or should have known*" that "interferes with or limits a student's ability to participate in or benefit from the services, activities or opportunities offered by the school."[285] The National School Boards Association's (NSBA) Counsel of School Attorneys (COSA) took issue with the Letter by responding to OCR's alteration[286] of the U.S. Supreme Court's ruling in *Davis*, which is discussed in the Title IX section above. *Davis* states that "a private damages action could be filed against a Title IX funding recipient for peer harassment only when the recipient acted with deliberate indifference to *known acts* of harassment in its programs or activities. An action would lie only for sexual harassment that was so severe, pervasive, *and* objectively offensive that it could be said to deprive the Plaintiff of access to the educational opportunities or benefits provided by the school, and the knowledge of the sexual harassment and that the funding recipient was deliberately indifferent to the harassment."[287]

Essentially, COSA's positions include two primary points, among others. First, that in *Davis* the U.S. Supreme Court held school districts to an "actual knowledge" standard, whereas OCR broadened the standard to hold school districts to a "knew or should have known" standard, which could subject school districts to greater litigation.[288] Second, where *Davis* requires unlawful harassment to be severe, pervasive, *and* objectively offensive (all three), the OCR Letter states that unlawful harassment is severe, pervasive, *or* persistent (one of the three). Additional areas of conflict are addressed in the letter. Assistant Secretary Ali's response from OCR to COSA stated that its standard is "not new and do[es] not expand the standard of liability for administrative enforcement of federal civil rights laws with respect to harassment, and that they apply in administrative enforcement and in court cases where plaintiffs are seeking injunctive relief." Ali further responded that "the standards OCR uses for administrative enforcement are different from liability standards established in

Davis for private lawsuits seeking monetary damages . . . the Court limited the liability standards established in *Gebser* and *Davis* to private actions for money damages."[289]

OCR and COSA do not appear to agree on the degree to which a school district can be held responsible for peer-to-peer bullying. Schools need to be cautious when they adopt language for their cyberbullying policies. In addition to federal laws, state harassment and anti-bullying laws need to be considered in this extremely complicated area. See also the letter from Eugene Volokh, professor of law, UCLA, to the U.S. Commission on Civil Rights on May 13, 2011, expressing concern, caution, and challenging the position taken by OCR in the Dear Colleague Letter.[290]

After the exchange of letters, generally courts have adhered to *Davis* for liability purposes. For example, shortly after the exchange of letters occurred, the U.S. District Court for the Eastern District of New York held a school district to the higher OCR standard in *T.K. and S.K. v. New York City Department of Education* (2011).[291] On the other hand, after *T.K.*, the U.S. Court of Appeals for the Eleventh Circuit in *Long v. Murray County School District* (2013)[292] followed *Davis*, rejecting OCR's authority to broaden the Section 504 statute by regulation. In *Long* and subsequent cases, the courts have stated that OCR's interpretations exceed controlling law, even where agency regulation is usually afforded deference.[293] See also the discussions of this issue and the *Long* case in chapter 3, "Cyberbullying in Social Media: Parents," in this book. To date, no courts appear to have adopted the reasoning of the *T.K.* decision.

The U.S. Department of Education's Office of Special Education and Rehabilitative Services (OSERS), on August 20, 2013, also issued a "Dear Colleague Letter." In the letter OSERS provided a summary of a school district's responsibilities under IDEA 2004 to address bullying of students with disabilities. The letter states that "bullying of a student with a disability that results in the student not receiving meaningful educational benefit constitutes a denial of a free appropriate education (FAPE) under the IDEA that must be remedied."[294]

In conclusion, school employees must respond to reports and notifications of incidents of cyberbullying and harassment in a legally appropriate manner. Educational institutions need policies to address unlawful harassment and cyberbullying based on numerous considerations, whether, as illustrated above, based on race, religion, sex, creed, national origin, disability, retaliation, false accusation, or some other basis. Harassment should not be defined too broadly or too narrowly. Cyberbullying is broader than harassment. Cyberbullying is not divided into classes or traits; not all students who violate a bullying/cyberbullying policy also violate an unlawful harassment policy. The basis of a cyberbullying case could be brought under Title IV, Title IX, the ADA, § 504, IDEA, equal protection, substantive due process, and state harassment laws, as well as child abuse, negligent reporting, wrongful death, intentional infliction of emotional distress, defamation, invasion of privacy, negligence, negligent supervision, extortion, and many other actions, depending on the facts of the particular case.

Invasion of Privacy Cases

The deliberate posting of another person's private information on a social media website could render the poster subject to civil liability under the torts of invasion of privacy, which include the following: (1) intrusion upon seclusion (e.g., posting nude or seminude photos, stolen documents);[295] (2) public disclosure of private facts (e.g., hidden camera images);[296] (3) false light (e.g., Photoshopped images);[297] and (4) appropriation of name and likeness.[298]

In *State of New Jersey v. Dharun Ravi* (2012), Dharun Ravi, a Rutgers University student and roommate of Tyler Clementi, used a camera to secretly film and stream his roommate's intimate sexual encounter with another student at Rutgers University on September 19 and 21, 2010. Ravi allegedly did this to intimidate Tyler Clementi and his friend (MB) because of Tyler's sexual orientation.[299] After Tyler Clementi committed suicide by jumping off the George Washington Bridge,[300] Ravi allegedly attempted to hinder the investigation by tampering with the electronic evidence. He was indicted on fifteen counts: four counts of invasion of privacy, four counts of bias intimidation, three counts of tampering with physical evidence, three counts of hindering apprehension or prosecution, and one count of witness tampering.[301]

Ravi was found guilty by a jury on March 16, 2012, of all counts in the indictment (four counts of invasion of privacy, four counts of bias intimidation, and seven counts of hindering and tampering), but he was acquitted of the subquestions of whether he had tried to intimidate Tyler Clementi's friend (MB) due to his sexuality.[302] On May 21, 2012, Ravi was sentenced to three years' probation, thirty days in county jail, three hundred hours of community service, counseling on cyberbullying and alternative lifestyles, and a $10,000 assessment.[303] Ravi appealed the case on May 23, 2012.[304] On June 19, 2012, Ravi was released from jail after serving twenty days of his thirty-day sentence.[305] See the above "Cyberbullying in Social Media: It Really, Really Hurts" section about Tyler Clementi and the formation of the Clementi Center at Rutgers University.

Tyler Clementi, the student-victim, had privacy rights from being secretly video recorded and published online. The court ruled the student-bully had invaded his privacy. In another student privacy case, *R.S. v. Minnewaska Area School District*, the court tackled the issue of whether a student has a right to keep her Facebook password secret from school district administrators who are conducting an investigation.

In *R.S. v. Minnewaska Area School District* (2012), a twelve-year-old sixth-grade student posted two messages on her Facebook "wall" for which she was disciplined by her school. The first post was meant to be read by her "friends" only. Essentially, the post stated that she hated a particular hall monitor because the woman was mean to her. The message was posted from home, outside of school hours, and was inaccessible from school computers. One of her friends viewed and recorded the post, which made its way to the principal, who considered the message to be "impermissible bullying."[306] The principal required her to apologize to the hall monitor and gave R.S. a detention for her "rude/discourteous" behavior. Her second post—"I want to know who the f%$# [*sic*] told on me"—also resulted in disciplinary actions. She received a one-day in-school suspension and was prohibited from attending a class ski trip for "insubordination" and "dangerous, harmful, and nuisance substances and articles."[307]

Later, school officials received a complaint from a male student's guardian that the boy and R.S. were communicating about sexual topics over the Internet. The school officials called R.S.'s mother, telling her that the boy had admitted to the conduct. Later that same day, the school officials called R.S. out of class to ask her about the communications, to which she admitted "talking about 'naughty things' with her classmate over the Internet, off school grounds, and outside school hours."[308] After returning to class, she claimed that she was called out of class again the same day for a meeting in an administrative office with the school's counselor, local deputy sheriff assigned to the school district, and a school employee whom R.S. did not know (her mother was not present), where she was questioned again about the communications and required to provide them with her email and Facebook usernames and passwords. R.S. stated that she did not remember them and claimed that the officials called her a liar and threatened her with detention if she did not provide them, so she disclosed them. The officials allegedly used them to view her public and private Facebook messages to find the naughty discussion, but she was "not sure if they searched her private email account because she could not see the computer screen."[309] However, R.S. maintained that they found additional messages in which R.S. had used profanity and had taken "Facebook fun and funny sex quizzes and had posted the results of those quizzes, and that the school officials examined her private correspondence."[310] Purportedly, they did not ask permission to search, and she was "intimidated, frightened, humiliated, and sobbing while she was detained."[311] Apparently, she did not return to school for two days, fell behind in school, and felt less safe and secure at school. She also claimed that she was not the only student for whom school officials acquired their private information and searched their private communications.[312]

R.S.'s allegations included "that school officials forced R.S. to involuntarily surrender her Facebook and e-mail passwords upon their learning that R.S. and one of her classmates had an out-of-school sex-related conversation,"[313] that school officials violated her Fourth Amendment rights by searching her private Facebook account, and that they violated her right to free speech. She also asserted additional claims of conspiracy, invasion of privacy, intentional infliction of emotion distress, and failure to train or supervise employees, among others. The school district argued that it did not violate her constitutional rights and that the school officials were entitled to qualified immunity because her rights were not clearly established at the time of her conduct.[314]

The U.S. District Court of Minnesota's decision was rendered in the early stages of the case, in which only the student's side of the facts were presented in a motion to dismiss. The U.S. District Court of Minnesota decided that the school district's motion to dismiss the case (because its employees were not motivated by and conducting themselves with a "continuing, widespread, persistent pattern of unconstitutional conduct") was denied (where R.S. alleged that multiple students were punished for off-school online activities and experienced similar searches of their private communications), and that, if the facts were true, the student's First Amendment speech and Fourth Amendment search constitutional rights were violated and that the school district's qualified immunity argument would not be successful because the law was clearly established through cases such as *Tinker*, *Morse*, *D.J.M.*, *Layshock*, *J.S. v. Blue Mountain School District*, *New Jersey v. T.L.O*, and others at the time of her conduct.[315]

As to the First Amendment speech claim, the court stated that if the facts were true, the school district violated the student's free speech rights because the "out-of-school statements by the students . . . [were] protected . . . and not punishable by school authorities unless they were true threats or [were] reasonably calculated to reach the school environment and [were] so egregious as to pose a serious safety risk or other substantial disruption in that environment."[316] The court found that, if true, the statements were not true threats, may have been reasonably calculated to reach the school environment, but could not reasonably be the cause of a substantial disruption to the school environment.[317]

As to the Fourth Amendment unreasonable search claim, the court stated that in order to determine whether the search was reasonable, the court must "consider first the scope of the legitimate expectation of privacy at issue"; second, "the character of the intrusion that is complained of"; and finally, "the nature and immediacy of the governmental concern at issue and the efficacy of the means employed for dealing with it."[318] Here, the court stated that R.S. had a reasonable expectation of privacy in her password-protected private Facebook account and email messages. As such, there was "no indication at this stage that [the school district] tailored its search in any way" and that it was difficult to determine "what if any, legitimate interest the school officials had for pursuing R.S.'s private communications."[319]

Finally, as to the other claims, the court permitted the student's "failure to train or supervise" claim and the student's "invasion of privacy" claims to proceed, but the court upheld the school district's motion to dismiss R.S.'s "conspiracy" and "intentional infliction of emotional distress" claims.[320]

Examination of Cyberbullying in Social Media Cases Filed, But Not Adjudicated

In addition to cyberbullying in social media cases that have been decided by the courts at both federal and state levels, numerous cases involving cyberbullying that occur in social media have been brought by students and their parents against other students for cyberbullying, but they have not been decided by the courts. Some have been settled, while others are still winding their way through the court system, and some are unresolved for various other reasons. Three examples of the numerous cases that have not been fully adjudicated provide illustrations.

First, Alex Boston (Cobbs County, Georgia),[321] a fourteen-year-old, filed suits against two classmates for defamation (libel) in 2012. She did not know why she was being harassed until she discovered that imposters had created a Facebook page with her name and information (including an altered photo to make her face bloated) that suggested she smoked marijuana, and that she spoke a made-up language called "Retardish." In addition, the website imposters included obscene comments and frequent sexual references, and posted a racist video from "Alex" on other friends' pages. In the case, the imposters were accused of posting derogatory messages about Alex. "I was upset that my friends would turn on me like that," she told the Associated Press. "I was crying. It was hard to go to school the next day." Alex learned of the page and told her parents, who soon contacted administrators at her middle school and filed a report with Cobbs County Police.[322]

Second, Jason Medley (Houston, Georgia) (2012) filed defamation suits against three of his daughter's classmates, who allegedly filmed themselves making false sexual remarks about his daughter and posting the video to Facebook.[323] The complaint was settled months later with apologies from the girls and a small donation to charity. "The girls involved likely now understand the wrongful nature of what they did and the harm that can come of such conduct," Medley's attorney stated. "They made a donation out of their allowances to a charitable organization that fights against cyberbullying."[324]

Third, *S.M., et al. v. Griffith Public Schools* (IN) (2012)[325] addressed the line between First Amendment off-campus speech and whether the acts of three eighth-grade students were true threats. Three students were expelled from school after they posted on Facebook a "hit list" of their peers and the best ways to kill them, as well as comments about some teachers. The school district expelled them for violating the school district's bullying and harassment policy. The students argued that they were joking and that it was apparent because they used emoticons, did not state any intent to harm anyone, and did not intimidate or threaten anyone. The parties settled the case.[326]

Conclusion

Students feel humiliated, ridiculed, and many other harmful emotions as they are cyberbullied in social media. Some of the cyberbullying occurs during times the students are not at school (e.g., texting while at home, at a friend's house, at a party, at a restaurant, or while they are driving, and more). Some cyberbullying starts while the student is not at school, but carries over into the school. Other cyberbullying may occur while the student is at school. The above cases illustrate how the courts have tackled these many different locations and means of cyberbullying. Where the cyberbullying does not occur at school and does not carry over to school, parents and guardians attend to the incidents. Where the cyberbullying carries over to the school or occurs in school, administrators must make decisions about dealing with the cyberbullying in social media.

Determining what type of speech is involved and applying the various standard(s) is important. The *Tinker* Court created a distinction between expression taking place out of school and in school when it stated that students do not "shed their constitutional rights to freedom of speech or expression at the schoolhouse gate," and it established its "material and substantial disruption of the work and discipline of the school" standard. Others, as illustrated in this chapter, have developed over the years. It is also a challenge.

Educational institutions should create and enforce good, useful, and tailored policies and plan(s) that consider their school district's unique needs, applicable federal and state courts' decisions, and applicable federal and state statutory and/or regulatory laws. In doing so, educational institutions must be mindful that some states delegate the responsibility for cyberbullying to school districts to create their own policy and plan, while other states specifically include in the state laws what school districts must include in their policy, and in still other states the state departments of education must create a model policy for local school districts to use. Violations of an educational institution's bullying/cyberbullying policy can result in a student being disciplined.

All parties need to be involved in providing a solution to the cyberbullying problem. Students need to take responsibility for their own actions. Parents need to confront issues in the home. Schools need to educate, intervene, and try to prevent cyberbullying where appropriate. Religious, mental health, medical, community law enforcement, juvenile services, and citizens, among others, need to collaborate and cooperate to attack the severe problem of cyberbullying in social media.

Educational institutions also need to be mindful that when investigating these matters not to cross the line and invade the perpetrators' privacy, and/or to be mindful of balancing the investigation with the severity of the allegations.

EMPLOYEES

2

Cyberbullying in Social Media: Employees

Cyberbullying issues for employees have garnered significant attention over the past few years and appear to be increasing. Media stories abound about educators who have posted inappropriate content online, placed their school districts in jeopardy by sending thoughtless and inappropriate emails, and been accused of online pornography, and, on the flip side, who have received harassing or slanderous emails from students, other employees, or parents.

EDUCATIONAL ASPECTS

Cyberbullying

The above types of issues were the catalyst for my dissertation study on uncomfortable and distracting email communication for school district employees (Horowitz, 2009). The use of email communication can have a significant effect on one's personal and professional roles and relationships by facilitating uncomfortable email communication between constituents and affecting an individual's sense of well-being and security. My research examined the demographic and career characteristics of educators who receive uncomfortable emails, their reported responses to emails in the context of their employment, and to what extent they report emotional reactions to emails that make them feel uncomfortable. I defined uncomfortable and distressing email inductively by one of the following categories:

1. impolite, insensitive, rude
2. angry, coercive, capricious
3. lies, slander
4. racist
5. unprofessional, inappropriate jokes, casual
6. repetitive, huge quantity
7. copies, blind copies
8. solicitations, fishing for personal information
9. spam

Educators are being inundated with emails that have rapidly become the most popular vehicle of communication. Emails arrive daily from a wide variety of constituents, and many demand a response (Horowitz, 2009). According to reports from educators (Horowitz, 2009), the tone and nature of some emails engender uncomfortable feelings. Educators react differently to emails, and some are uncertain how to respond. Regardless, emails can cause consternation in the workplace environment, such as when educators receive uncomfortable emails via their school district server.

My online dissertation survey (2009) described synonyms for the word *uncomfortable*: "annoying; embarrassing; including offensive language; insulting; threatening, harmful, untrue, cruel; defaming or denigrating one's reputation; sexually explicit; sexually suggestive, posted on the Internet." As part of the survey, educators checked off if they had received emails containing content that made them feel uncomfortable, as described by any of the above synonyms. The responses were then tabulated as follows:

- 92.1 percent reported receiving annoying emails.
- 38 percent reported receiving insulting emails.
- Between 18 percent and 38 percent reported receiving emails that were along the following scale: insulting; embarrassing; including offensive language; sexually suggestive; harmful, untrue, or cruel; sexually explicit; and demeaning and denigrating to one's reputation.
- 12 percent reported receiving emails that were threatening.

As part of the study (Horowitz, 2009), educators reported the following examples from parents that demonstrate a threatening and denigrating tone: "I will have you fired, I will go to the newspaper and I will sue you," and "You are an awful teacher and have ruined my son's life." A few examples from colleagues that are sexually suggestive are "I am going to miss seeing your pretty face in my classroom every day," and "A female co-worker took a photo of me and made a top 10 list that had various sexual innuendoes." A few examples from students that are threatening and denigrating are "You can go to hell for sending an email to my parents," and "F—k you, you gray haired f—k."

Email Usage: Friend or Foe

Online harassment is emerging as one of the more challenging issues facing educators as adolescents and adults have embraced the Internet. While much of this activity occurs away from the school environment, the impact on the emotional well-being of educators can be significant. Conn (2004) expressed the concern that

> with districts releasing email addresses of teachers and administrators to students, parents and community members and requiring educators to post responses within certain limited time periods, schools and districts may be

> exposing educators as targets for unwarranted harassment, parents who demand constant progress updates for their students regardless of justifiable educational needs, parents who dislike certain teachers for valid or invalid reasons, or any unreasonable individuals with email access may become thorns in the sides of educators trying to do their best in a landscape of ever-increasing demands on their time. (163)

Administrators and teachers are acknowledging the necessity of checking their work email on a daily basis to communicate with each other, students, and parents (Horowitz, 2009). Although email certainly stands near the top of the list of important modern inventions (Suler, 2003), it comes with a price, as do many (if not all) inventions. In our complex and harried world, email can add to the stress of everyday work. A variety of factors contribute to email-induced stress (Suler, 2003; Joinson, 1998), including the following:

- social and information overload—being overwhelmed by the fast pace and heavy bombardment of incoming messages, necessitating work multitasking to evaluate what is valuable and how to respond
- social ambiguity—the missing face-to-face cues of email make it potentially ambiguous and may generate miscommunication
- disintegrated work/leisure boundaries—the boundaries between work and leisure break down, as educators can access email from home; this can also cause a breakdown between stress and relaxation
- emotional intensity—people may be disinhibited; they may say and do things that they ordinarily would not say or do in face-to-face communication; they may reveal a great deal about themselves, may eventually regret self-disclosure, and feel exposed and vulnerable
- tenuous privacy—an email message is a record of a conversation that can be accessed by a third party, forwarded to a third party, or unintentionally sent to a third party or an entire group; the disruption of privacy may feel like a personal violation and may result in humiliation
- black hole experiences—receiving no reply makes one wonder because of the ambiguity of cyberspace and can cause anxiety and insecurity
- spam trickery and disruption—spam has reached voluminous proportions; spammers attempt to lie, induce guilt and anxiety, and/or pretend to be someone else, all in order to trick us into opening their message; spam causes individuals to distrust email and the Internet in general

Although Suler (2003) and Joinson (1998) were two of the first researchers to discuss email-induced stress, they did not use the terms *bullying* and *harassment*. Those terms are more prevalent today than when the authors' research was conducted.

Email can be either a friend or a foe for educators. A Massachusetts teacher and dean of students shares that

> three factors can make email a problem for teachers: volume, content and choice of medium. Volume is when teachers have too many emails to respond to; content is that emails can be rude, unclear or of painful grammar; choice of medium refers to the fact that by using email, teachers run the risk of avoiding the phone call or face-to-face communication that would do the job better. (Libman, 2008)

Friendly email correspondence is always welcome for educators. Teachers particularly enjoy learning that a parent is pleased with the progress a student is making in his/her classroom. And it is rewarding for guidance counselors and teachers to learn that a senior got into the college or university of his/her choice.

On the flip side, email can be a foe for educators. A number of administrators throughout the United States have experienced vicious, personal attacks waged by the public via Internet postings (Horowitz, 2009). Disgruntled students, colleagues, parents, and school board directors have attempted career assassination of administrators. Some superintendents have coped with daily personal attacks against them, requesting their removal from their position. Others have been demeaned, vilified, and humiliated. Many of these attacks are anonymous, and the speech is protected by the First Amendment (Horowitz, 2009).

Cyberbullying is also experienced by teachers in the United Kingdom, according to BBC News: "Figures obtained by the Associated Press news agency show a steadily rising tally of prosecutions for electronic communications that are grossly offensive or of an indecent, obscene or menacing character from 1,263 in 2009 to 1,843 in 2011. The number of convictions grew from 873 in 2009 to 1,286 in 2011" (BBC News, 2012).

Social Media

The ubiquitous rise of social media has changed the way that society communicates. Online communication is a daily ritual for just about everyone. Social media sites have permeated every facet of our lives, including our personal and work environments. School districts must also adapt to these new technologies and strongly consider policies that address privacy, protection, and responsibility.

Social media can enhance learning opportunities and engagement for today's tech-savvy students. Adolescents' lives often revolve around social media, so it behooves school districts to find positive, constructive ways to channel social media into instructional practices. School districts can launch website pages that serve as community message boards. Educators can initiate wikis and blogs in which only group members can post content or videos related to a classroom research project or discussion. Students can also collaborate with students in other states or countries on classroom projects.

New Jersey technology coordinator Frank Pileiro developed Three Simple C's of Social Media Success for Educators that are very worthwhile to consider:

- Connect: Connect to the right social media that works for you. Do the research, sign up, and spend time playing with them.
- Collaborate: Leverage the social aspect that social media offers. Join a site and consume the information that is being shared. By contributing, you will gain followers and valuable resources.
- Curate: Utilize tools that allow you to sort things out and remain organized. Use free social media dashboards that include multiple social media sites in one location. You can consume, contribute and curate information (Careless, 2012).

Disciplinary Actions

School district policies need to establish rules and guidance for the use of social media for students and employees, as well as for any guests accessing social media through the district's communications and information systems. These systems consist of, but are not limited to, computers, logical and physical networks, the Internet, electronic communications, information systems, databases, files, software, peripherals, interactive devices, and media. Users are responsible for their own behavior when communicating through social media. They should be held accountable for the content of the communications that they state or post on social media locations.

Social media policies may include language that will enable school districts to take disciplinary action against employees who act inappropriately. Those policies specifically state the consequences for particular actions. News media and state department of education reports demonstrate specific examples of the behaviors and actions taken by schools or school districts. Below are examples primarily from Pennsylvania, but they reflect actions of employees and responses by school districts and departments of education across the country:

- A Pennsylvania secondary mathematics teacher sent sexually explicit material/photographs to a student. He surrendered his teaching certificate in lieu of discipline (Pennsylvania Department of Education Field Notices, 2010).
- A Pennsylvania high school chemistry teacher posted a nude photograph of himself on an adult website and used his school computer to access inappropriate content. His teaching certificate was suspended for three years (Pennsylvania Department of Education Field Notices, 2010).

- A Pennsylvania special education teacher sent inappropriate and sexually explicit text messages to female students, stored a nude photograph of a female student on his cell phone, and arranged to meet a student outside of school to engage in sexual activity. His teaching certificate was revoked (Pennsylvania Department of Education Field Notices, 2010).
- A Pennsylvania private school secondary English teacher posted her thoughts about a student's presentation in the English class by criticizing its tone and political outlook. Two months later she was suspended, and then fired (Hardy, 2010).
- A Michigan middle school teacher participated in a bachelorette party and was photographed simulating a lewd act with a mannequin. The photos were posted on a website without her consent. Two years later rumors surfaced about the photos. She was recommended for dismissal by the district. That recommendation was overturned by the Michigan Tenure Commission and the Michigan Court of Appeals (*School Superintendent's Insider*, 2010).
- A Pennsylvania secondary English teacher exchanged inappropriate emails, text messages, and other interpersonal communication with a student. He surrendered his teaching certificate in lieu of discipline (Pennsylvania Department of Education Field Notices, 2010).
- A Pennsylvania secondary music teacher exchanged inappropriate text messages with a student. His teaching certificate was suspended (Pennsylvania Department of Education Field Notices, 2010).
- A Pennsylvania secondary social studies teacher engaged in inappropriate conduct with several female students, which included sending sexually explicit messages to a student, exchanging nude photographs with a student, and making inappropriate comments to several students. His teaching certificate was revoked (Pennsylvania Department of Education Field Notices, 2010).
- A Pennsylvania high school special education teacher sent sexually explicit text messages to a female student. He surrendered his teaching certificate in lieu of discipline (Pennsylvania Department of Education Field Notices, 2010).
- A Pennsylvania secondary Spanish teacher was tagged in a photo on Facebook with a male stripper at a bachelorette party. She was suspended (Sostek, 2011).
- A Pennsylvania secondary English teacher used her blog to lambaste some students with derogatory comments. She was suspended (Hardy, 2011).
- A California middle school administrator placed an ad on Craigslist stating in obscene, vulgar, and albeit misspelled and grammatically incorrect phrases that he wished to engage in sexual relations with another adult. His termination was supported by the California Court of Appeal (Rogers, 2011).

- A Florida secondary social studies teacher made anti-gay comments on Facebook and repeatedly expressed his views, which made students in his class uncomfortable and fearful (eSchool News, 2011).
- A California high school band director posted more than 1,200 messages on a sixteen-year-old female student's Facebook page. He pleaded guilty to sexual misconduct (*Los Angeles Daily News*, 2012).

Privacy Issues

Communicating in an online world can be helpful in many ways, but it potentially could infringe upon someone's privacy. Where some teachers are very comfortable posting assignments online and communicating with students via email and in social media education sites authorized by the school district, other employees are hesitant, have questions, and are circumspect. Concerns have been expressed by administrators about which emails from staff are privileged and which are not (Horowitz, 2010) and about sending the wrong message to the wrong person—for example, what if a student's information goes to the wrong parent?

Educators must refrain from sharing inappropriate private information (personal, family, sexual preferences) with students, parents, colleagues, and school board directors. Educators should exercise caution when posting comments on social media sites that would damage the integrity of the teaching profession, reflect poorly on them as employees, or disrupt the school environment for students, colleagues, and administrators. The nature of the education profession suggests that educators exercise more decorum in their personal lives than other professions, as educators are held to a higher standard.

School employees across the country have been disciplined for not maintaining proper, professional decorum in the online, digital world. As illustrated above, some educators have posted photos that are sexually explicit or involve drinking alcohol at parties, stated sexually suggestive comments to students, and posted derogatory comments about students, colleagues, and administrators. In some cases, relationships that began between teachers and students on social media sites became sexual or inappropriate (Horowitz, 2009).

Use in Higher Education

Similar to K–12 educators, college and university faculty are now using social media personally, professionally, and in the classroom. Pearson, an education services company, and the Babson Survey Research Group surveyed 3,875 higher-education faculty from across the country in 2012 (Liss, 2012). Their survey found that "about 45% of faculty use social media professionally on a monthly basis and about 65% use it for personal purposes." The study also found that "social media use drops off with age: faculty under the age of 35 had the highest usage rate for personal, professional and teaching use, followed by professors aged 35–44." College and university faculty also reported that using video in the classroom has become quite popular (Liss, 2012).

LEGAL ASPECTS

Whether at the K–12 school district level or at the higher-education level, in most instances, the principle course of action taken by victims of cyberbullying has involved challenging the educational institutions' established school policies and the administrators' disciplinary procedures. However, it is important to consider how the victim of cyberbullying structures the nature of the available relief. Offensive or disparaging Internet content aimed at school administrators or faculty members may be legally distinct from cases in which the cyberbullying is directed toward another student. Because attacks on teachers and administrators may create a greater possibility of "material disruption" in the educational environment, courts have been willing to support an educational entity's actions regulating this type of speech. Essentially, the critical determinations in upholding school district disciplinary actions against students are:

- whether the student is being punished for his or her on-campus conduct, not for his or her off-campus speech;
- whether the student is violating an educational institution's policy;
- whether there is a sufficient nexus to cause substantial disruption to the educational environment;
- whether the facts might reasonably have led school authorities to forecast substantial disruption of, or material interference in, school activities;
- whether the educational environment has been disrupted; or
- whether the student's conduct threatened, harassed, and/or intimidated school employees.

Students Allegedly Cyberbullying Educators and Educators Allegedly Cyberbullying Students

State statutes, decided cases, and educational institutions' policies form the basis for employees' legal actions when they are victims of students' offensive and disparaging Internet content. Conversely, cases are beginning to be brought and decided against employees who post repulsive, insulting, or intemperate comments about students in their online social media. Below is an examination of both.

Statutes: Students Cyberbullying Educators

Within statutory mandates, some states prohibit cyberbullying not just against other students but also against school district employees. Nine states have enacted school code statutes that protect employees from cyberbullying.[1]

Arkansas Arkansas prohibits electronic acts directed at personnel that result in substantial disruption, are maliciously intended to disrupt, and have a high likelihood of succeeding for that purpose.[2]

California California's current statute provides that, in addition to numerous enumerated grounds in its education law, "a pupil enrolled in any of grades 4 to 12, inclusive, may be suspended from school or recommended for expulsion if the superintendent or the principal of the school in which the pupil is enrolled determines that *the pupil has intentionally engaged in harassment, threats, or intimidation, directed against school district personnel* . . . that is sufficiently severe or pervasive to have the actual and reasonably expected effect of materially disrupting classwork, creating substantial disorder, and invading *the rights of either school personnel* or pupils by creating an intimidating or hostile educational environment" (*emphasis added*).[3] Additionally, the California Assembly is considering Bill No. 256, California 2013 to 2014 Regular Session, which proposes to amend this section of California's Education Code by adding "or bullying by means of an electronic act, as defined in the [statute]."[4]

Colorado Colorado requires that each year each school must submit a report in a format approved by the state board to their board of education that in turn must be submitted to the state's department of education and made available to the public. Among the items that must be included in the report are the number of conduct and discipline code violations of "behavior on school grounds, in a school vehicle, or at a school activity or sanctioned event that is detrimental to the welfare or safety of . . . *school personnel*, including but not limited to incidents of bullying." Electronic acts and gestures are included in the definition of bullying (*emphasis added*).[5]

Florida Florida's education law prohibits bullying (including cyberbullying) and harassment of any K–12 public *school employees* during any school district education program or activity; any school-related or school-sponsored program or activity or on a school bus; "through the use of data or computer software that is accessed through a computer, computer system, or computer network within the scope of a public K–12 educational institution"; or "through the use of data or computer software that is accessed at a non-school-related location, activity, function, or program or through the use of technology or an electronic device that is not owned, leased, or used by a school district or school, if the bullying (including cyberbullying) substantially interferes with or limits the victim's ability to participate in or benefit from the services, activities, or opportunities offered by a school or substantially disrupts the education process or orderly operation of a school" (*emphasis added*).[6]

Cyberbullying is defined to include, among others, the use of technology or electronic communications transmitted by electronic mail, Internet communications, instant messages, or facsimile communications, and the creation of a web page or web log in which the creator assumes the identity of another person, or impersonates another person as the author of posted content or messages, if they meet the definition of bullying.[7]

"Harassment means any threatening, insulting, or dehumanizing gesture, use of data or computer software, or written, verbal, or physical conduct directed against a student or *school employee*" that places a *school employee* in reasonable fear of harm to his or her person or damage to his or her property, and has the effect of substantially disrupting the orderly operation of a school.[8] Stalking (including cyberstalking) also applies (*emphasis added*).[9]

Under Florida's criminal law, a person who willfully, maliciously, and repeatedly follows, harasses, or cyberstalks another person commits the offense of stalking, which is a misdemeanor of the first degree. If a person additionally makes a credible threat against that person, he or she commits the offense of aggravated stalking, a felony of the third degree.[10]

Hawaii Hawaii law provides that cyberbullying can occur "through an off campus computer network that is sufficiently severe, persistent, or pervasive that it creates an intimidating, threatening, or abusive educational environment for the other student *or school personnel, or both.*" Cyberbullying, as defined by Hawaii, includes "electronically transmitted acts, i.e., Internet, cell phone, personal digital assistance (PDA), or wireless hand-held device that a student has exhibited toward another student *or employee of the department* which causes mental or physical harm to the other student(s) *or school personnel* and is sufficiently severe, persistent or pervasive that it creates an intimidating, threatening, or abusive educational environment" (*emphasis added*).[11]

Mississippi Mississippi law includes an education code requirement and a criminal code offense relevant to employees. In the education code, no *employee* may be subjected to cyberbullying or harassing behavior by students or other school employees. Cyberbullying involves placing a *school employee* in actual and reasonable fear of harm to his or her person or damage to his or her property. Mississippi defines cyberbullying as "any pattern of gestures or written, electronic or verbal communications, or any physical act or any threatening communication, or any act reasonably perceived as being motivated by any actual or perceived differentiating characteristic, that takes place on school property, at any school-sponsored function, or on a school bus."[12] A *school employee*, student, or volunteer who has witnessed or has reliable information that a student or *school employee* has been subject to any act of bullying or harassing behavior must report the incident to the appropriate school official. Additionally, each school district must include in its personnel and student policies a prohibition against bullying or harassing behavior and adopt procedures for reporting, investigating, and addressing such behavior (*emphasis added*).[13]

As to the criminal offense, an electronic communication involving "any person who knowingly and without consent impersonates another actual person through or on an Internet website or by other electronic means for purposes of harming, intimidating, threatening or defrauding another person" could be guilty of a misdemeanor. Electronic means under Mississippi law includes opening an email account or an account or profile on a social networking Internet website in another person's name.[14]

North Carolina North Carolina law, like Mississippi law, includes an education code requirement and a criminal code offense relevant to employees. In the North Carolina education code "*no employee* shall be subjected to bullying or harassing behavior by . . . students." Bullying involves "placing a . . . *school employee* in actual and reasonable fear of harm to his or her person or damage to his or her property" (*emphasis added*).[15] Cyberbullying is included in North Carolina's definition of bullying as electronic communications, which states, "Bullying or harassing behavior is any pattern of gestures or written, electronic, or verbal communications, or any physical act or any threatening communication, that takes place on school property, at any school-sponsored function, or on a school bus," and "includes, but is not limited to, acts reasonably perceived as being motivated by any actual or perceived differentiating characteristic, such as race, color, religion, ancestry, national origin, gender, socioeconomic status, academic status, gender identity, physical appearance, sexual orientation, or mental, physical, developmental, or sensory disability, or by association with a person who has or is perceived to have one or more of these characteristics."

A school employee, student, or volunteer who has witnessed or has reliable information that a student or *school employee has been subjected to any act of bullying or harassing behavior* must report the incident to the appropriate school official (*emphasis added*). Also, if a student is convicted under North Carolina's criminal statute of Cyberbullying a School Employee by Student, the student must be transferred to another school within the school administrative unit, unless there is no other appropriate school within the school administrative unit, in which event the student must be transferred to a different class or assigned to a teacher who was not involved as a victim of the cyberbullying. Notwithstanding these requirements, the superintendent may modify, in writing, the required transfer of a student on a case-by-case basis.[16]

North Carolina's criminal law states that it is unlawful for any student to use a computer or computer network to:

- intentionally intimidate or torment a school employee by building a fake profile or website; posting or encouraging others to post on the Internet private, personal, or sexual information pertaining to a school employee; posting a real or doctored image of the school employee on the Internet; accessing, altering, or erasing any computer network, computer data, computer program, or computer software, including breaking into a password-protected account or stealing or otherwise accessing passwords; and using a computer system for repeated, continuing, or sustained electronic communications, including electronic mail or other transmissions, to a school employee.
- make any statement (whether true or false) that is intended to immediately provoke, and that is likely to provoke, any third party to stalk or harass a school employee.
- "[c]opy and disseminate, or cause to be made, an unauthorized copy of any data pertaining to a school employee for the purpose of intimidating or tormenting that school employee (in any form, including, but not limited to, any printed or electronic form of computer data, computer programs, or computer software residing in, communicated by, or produced by a computer or computer network)."
- "[s]ign up a school employee for a pornographic Internet site with the intent to intimidate or torment the employee."
- "[w]ithout authorization of the school employee, sign up a school employee for electronic mailing lists or to receive junk electronic messages and instant messages, with the intent to intimidate or torment the school employee."[17]

A student found guilty of cyberbullying a school employee is subject to a Class 2 misdemeanor penalty. However, the court may, without entering a judgment of guilt and with the consent of the student, defer further proceedings and place the student on probation subject to reasonable terms and conditions that the court may require. If the student fulfills the terms and conditions of the probation, the court must discharge the student and dismiss the proceedings against the student. Discharge and dismissal must be without court adjudication of guilt and must not be deemed a conviction for this offense or for purposes of disqualifications or disabilities imposed by law upon conviction of a crime. Upon discharge and dismissal, the student may apply for an order to expunge the complete record of the proceedings resulting in the dismissal and discharge.[18]

The ACLU claims that students' speech rights may be violated by the North Carolina criminal law because it is too broad and vague, potentially unconstitutional, and the charges are disproportionate to the offense.[19] No case has addressed the statute at this time. The National Education Association (NEA), in supporting protections for school employees, reported that according to a National Survey of Violence Against Teachers developed by a special task force of the American Psychological Association, 50 percent of the 4,735 kindergarten through twelfth-grade teachers surveyed were victims of students, parents, or colleagues, many by cyberbullying, within the previous year.[20]

Oklahoma Oklahoma's school code directs school districts to establish a policy that specifically "prohibit[s] threatening behavior, harassment, intimidation, and bullying by students at school and by electronic communication, whether or not such communication originated at school or with school equipment, if the communication is specifically directed at students *or school personnel* and concerns harassment, intimidation, or bullying at school" (*emphasis added*). Bullying is defined to incorporate electronic communication, which includes any written, verbal, or pictorial information communicated by an electronic device, such as a telephone, a cellular telephone or other wireless telecommunication device, or a computer.[21]

Utah Utah's school code obligates school districts to establish a "bullying, cyberbullying, harassment, and hazing policy" that is consistent with Utah law. The law mandates that "no school employee or student may engage in cyberbullying, or hazing a *school employee* . . . at any time or in any location . . ." and that students "may not engage in bullying or harassing a school employee . . . on school property; at a school related or sponsored event; on a school bus; at a school bus stop; or while the school employee or student is traveling to or from a location or event described previously in this sentence" (*emphasis added*).[22]

Bullying is defined as "intentionally or knowingly committing an act that endangers the physical health or safety of a *school employee* or student." *Cyberbullying* is defined as "using the Internet, a cell phone, or another device to send or post text, video, or an image with the intent or knowledge, or with reckless disregard, that the text, video, or image will hurt, embarrass, or threaten an individual, regardless of whether the individual directed, consented to, or acquiesced in the conduct, or voluntarily accessed the electronic communication." Electronic communication is defined as conveying a message electronically.[23]

Cases: Students Allegedly Cyberbullying Educators

For several years, schools have disciplined students for their comments about teachers in social media and on their websites. In response, students and their parents have sued school districts. Numerous cases in which students claimed they were cyberbullied by employees of educational institutions are discussed in the student cyberbullying section of this book. Some cases brought against students by educational entities and employees were successful; others were not. Examples follow.

Cases Where the Employees and Educational Entities Were Successful

- *Requa v. Kent School District* (student who surreptitiously video recorded his teacher in the classroom, edited the video, and placed it on YouTube was punished for violating the school district's policies and on-campus conduct, not for his off-campus speech).[24]
- *J.S. v. Bethlehem Area School District* (student who established a website depicting his teacher in hateful ways and offered to pay a hit man to kill her was expelled for his off-campus speech that the court considered on-campus speech because it was viewed or accessed on school property; was aimed at a specific school district, personnel, and/or student audience and others connected with the particular school district [not a random audience]; and was brought onto the school district's property, and because there was a sufficient nexus between the website and the school campus).[25]
- *Wisniewski v. Board of Education* (a student's created and transmitted drawing depicting the shooting of a teacher posed the reasonably foreseeable risk that the drawing would come to the attention of school authorities and would materially and substantially disrupt the work and discipline of the school).[26]
- *Doninger v. Niehoff* (court found that the school district could reasonably forecast that a substantial disruption or material interference would occur when the student called administrators "douchbags" and asked people to contact the superintendent "to piss her off more" in her livejournal.com blog after she was denied the opportunity to run for senior class secretary because she violated a school policy).[27]
- *Barnett v. Tipton County Board of Education* (two high school students' fake profiles about their assistant principal and coach [which included sexually suggestive comments] believed to be true by parents and a local reporter were not parodies; therefore, it was not protected speech, so the school district's discipline was upheld).[28]
- *Bell v. Itawamba County School Board* (student's song that had many vulgar verses insulting and criticizing two coaches and one of their wives, specific allegations of improper conduct with female students, and two threatening lyrics was found to cause a material and/or substantial disruption, and it was reasonably foreseeable that such a disruption would occur).[29]

Cases Where the Students Were Successful

- *Evans v. Bayer* (a student's suspension for creating a Facebook group that focused on "express[ing] your feelings of hatred" about a teacher was not upheld by the court because the expressions were opinions [protected speech], they did not cause any disruption at school, and no reasonably foreseeable disruption could be found).[30]

- *Barnes v. Zaccari* (a student's expulsion by the university president because of the student's distribution and posting of information on Facebook about a campus parking structure he opposed but that the president had proposed and supported was determined to be protected speech).[31]
- *Layshock v. Hermitage School District*[32] and *J.S. v. Blue Mountain School District*[33] (students' off-campus creation of MySpace profiles of principals that included vulgar, lewd, and offensive expressions could not be disciplined by the school districts because they could not establish a sufficient nexus between the students' speech and a substantial disruption of the schools' environments).

In *J.S. v. Blue Mountain School District*, Judge Fisher's dissent, joined by five additional judges, disagreed with the majority's ruling that J.S.'s speech did not pose a substantial disruption to the educational environment. J.S. impersonated her middle school principal on Facebook by posting lewd, vulgar, and offensive expressions that she intended to be a joke. The dissenting judges stated:

> The majority failed to recognize the effects of accusations of sexual misconduct . . . such accusations interfere with the educational process by undermining the authority of school officials to perform their jobs . . . they divert school resources required to correct misinformation and remedy confusion, and overlooks the substantial disruption to the classroom environment that follows from personal and harmful attacks on educators and school officials.[34]

Citing and summarizing numerous studies on cyberbullying, harassment, and teacher-student relationships, Judge Fisher stated, "It may cause teachers to leave the school and stop teaching altogether, and those who stay are oftentimes less effective. Educators become anxious and depressed and feel unable to relate to their students. They lose their motivation to teach, and their students suffer as a result." Judge Fisher also cited two cases consistent with the studies.[35]

Cases Filed, But Not Adjudicated West Mifflin Area School District (PA) filed suit in Mifflin County Common Pleas Court on behalf of the school district's union president and a teacher against John Doe 1 and John Doe 2, anonymous individuals who sent allegedly defamatory email messages to them. A previous suit was also filed a month earlier by the school district on behalf of a school board member against anonymous individuals who allegedly threatened and defamed him on an Internet discussion board.[36] Decisions on these cases have not been rendered at the time of preparing this book.

Cases: Educators Allegedly Cyberbullying Students

Employee-to-student cyberbullying is not alleged as often as student-to-employee cyberbullying. However, a few decided and undecided cases do exist.

Many different kinds of actions can be brought against school employees by many different parties—for example, students, parents, the school district, and others. As demonstrated in the cases below, a defense often asserted by employees is that "they are protected by the First Amendment." In those types of cases, it is essential to determine whether the employees' expression addresses a matter of public concern, or private concern, or whether, even if one could find that the employee was addressing a matter of public concern, her right to express her views was outweighed by the school district's need to operate its schools efficiently.

Case Where Employee Was Disciplined, But Not Terminated In *Rubino v. City of New York* (2012),[37] the Supreme Court, New York County, addressed a teacher's Facebook postings about her students. A New York City public school student fatally drowned during a field trip to the beach. The next day a teacher, while at home, posted, "After today, I am thinking the beach sounds like a wonderful idea for my 5th graders! I HATE THEIR GUTS! They are the devils [*sic*] spawn!" One of her Facebook friends then posted, "Oh you would let little Kwame float away!" to which the teacher responded, "Yes, I wld [*sic*] not throw a life jacket in for a million!!" After an investigation and report, the teacher was recommended for termination.[38]

When the principal presented the teacher with the final report, she claimed to not remember the postings and said that a friend had access to her Facebook account. When the investigator interviewed the friend about the postings, she initially said that she made the postings; however, the investigator did not believe her and warned her that she could be incarcerated for perjury if she lied. She recanted, saying that the teacher had asked her to take the responsibility so that she would not lose her job. The teacher was found to have interfered with an official investigation by directing her friend to provide false information to investigators. The investigator again recommended that the teacher be terminated. The Department of Education charged her with misconduct, neglect of duty, and conduct unbecoming her profession.[39]

During the hearing, the teacher admitted to posting the comments, said that she removed them three days after posting them, and apologized for the postings. The hearing officer issued her opinion finding that the teacher be terminated, highlighting the public nature of the online postings and that the teacher had breached the school's trust by conspiring with her friend. She concluded that the teacher had "attempted to obstruct the investigation by continuously denying knowledge of the comments and by pointing to [her friend] as the likely or possible source."[40] The hearing officer did not make a First Amendment ruling, but did state that "having referred to her students in her postings, [she] was acting as a teacher, not a private citizen, and that while the drowning itself was a matter of public concern, the postings were not."[41] Finally, the hearing officer stated that teachers should instill in their students the importance of taking responsibility for their actions and found that the teacher did not apologize fully; instead she only apologized "begrudgingly" for the postings.[42]

The teacher appealed the hearing officer's decision, asserting that it was arbitrary and capricious, that it shocked one's senses of fairness since she had a fifteen-year unblemished employment history with the school district, that her offense did not relate to her teaching ability, that the hearing officer focused on her alleged lack of remorse, and that her First Amendment free speech rights were violated because she spoke on a matter of public concern as a private citizen.[43]

Conversely, the school district supported the hearing officer's decision, stating that the teacher's termination was proportionate to her offense because the hearing officer was entitled to consider her lack of remorse, that the teacher was speaking in her capacity as a teacher in posting the comments on Facebook, and that her termination did not violate her First Amendment rights.[44]

In reacting to the school district's position, the teacher stated that the penalty was disproportionate to her offense because "it was made in a small, private, adults-only audience, and the hearing officer disregarded her apology for her actions." Then the school district responded to the teacher's reply, stating, "Termination was the appropriate penalty, emphasizing that [the teacher] was also found guilty of conspiring to mislead the . . . investigator and that Facebook is a public forum insofar as anything posted on it may be copied and publically [*sic*] disseminated."[45]

The court did not take issue with the hearing officer's First Amendment conclusion, and it upheld the hearing officer's findings of misconduct, neglect of duty, and conduct unbecoming her profession by posting the alleged comments and interfering with an official investigation.[46]

However, the court found the penalty of termination of employment to be so disproportionate to her offense as to shock one's sense of fairness, and it remanded the case to the New York City Board of Education to impose a lesser penalty. The court reasoned that (1) the teacher's fifteen-year employment history was unblemished before her postings, which she made outside of school and after school hours, and (2) nothing in the record stated that her postings affected her ability to teach, (3) that the postings injured her students, (4) that the teacher intended any injury, that the "electronic footprint" of the postings would affect past or future students, (5) that the racism emerging from the postings did not originate with the teacher, and (6) that she was intolerant or it affected the way she teaches or treats students.[47] Although the court did not overturn the hearing officer's First Amendment conclusion, the court stated:

> In these circumstances, termination of [her] employment is inconsistent with the spirit of the first amendment. . . . Indeed, with Facebook, as with social media in general, one may express oneself as freely and rapidly as when conversation on

> the telephone with a friend. This, even though [she] should have known that her postings could become public more easily than if she had uttered them during a telephone call or over dinner, given the illusion that Facebook postings reach only Facebook friends and the fleeting nature of social media, her expectation that only her friends, all of whom are adults, would see the postings is not only apparent, but reasonable. While her reference to a child's death is repulsive, there is no evidence that her postings are part of a pattern of conduct or anything other than an isolated incident of intemperance.[48]

The court also stated that it had no reason to believe that the teacher would again post inappropriate or offensive comments online because she apologized for her posts, and that even though she was found to have violated the school district's trust by interfering with the investigation (which she denied but the hearing officer did not find credible), it was reasonable that she would not apologize for what she believed she did not do, and that "her [actions were a] clumsy attempt at a cover-up [that] reflects panic, not planning."[49] Finally, the court stated:

> While students must learn to take responsibility for their actions, they should also know that sometimes there are second chances and that compassion is a quality rightly valued in our society. Ending [her] long-term employment on the basis of a single isolated lapse of judgment teaches otherwise. While I do not condone [her] conduct and acknowledge that teachers should act as role models for their students, termination on these circumstances does not correspond with the measure of compassion a teacher should show her students. Rather, it places far too great a strain on the right to express oneself freely among friends, notwithstanding the repulsiveness of that expression.[50]

On appeal to the New York Supreme Court, Appellate Division,[51] the appellate court added that, although the comments were clearly inappropriate, "it is apparent that petitioner's purpose was to vent her frustration only to her online friends after a difficult day with her own students. None of her students or her parents were part of her network of friends and, thus, the comments were not published to them, nor to the public at large, and [she] deleted the comments three days later." The appellate court unanimously upheld the court's decision that the penalty of termination was so disproportionate to her offense as to shock one's sense of fairness.[52]

Case Where the Employee Was Terminated In *In the Matter of the Tenure Hearing of Jennifer O'Brien* (2013),[53] the Superior Court of New Jersey heard an appeal from the New Jersey Commissioner of Education, who affirmed the administrative law judge's decision to uphold a teacher's dismissal because of her posts on Facebook. Jennifer O'Brien was employed in the school district of the city of Paterson as a first-grade teacher. She posted two statements on Facebook: (1) "I'm a warden for future criminals!" and (2) "They had a scared straight program in school—why couldn't [I] bring [first] graders?" An administrator was appalled and some parents were angry and made irate calls to the school. Also, a protest occurred outside of the school, reporters and camera crews arrived, and a large number of parents attended and spoke of their outrage concerning the postings. The deputy superintendent filed a complaint against the teacher for conduct unbecoming a teacher, which the superintendent upheld. She was suspended without pay. The superintendent stated that, if the facts as alleged were sufficiently established, she was subject to dismissal.[54]

The commissioner of education appointed an administrative law judge (ALJ) to hear the case. During the hearing, the teacher stated that she had posted the comments "because of their behavior, not because of their race or ethnicity." One student had struck her, another stole from her and other students, and some students hit each other. Purportedly, she reported the behavior problems to the administration, but she did not believe they were addressed adequately. Further, she claimed that she did not think of her students as "future criminals." She explained that she was speaking out of frustration over her students' behavior and did not anticipate that they would be interpreted as racist. She claimed that her comments were protected by the First Amendment.[55]

The ALJ ruled against her, stating that her comments were not protected by the First Amendment because they were not addressing a matter of public concern, and even if one could find that they were addressing a matter of public concern, her right to express her views was outweighed by the school district's need to operate its schools efficiently. Essentially, the ALJ stated that Facebook is not the place to begin a conversation about classroom discipline, that a "description of first-grade children as criminals with their teacher as their warden is intemperate and vituperative," and that "it becomes impossible for parents to cooperate with or have faith in a teacher who insults their children and trivializes legitimate educational concerns on the internet."[56] As to the First Amendment, the ALJ stated, "In a public school setting thoughtless words can destroy the partnership between home and school that is essential to the mission of the schools."[57]

In all, the ALJ found that the teacher "failed to maintain[] a safe, caring, nurturing, educational environment," that she breached her duty as a professional teacher, that her conduct endangered the mental well-being of the students, and that her actions supported her removal even though her prior record was unblemished. The acting commissioner's decision reflected the hearing officer's decision. The teacher appealed to the Superior Court of New Jersey, Appellate Division. The court affirmed the decisions of the ALJ and acting commissioner.[58]

Case Filed, But Not Adjudicated In *Munroe v. Central Bucks School District*,[59] a high school English teacher filed a suit against her high school principal and superintendent claiming that the school district terminated her in retaliation for her engaging in protected, constitutional speech. The teacher created a blog titled "Where Are We Going and Why Are We in This Handbasket?" In the blog, she criticized students, parents, and school officials without reference to specific individuals or locations where she worked or lived. She claimed that she intended the blog to be anonymous, except to her friends she invited to be followers. According to an interview with the teacher on ABC *Good Morning America*, she admitted to including in her blog comments that she would like to write about her students on their report cards instead of the "canned comments" that were provided by the school district—for example, "frightfully dim," "rat-like," and "dresses like a street-walker," among others—and that she complained about the students for a year, posting phrases such as "lazy," "rude," "I hate your kid," and "out of control."[60]

In her amended complaint before the U.S. District Court for the Eastern District of Pennsylvania, the teacher claimed that:

- she was terminated after the principal confronted her about her blog, but that prior to the event she received excellent performance evaluations;
- her blog generated national media interest, and that she defended herself in interviews for television and print, and that she refused to apologize when she was focusing attention on the education debate to supporting teachers;
- while she was blogging, the school district did not have a policy prohibiting an employee from maintaining a blog;
- she was given unsatisfactory performance evaluations, placed on a performance improvement plan, and required to prepare daily lesson plans, all in retaliation for exercising her free speech rights, and the administrators targeted her for "ridiculous and untrue criticism at every opportunity"; and
- her blogging activity was done as a private citizen; therefore, it was protected under the First Amendment.

She is seeking reinstatement, back pay, front pay, and punitive damages for civil rights violations, emotional distress, and damages to her reputation.[61]

According to the school district's Answer with Affirmative Defenses to her Amended Complaint, before the publication of her blog, her performance drifted downward, and that after the flurry of the publication of the blog and her media tour, her performance began to suffer. To help her, the school district stated that she was given opportunities to improve her performance and was assigned a mentor, but she failed to comply with directives and resources. According to the school district, the teacher could not have intended to have her blog remain anonymous because she challenged her students to "find" the blog entry and it was clear that the teacher intended to publish her identity as the author of the entries. The school district also stated that the teacher's blog entries were conducted in a public capacity as a public school teacher and therefore were not protected under the First Amendment. As to her having to prepare daily lesson plans, the school district stated that all teachers are required to prepare daily lesson plans.[62]

Defendant filed a motion for summary judgment on October 30, 2013; the plaintiffs filed its response in opposition to the motion for summary judgment on November 22, 2013. Thereafter, the defendant filed a motion for summary judgment on December 6, 2013. No decision by the court has occurred at the time of publishing this book.

Conclusion

Students allegedly cyberbully educators and educators allegedly cyberbully students. State statutes protect educators from being cyberbullied, and state statutes protect students from being cyberbullied. Cases have been decided in which educational institutions and employees were successful against the cyberbullying of students, and cases have been decided in which students were successful in defending their actions when disciplined by the educational institution and/or employees. An educator was terminated for her online statements against students, and an educator was not terminated for her online statements against her students. What is an educator to do?

Employees of educational institutions have a formidable responsibility to be knowledgeable about what they can and cannot do and say in social media, what they should do and not do to protect their students from hurtful and injurious statements sent out against them in social media, and when they have the right to protect themselves from statements by students or other employees publicized in social media. Offensive and disparaging Internet content has emerged into a multifaceted and complex challenge for educational institutions to tackle.

PARENTS

3

Cyberbullying in Social Media: Parents

Communication with educators has significantly changed in the twenty-first century with increasing use of the Internet. Parents and key stakeholders clearly are using technology in record numbers to communicate with teachers, to research schools, to investigate new programs, to raise money for the PTA, and to check their children's grades and homework assignments (Zieger & Tan, 2012; Murray, 2011; Gielen, 2010; Carr, 2006). While the traditional backpack method for parent communication still has its place for some school-based information, such as family nights and field trip notices, it is a growing trend for educators to shift more time and resources toward electronic communication.

EDUCATIONAL ASPECTS

Parent involvement in a child's education improves learning, attendance, behavior, and graduation rates. Increased and meaningful communication between parents and educators enhances parent involvement. Research studies (Zieger & Tan, 2012; Gielen, 2010; Glanz, 2006; Marzano, 2003; Cotton & Wikelund, 1989) overwhelmingly demonstrate that parent involvement in their children's learning is positively related to student achievement. The research also shows that the more intensively parents are involved, the more beneficial are the achievement effects. Swap (1993, as cited by Glanz, 2006) reports that "parent involvement in students' education is directly related to children's achievement" (17). Communication is most effective when parents are encouraged to become involved with their child's learning. Equally important is communication that helps parents support their child's learning at home, such as classroom assignments, homework, student progress, attendance, and recommendations for how to help a child at home.

Carter (2002) reports that the earlier in a child's educational process parent involvement begins, the more powerful the effects will be. Although parent involvement has been shown to benefit students at all grade levels, the nature of the involvement that is most beneficial to children changes as they reach adolescence. Parents generally become less involved with the daily aspects of their children's education as the children grow older. Their involvement then is likely to take different forms, such as monitoring homework, helping with college or career plans, and participating in extracurricular activities (Cotton & Wikelund, 1989).

The use of technology has increased the frequency and effectiveness of communication between parents and schools, which has enhanced parent involvement. The digital age has opened up new ways for educators to communicate with parents, such as email, online newsletters, websites, and web access to useful information. In addition, when used properly, they are valuable public relations tools that generate involvement and good will. Although parent involvement tends to drop off after the elementary school years, technology affords parents the opportunity to stay involved in the progress their children are making in school. Parents can access their students' attendance, grades, and assignments via websites or parent portals and email teachers and administrators with questions and concerns. Zieger and Tan (2012) report, "Technology has given parents and teachers the opportunity to explore ways of communicating. New technologies have the power to improve the parent-teacher relationship by providing easy, efficient methods of transferring information. Online gradebooks have become widely used in many school districts, giving parents and students 24-hour access to their grades and information about upcoming assignments."

Cyberbullying

U.S. Concerns

While parent involvement has a positive influence on child and adolescent learning and achievement, there are downsides to excessive parent involvement. Parents of today's "millennial generation" are very protective of their children (Strauss, 2006). They are accustomed to close contact with their children and vice versa. Parents who previously spent more time in classrooms or frequently called teachers are now emailing them, seeking new ways of staying involved in their child's education. The option to email their teachers with questions or concerns can make a huge difference in their ability to stay in touch (Carr, 2004). Of particular concern are parents who are dubbed "helicopter parents" because of their tendency to hover over their children. According to teachers, helicopter parents email them with messages that are often excessive or abusive, or both (Williams, 2008). The prevalence of harassing emails from helicopter parents contributed to the Howard County, Maryland, school system's decision to implement a civility policy in 2007 and prompted the PTA to send a warning to parents about email at the beginning of the school year. A spokeswoman for the Howard County schools shared that teachers and administrators were receiving frequent and multiple upsetting emails from the same parents so frequently that employees felt they were being harassed (Williams, 2008).

Many special education teachers are seeing a rise in annoying and uncomfortable behavior from litigious parents. Demands placed on these teachers may have hurt retention. The wide use of email and other advances such as parent portals to view attendance, grades, and assignments have equipped special education parents with tools to better monitor their children's academic performance and communicate concerns more often with teachers. "Nearly 9 in 10 superintendents and 8 in 10 principals say that special education laws give parents a sense of entitlement and make them too quick to threaten legal action, sometimes through email, to get their way" (Public Agenda, 2003). Conflicts are worsened when parents and school staff are hostile to each other through email communication. When parents' and teachers' behaviors become disrespectful and angry, relationships can become so strained that the child can suffer emotionally and academically. Hostile relationships can develop, in which:

- parents and/or teachers do not respect one another;
- teachers, administrators, or parents refuse to make changes to accommodate the child;
- parents make unrealistic demands in an angry, confrontational manner;
- parents or teachers feel that they are not valued, that their input is not wanted, and that the child is not receiving an appropriate education; and
- the school or home environment is negative, unsafe, rigid, or unsupportive (Logsdon, 2007).

My dissertation online survey (Horowitz, 2009) explored the frequency of several issues, including email communication with parents, students, and colleagues; uncomfortable emails; harassing emails; and how educators responded to email communication. One-third of educators reported emailing parents one to two times a week. Another third reported emailing parents one to two times a month. A greater percentage of educators reported feeling uncomfortable after the receipt of an email from parents than from colleagues or students. With respect to uncomfortable email from parents, 45 percent of educators report that they considered it a form of cyberbullying or harassment. When responding to uncomfortable emails from parents, 70–78 percent of educators reported they responded to the sender, shared the emails with colleagues, shared them with an administrator, sought advice from a colleague, or sought advice from an administrator. Within the sample, 8 percent reported receiving uncomfortable online communication via social media, and 49 percent said they considered it a form of cyberbullying or harassment.

After an extensive analysis of the severity of reactions to uncomfortable email communications, the Horowitz RUDE (Responses to Uncomfortable and Distracting Email) Scale was developed. The first factor in the scale involved offensive email reactions (the educator found them offensive), including:

sexually suggestive, sexually explicit, offensive language, embarrassing, and annoying. The second factor involved threatening email reactions (the educator found them threatening), including: defaming and denigrating, harmful, untrue or cruel, threatening, and insulting. Not surprisingly, respondents in the fifty and older group of educators reported higher mean levels of reactions than those of younger educators for the offensive factor. Also not surprisingly, educators who work in more affluent school districts reported higher mean levels of reactions from parents than in less affluent school districts for both offensive and threatening factors. I believed that this was likely because parents in more affluent school districts are typically college educated and professional, precipitating more aggressive questions and threats of litigation (Horowitz, 2009). A very interesting finding was that male educators reported a greater number of offensive and threatening email reactions as compared to female educators.

Additionally, the school-level data presented the finding that middle school educators received more uncomfortable emails from parents than educators from the other levels. One may speculate that the challenge of raising and educating adolescent children precipitates emails of this nature. Another interesting finding was that educators who work across two or more levels in a K–12 system reported higher mean levels of both offensive and threatening email reactions than those who work at one level in a school district. These educators may be administrators or pupil services personnel who serve more than one level in a school district.

As a school district superintendent, I personally receive aggressive emails from parents on a biweekly basis, unhappy about the education or discipline of their child. In most cases, these emails arrive in my email inbox or spam filter. Frequently, the parents copy themselves, and in some instances, they copy an attorney or educational advocate. From time to time, I am blind copied on an email to a school administrator, teacher, or guidance counselor. Rarely will I respond to these emails. I prefer to contact the parent via telephone or meet in person.

International Concerns

In addition to events occurring in the United States, internationally, there is a growing population of parents who cyberbully educators. The Association of Teachers and Lecturers in the United Kingdom stated that more than one in seven teachers has been the victim of cyberbullying by pupils or parents, and almost half know a colleague who has been targeted (Williams, 2010). The Association's survey found that 15 percent of educators had been bullied online with tactics ranging from abusive messages to hate sites and photographs or videos being posted. Some 45 percent of them knew a colleague who had been a victim, and 17 percent were aware of hate groups being set up to target others.

According to a study conducted in the United Kingdom (Evans, 2011; Chew, 2011), one-third of teachers have been victims of cyberbullying or know a teacher who has been cyberbullied, and 26 percent of the cyberbullying was reported to come from parents. The majority of those claiming abuse were women. Some of those educators have been left suicidal or needing psychological treatment after campaigns have been launched about them on Facebook or Twitter. This was considered public defamation of character as reported by Evans (2011) and Chew (2011).

A commentary about the Evans and Chew survey (Garling, 2011) reported that the walls and protection of the Internet seem to be catalyzing the viciousness. Teachers reported that Facebook groups, chat rooms, Twitter accounts, and a variety of additional online forums were set up to harangue and smear them. The cases of outright libel and mean-spirited slander were not normal means of expressing displeasure, as reported by Garling (2011).

Another more recent survey in the United Kingdom (Mulholland, 2012) reported that teachers have received death threats, were accused of serious crimes, and were subjected to sexist and racist abuse by students and parents from social networking sites. Sixteen percent of the teachers reported that parents were commenting about them. Almost half the teachers who were subjected to abusive comments by parents reported they did not feel supported by their schools because the schools did not take any action. The leader of the teachers' union shared that the survey findings exposed the way employers were failing in their responsibility toward educators by not having appropriate policies in place or by not taking incidents seriously when reported (Mulholland, 2012).

Social Media

Social media is providing a growing variety of methods for parents to communicate with educators. Many school districts have parent portals for 24-7 communication about students' attendance, grades, and assignments. Some school districts or individual schools have Facebook pages and/or Twitter accounts. The expectation is that parents will become more engaged in their children's education and support the educational establishment. Many school districts have online emergency communication systems to notify parents of things such as school closings and other emergencies or important announcements (Horowitz, 2010).

Local and state education associations are cautioning educators to control access to their personal information on social media sites. They have been advised not to accept friend requests from students or their parents (PSEA, Social Networking, 2012). Educators should not accept someone they do not know as their friend or join groups that may be considered unprofessional or inappropriate. They should not use obscene or vulgar language or post photos or materials that could be considered inappropriate or unprofessional on sites in which they communicate with students and parents (PSEA, Social Networking, 2012).

Health Benefits and Concerns

"The digital landscape is a positive place for kids," states Dr. Gwenn O'Keeffe, lead author of the American Academy of Pediatrics 2011 report on the impact of social media on children, adolescents, and families. It promotes a variety of healthy habits like socialization and a sense of connectedness to the greater world and to causes (Listfield, 2011). However, children need guidance from their parents regarding such issues as privacy and security online, friending others on Facebook, cyberbullying, plagiarism, and being totally consumed by the technology itself, such as texting and playing video games. Listfield (2011) reports that "we are just beginning to assess how this nonstop connectivity is affecting our children's social and intellectual development. It is changing the nature of the relationships to each other, to their families and to the world around them."

The American Academy of Pediatrics Council on Communications and Media led a panel at their annual 2012 conference called "Social Media: The Good, the Bad and the Ugly." The goal was to get pediatricians to discuss social media issues with adolescents and parents. The panel was established in 2007 with the recognition that social media touches on numerous health concerns: aggression, sex, drugs, obesity, self-image, eating disorders, depression, suicide, learning disorders, and academic achievement (Etheridge, 2012). According to estimates from a 2012 Nielsen survey, "The average teenager sends an astonishing 3,400 texts a month: more than 100 a day. Many learn the hard way that once they hit send, there is no such thing as an erase button" (Etheridge, 2012). The American Academy of Pediatrics encourages parents to monitor their adolescent's computer and cell phone usage. Parents need to provide a safety net for their children and look out for them. Etheridge (2012) advises parents to be a good digital role model for their children. Parents should use teachable moments in the media headlines to counsel their children.

Main Line Health, a large hospital system in suburban Philadelphia, advises parents of specific safety strategies in their monthly magazine, *Women's Health Source* (Spring 2013):

- Teach your child to keep private information private and never reveal his or her name, age, sex, or location online.
- Discuss the consequences of sending inappropriate messages and pictures that can include legal action.
- Set up browser filters for language, nudity, and violence, or use a browser created just for kids.

- Create your own profile on the social networking sites your child uses and require your child to "friend" you on Facebook. Check the privacy settings on your child's account.
- Check your computer history and your child's cell phone. Be transparent and let your kids know what you're doing.
- Set family time limits for using the Internet and electronic devices.

Public Health Approach

John Culhane, professor of law and director of the Health Law Institute at Widener University School of Law, recommends a public health approach to school bullying for school administrators. He defines public health as the practice of preventing disease and promoting good health within groups of people, from small communities to entire countries. Professor Culhane draws a parallel to a population-based approach in which all populations are affected by bullying: bullies, victims, and all students and staff in the learning environment and the larger school community. This approach would use the best available evidence to determine how to address the problems: using qualitative and quantitative data, as well as considering the effects of types of bullying, populations most at risk, complex effects, and the effectiveness of interventions. Culhane suggests that success can be measured by a reduction of the incidence and prevalence of bullying. Culhane's approach should be seriously considered by school administrators and pupil services personnel.

Responses to Parent Cyberbullying or Harassment

The Horowitz doctoral research study demonstrated the need to provide guidance to educators as to how to respond to electronic cyberbullying or harassment by parents. The following document was developed by Merle Horowitz, EdD, and Dorothy M. Bollinger, Esquire, to address this need.

Continuum of Actions and Consequences for Electronic Harassment by Parents[1]

BACKGROUND

The volume of electronic communications that an administrator receives has grown, and more of it than ever carries a hostile or threatening tone.[2] These electronic communications are received from parents, students, and others and have been classified into two reactions that administrators feel—fear or embarrassment—based on two factors. First, they were classified by whether the electronic communication is offensive and includes offensive language, embarrassing and annoying messages, and content that are sexually explicit or suggestive. Second, they were classified by whether the message is threatening and includes messages that are defaming or denigrating; harmful, untrue, or cruel; or insulting or threatening.

An overwhelming number of administrators express concern that they are not provided with guidance about how to deal with online hostile and threatening electronic communications.

PURPOSE

This document is an attempt to help central- and building-level administrators, as well as professional staff, to address parents' electronic communication issues, which include a hostile or a threatening tone, or both, and that cause the administrators or professional staff members to be fearful or embarrassed in the school district atmosphere today. First, a continuum of the hostile and threatening electronic communications is defined and an example offered. Second, considerations, including consequences for handling the electronic communications, are presented.

Continuum

1. Emails That Are Annoying

⊠ Definition

annoy: to disturb or bother (a person) in a way that displeases, troubles, or slightly irritates; to be bothersome or troublesome. www.dictionary.com (2010)

⊠ Example

"I have many complaints about the grades you have given my child."
"Here is how to write my child's GIEP."
"Alter his grade so he can graduate."

2. Emails That Are Embarrassing

⊠ Definition

embarrass: (1) to cause confusion and shame to; make uncomfortable, self-conscious; disconcert; abash; (2) to make difficult or intricate, as a question or problem; complicate; (3) to put obstacles or difficulties in the way of; impede. www.dictionary.com (2010)

⊠ Example

"I question your ability to teach."
"You don't like my child and we all know it."
"What are your credentials?"
"I question your professional judgment on homework completion and student responsibility."
"You are an embarrassment to your profession."

3. Emails That Include Offensive Language

☒ Definition

offensive language: causing displeasure, anger, or resentment, especially repugnant to the prevailing sense of what is decent or moral. *Black's Law Dictionary*, 9th ed. (2009)

☒ Example

"You are a f--king asshole."

"Why don't you help my f--king kid?"

4. Emails That Are Insulting

☒ Definition

insulting: (1) to treat or speak to insolently or with contemptuous rudeness; affront; (2) to affect as an affront; (3) offend or demean; (4) to attack; assault; (5) to behave with insolent triumph; exult contemptuously; (6) an insolent or contemptuously rude action or remark; affront. www.dictionary.com (2010)

☒ Example

"I told my child to disregard your assignment because I do not agree with your discipline."

"I question your authority to discipline my child."

"Your teachers are incompetent."

"Was race a factor in your assigning that grade?"

"My daughter is not a liar so you have to be."

5. Emails That Are Threatening

☒ Definition

threat: a communicated intent to inflict harm or loss on another or another's property, especially one who might diminish a person's freedom to act voluntarily or with lawful consent; a person or thing that might well cause harm. *Black's Law Dictionary*, 9th ed. (2009)

☒ Example

"I will post this on a list serve if you do not give me services."

"You will address the following numbered items."

"I am going to tell the principal you are not doing your job."

"I am hiring a lawyer to have you fired."

"Make sure my child passes."

"Your teaching certificate ought to be revoked."

"You threatened my child."

"You will be responsible if my child commits suicide."

"You have not followed my son's IEP and have violated his rights as a student."

"I will get you fired."

"I demand the release of that teacher. She is incompetent."

6. Emails That Are Harmful, Untrue, or Cruel

⊠ Definition

harmful: (1) causing or capable of causing harm; injurious; (2) physical injury or mental damage; hurt; (3) to do bodily harm; (4) moral injury; evil; wrong; (5) to do or cause harm to; injure; damage; hurt: to harm one's reputation. www.dictionary.com (2010)

untrue: not correct; inaccurate. *Black's Law Dictionary*, 9th ed. (2009)

cruelty: the intentional and malicious infliction of mental or physical suffering on a living creature, especially a human; abusive treatment; outrage. *Black's Law Dictionary*, 9th ed. (2009)

⊠ Example

"You hate my child."

"You have hurt my son."

"You are harming my child's ability to learn."

"I find your decision to be based on lies and inaccuracies."

"You have been unjust to my child."

"Your decision will be your negative legacy."

7. Emails That Defame or Denigrate One's Reputation

⊠ Definition

defamation: the act of harming the reputation of another by making a false statement to a third person; a false written or oral statement that damages another's reputation (includes both libel and slander). *Black's Law Dictionary*, 9th ed. (2009)

denigrate: to speak damagingly of; criticize in a derogatory manner; sully

defame: to denigrate someone's character; to treat or represent as lacking in value or importance; belittle

disparage: to denigrate someone's contributions to a project. www.dictionary.com (2010)

⊠ Example

"You have made unfair, biased decisions."

"You are not qualified to teach my child."

"You are wrong in your thinking and stupid."

"You don't know what is best for my child."

"You are a racist."

"Your lesson choice was politically motivated and inappropriate for children."

"You are an awful teacher who has ruined my son's life."

"You don't care and are sabotaging my child's education."

8. Emails That Are Sexually Explicit

⊠ Definition

sexually explicit:

sex: the sum of the peculiarities of structure and function that distinguish a male from a female organism; gender. *Black's Law Dictionary*, 9th ed. (2009)

explicit: (1) fully and clearly expressed; leaving nothing implied; fully and clearly defined or formulated; (2) forthright and unreserved in expression; (3) readily observable; an explicit sign of trouble; describing or portraying nudity or sexual activity in graphic detail. *The American Heritage® Dictionary of the English Language*, 4th ed. (2009)

⌧ Example

"You are gay and should not be teaching children."

9. Emails That Are Sexually Suggestive

⌧ Definition

sexually suggestive:

sex: the sum of the peculiarities of structure and function that distinguish a male from a female organism; the character of being male or female. *Black's Law Dictionary*, 9th ed. (2009)

suggestion: an indirect presentation of an idea. *Black's Law Dictionary*, 9th ed. (2009)

⌧ Example

"Express your opinions about this national event on homosexuality."

"You have shown a movie to your class that sexually exploited women."

Considerations and Consequences for Handling Problems

Each electronic communication incident must be addressed within the uniqueness of the school district's policies, regulations, rules, procedures, contracts, and culture, and if appropriate, on a case-by-case basis. Administrators may need to progressively respond based on the degree of hostile and threatening communication and the harm caused, such as fear and embarrassment.

For Example

When *professional staff members* need assistance because they have attempted to politely and professionally resolve the matter and to address the content of the electronic communication but have been unsuccessful, or because it is not appropriate for the professional staff member to confront the parent, principals may need to speak to the parent either in a telephone conversation or in a face-to-face meeting, and then follow up with a letter to the parent(s). With some incidents, it may be appropriate for the principals to immediately prepare a written letter to the parent(s).

When *principals* need assistance because the actions they have taken on behalf of the incidents experienced by their professional staff members have not resolved the situation, or because the electronic communications are directed to the principals and the principals' polite and professional attempts to address the content of the electronic communications have not been successful, or because it is not appropriate for the principals to confront the parent(s), the superintendent may need to speak to the parent(s) either in a telephone conversation or in a face-to-face meeting, and then follow up with a letter to the parent(s). With some incidents it may be appropriate for superintendents to immediately prepare a written letter to the parent(s).

When *superintendents* need assistance because the actions they have taken on behalf of the incidents experienced by their professional staff members and administrators have not resolved the situation, or because the electronic communications are directed to superintendents and the superintendents' polite and professional attempts to address the content of the electronic communications have been unsuccessful, or because it is not appropriate for superintendents to confront the parents, superintendents may need to (i) speak to the board president to consider taking further action based on the policy, legislative, and quasi-judicial authority legally authorized to the board of school directors as a whole, or (ii) speak to the school solicitor about what further legal action(s) the school solicitor recommends, and then present the situation and possible legal actions[3] to the school board to determine the course of action the school district desires to take, or (iii) contact law enforcement to investigate the incident and, where justified, bring criminal actions. It may be appropriate with some incidents for superintendents to immediately prepare a written letter to the parent(s).

Educators should be aware that their electronic communications may be considered a discoverable item and useable as evidence in a case.

These considerations are intended as neither legal advice nor a recipe for all incidents.

Dr. Merle Horowitz is the superintendent of the Marple Newtown School District (www.mnsd.org) located in Newtown Square, Pennsylvania. You may contact her by email at mhorowitz@mnsd.org, by telephone at 610-359-4256, or by first-class mail at 40 Media Line Road, Newtown Square, PA 19073.

Dorothy M. Bollinger, Esquire, is an attorney at the Bollinger Law Firm, LLC (www.bollingerlawfirm.com) located in Radnor, Pennsylvania. You may contact her by email at dbollinger@bollingerlawfirm.com, by telephone at 610-688-6883, or by first-class mail at 104 Rock Rose Lane, Radnor, PA 19087.

LEGAL ASPECTS

Educational institutions are challenged today to handle cyberbullying and social media behaviors of not only students and employees but also parents. That being said, today parents also are challenged to control the cyberbullying and social media conduct of their children at home, at school, and in the wider cyberspace. Both have intricate and thorny responsibilities to help themselves and someone else in an increasingly communicative, informational, exposed, and technological world, whether from using social media websites or social media apps or other technological means. Educational institutions and parents need to understand each other's responsibilities and work together to conquer cyberbullying, including sexting, harassment, defamation, impersonation, and other unacceptable and illegal means of cyberbullying and social media misuse.

Sometimes there are clashes, as described in the Horowitz study; they are summarized earlier in this chapter. These indirect confrontations from the parent to the educator through electronic transactions at any level (preschool through higher education) are sometimes hateful, sometimes misinterpreted, and other times unproductive. As illustrated below, a mother hides behind the computer, a larger-than-life intruder, claiming, "Professor, you are . . . unfair! Wrong! Awful! Stupid!" while the professor sits shocked, hurt, and cyberbullied. At the same time, the student feels powerful, getting the best of her professor through her "#1 Mom."

Other times electronic transactions are useful because they precisely state the parent's valuable position that would not have been voiced face to face or during a live telephone conversation.

When educational approaches, communications, preventions, interventions, and other attempts fail to help students and employees of the educational institution to steer clear of cyberbullying in social media, administrators have a duty to discipline students and employees through the school's disciplinary hierarchy. Conversely, administrators have little administrative recourse against parents. Legal actions may be brought by the educational institution against the parent as a last resort—that is, for truancy or for defamation. Further, the school district can refer a case to law enforcement—for example, assault, battery, or harassment. Employees, too, may bring actions against the parent—for example, a defamation action. In addition, parents can sue the educational institutions and their employees when they are dissatisfied with the educational institution's decision to discipline their child. Examples of these cases were discussed in the student section of this book.

In this parent section, we examine some of the administrative and legal actions parents took against educational institutions and social media sites when the parents believed they or their children (alive or deceased) were the victims of cyberbullying, as well as administrative and legal actions that educational institutions and/or their employees took against parents and/or students when the educational institution and/or employees believed they were the victim of cyberbullying.

Finally, there are many times when the cyberbullying matter is between one parent/child and another parent/child or friend, without any reason for the school to be involved in the matter, even though one of the parents seeks discipline from the school for the other parent's child. Just as parents seek help with discipline from the school, they also at times must pursue assistance with social media cyber-issues in other jurisdictions, such as with law enforcement, with judicial actions, and with social media sites. Matters faced by parents beyond the educational institutions' jurisdiction raise privacy issues, too. To finish, we examine a privacy rights case confronted by a parent beyond the educational institution's jurisdiction.

In addition to legal actions, civil and criminal statutes, regulations, and contractual agreements—such as a website's terms of service and/or a website's privacy policy that are available to the general public—may be applicable for educational institutions and/or employees to punish or redress parents for their cyberbullying in social media. These, of course, depend on the facts and circumstances, jurisdiction, individuals, action(s), and issue(s), among others.

Civil and Criminal Statutes and Regulations

As discussed in chapter 2 and illustrated in appendix A, "Table of State Bullying and Cyberbullying Laws," numerous statutes and regulations have been enacted by Congress and federal agencies, as well as state legislatures and state administrative agencies. Some of these statutes and regulations require school districts to create and enforce bullying and cyberbullying policies, other statutes and regulations are designed to apply generally in civil actions, and still others are designed as criminal statutes.[4]

Parent/Student as Victims versus Educational Institutions

Parents, on behalf of their deceased child(ren), believe they are the victim, and what happened under the educational institution's auspices was the cause of the cyberbullying or could have prevented it. Under these circumstances, parents challenge or sue the educational institution.

Parents may challenge the educational institution's enforcement of its bullying or cyberbullying policy, or they may bring actions under federal statutes and regulations such as the Individuals with Disabilities in Education Act (IDEA 2004) or various Office of Civil Rights sources. Parents could decide to bring an action against an individual bully/cyberbully under a state's defamation, harassment, and/or unauthorized computer use statute, or parents may report cyberbullying actions to law enforcement where criminal actions generally available in most states, such as battery, stalking, harassment, extortion, or assault, can be pursued.

Rebecca Ann Sedwick, a twelve-year-old girl, jumped to her death on September 9, 2013, at an old cement business in Lakeland, Florida, after hate messages were posted about her online through social media messaging and photo apps.[5] The incident reportedly started over a boyfriend issue, with messages from a group of middle school girls stating, "You should die" and "Why don't you go kill yourself?" Reportedly, the cyberbullying started during the school year before her death. Investigators found her diaries, in which she talked about her terror, torment, and depression. During that year, Rebecca's mother withdrew her from school, homeschooled her, and helped her find and undergo therapy and counseling. She was hospitalized for cutting her wrists. Law enforcement became involved during the remainder of that school year. At the start of the next school year (the one during which she took her life), she transferred to a new school that she liked, but the bullies found her and continued to bully her online.[6]

Florida has multiple statutes that address cyberbullying, cyberstalking, and other unlawful computer actions. Examples include criminal statutes[7] and the Jeffrey Johnston Stand Up for All Students Act (located in Florida's education code) that became effective on July 1, 2013, and covers cyberbullying in schools.[8] In this matter, a Florida sheriff reportedly filed criminal charges against a twelve-year-old girl and a fourteen-year-old girl, but the charges were dropped.[9] Rebecca Sedwick's mother, Tricia Norman, is reportedly "considering a lawsuit against school officials and the parents of her tormentors."[10]

Educational Institution Victim versus Parent(s) and/or Student(s)

Employees of educational institutions at any level (preschool through higher education) also believe that they are bullied and/or cyberbullied by parents.[11] They receive electronic communication and transactions that are sometimes hateful, threatening, harassing, excessive, and disruptive.

Two school district attorneys, Patricia J. Whitten and Jennifer Smith, wrote about their experience with a parent of a student with disabilities sending excessive email communications to a special education teacher.[12] Faced with excessive parent communications, they asked "when is enough enough," "what limits can be imposed," and "what rights are violated when limits are imposed?" Not having legal decisions available on the issue, they took a thoughtful and measured approach. Considering a student's Individualized Education Program (IEP) and the federal 2004 statutory requirements as a means of addressing the communications, Whitten and Smith suggested:

> If a student's IEP calls for daily communication with the parent, a hearing officer or the OCR [U.S. Office of Civil Rights] could find that limitations on communication that call for less than that required in the IEP constitute noncompliance with the IEP. Thus, the provisions of a student's IEP should be reviewed before restrictions are imposed. If there is the potential of a violation, the IEP team should reconvene and revise the IEP to either reflect a reduced amount of communication, establish an alternative form of communication [communication logs, monthly meetings, etc.], or a more vague statement [if any] about communications with the parent.[13]

In Whitten's and Smith's experience with an OCR complaint that dealt with "a district's ban on parent emails that were excessive in number and constantly critical of the staff," OCR did not find that the school district violated the law.[14]

> Consequently, OCR determined that the District's restriction on email communication that was implemented from October 15, 2007, to January 23, 2008, did not significantly disadvantage the Complainant or Student A. OCR also determined that the restriction on email communication was not likely to deter or preclude the Complainant from engaging in further protected activity. In addition, the evidence indicated that the restriction was a reasonable attempt by the District to relieve District staff from the burden of reviewing and responding to the Complainant's excessive email communications, rather than an act of retaliation for the Complainant's lawsuit. As such, OCR determined that a prima facie case of retaliation was not established with respect to the restriction on email communication.[15]

Parents may sue and be sued when their cyberbullying and/or their child's cyberbullying violates specific statutes and/or regulations relevant to the cyberbullying and/or general, more traditional laws.

Contract Terms

In addition to statutes and regulations, contractual agreements that are available to the general public may be applicable for educational institutions, employees, parents, and/or students to punish or redress cyberbullying in social media. Contractual terms between websites and apps, on the one hand, and their users, on the other hand, are found in privacy policies and terms of service or terms of use, which are referred to by different names. For example, Facebook's terms of service is titled "Statement of Rights and Responsibilities" and incorporates a "Data Use Policy" and "Community Standards."

Social media websites typically provide terms that users are required to comply with in order to use the website. The terms are agreed to by the user in one of two ways: (1) by expressly agreeing through a "clickwrap agreement" (such as by clicking "I agree"); or (2) through a "browsewrap agreement" (by using the website).[16] Both the social media website and the website user can breach the terms of service, which activates an enforcement, cure, litigation, or other civil action. For example, most terms of service prohibit the use of false credentials to create or open an account, provide procedures for a user to identify the fraudulent account, and ask that the social media website shut the fraudulent account down. Falsely assuming the name of another person to create an account, and then posting inappropriate, false statements and photos about a student or employee could involve a parent, a student, and/or an employee. Therefore, the terms of service can sometimes be used to address cyberbullying and harassment online from both a parent-victim and a parent-cyberbully position.

Parent/Student Victim, Parent of Another Student, and Social Media Website

U.S. v. Drew (2009)[17] is often referred to as a cyberbullying case because the facts involved a repulsive cyberbullying incident. In this case, the parent of a middle school student, Lori Drew, created a fake MySpace account that she used to interact with Megan Meier, a classmate of her daughter's. Through the course of the interaction, the parent misrepresented herself as a boy named Josh Evans, leading Megan to believe Josh was infatuated with her. Lori Drew then abruptly sent a message from Josh to Megan stating that the world would be a better place without her. The same day Megan received this message, she hung herself.[18] The prosecution filed an indictment against Lori Drew under the Computer Fraud and Abuse Act (CFAA),[19] charging her with conspiracy[20] and with three counts of violating a felony portion of the CFAA,[21] which prohibits accessing a computer without authorization or in excess of authorization and obtaining information. Lori Drew claimed violations of her constitutional rights in her defense. The court originally found that the CFAA overcame the parent's constitutional challenges and arguments.

Later, a jury acquitted the parent of the felony counts but convicted her of misdemeanor CFAA violations. Once acquitted by the jury of the felony provisions, this case was no longer about "cyberbullying," but was instead concerned about the proper scope of the application of the CFAA in the context of violations of a website's Terms of Service. The prosecution had also claimed that Lori Drew breached the MySpace Terms of Service.

As to this claim, the court was required to examine whether the parent's intentional breach of the website's terms of service, without more, was sufficient to constitute a misdemeanor (criminal) violation of the CFAA, and, if so, would the statute, as so interpreted, survive constitutional challenges on the grounds of vagueness and related doctrines.[22]

In the final ruling in the case, the U.S. District Court for the Central District of California held that violating the MySpace Terms of Service could not constitute a criminal (misdemeanor) violation under the CFAA because terms in the Terms of Service were vague, failed to clearly spell out which violations would result in a loss of previously granted authorization to use the website, did not fairly inform users which acts may result in criminal liability, did not provide a notice of "fair warning" of prohibited conduct, and lacked minimal objective criteria for law enforcement to follow.[23]

Users may be denied the privilege of using a website because of their breach of the terms of service. Civil cases exist in which either websites or users have been found liable for their breach of the terms of service but not criminalized for their misuse.

Parent/Student Victim, Other Students, and Social Media Website

In another more recent Italian cyberbullying incident, a parent alleged violations of Facebook's Terms of Service (Statement of Rights and Responsibilities). Cyberbullying is not just a problem faced by parents in the United States; it is an international problem. One of the many examples involving tweens and teens in other countries involves Carolina Picchio, a fourteen-year-old girl from Novara, Italy, who committed suicide in January 2013 after a gang of teenage boys, who were allegedly friends of her ex-boyfriend, reportedly posted a video on Facebook of her drunk in a bathroom at a party. She had broken up with her boyfriend after he insulted her on Facebook days earlier. Before she took her life, she wrote on Facebook, "Forgive me if I am not strong. I cannot take it any longer." The ex-boyfriend and his friends reportedly posted a barrage of abusive, offensive messages aimed at Carolina that became too much for her to handle. She jumped headfirst out of her bedroom window, landing on the concrete below.[24]

Carolina's friend and sister reported the posts to Facebook, but they were not removed. Novara's prosecutor, Francesco Saluzzo, in addition to investigating the boys' actions, is reportedly placing Facebook staff under investigation, probing how the videos had stayed online "for days" even after her friends requested that they be removed, and is looking into filing a criminal complaint against Facebook for failing to remove the offensive content that led to her suicide. In addition to the Facebook posts, on the day leading up to her suicide, Carolina purportedly received 2,600 vulgar messages through the messaging service WhatsApp.

Facebook's spokesperson's response was as follows: "We are deeply saddened by the tragic death of Carolina Picchio and our hearts go out to the family and friends. Harassment has no place on Facebook and we actively encourage teens and parents to report incidences of bullying using the links located throughout the site. We remove content reported to us that violates our Statement of Rights and Responsibilities and we escalate reports of harassment and bullying to law enforcement where appropriate."[25]

The Italian Parent's Association filed a criminal complaint in Rome against Facebook. Antonia Affinita, director of the Italian Parent Association, said that "Italian law forbids minors under 18 signing contracts, yet Facebook is effectively entering into a contract with minors regarding their privacy, without their parents knowing."[26] For additional information about the cyberbullying of Carolina, see CNN's interview with her mother, Christina Zocca, by Ben Wedeman, "Online Bullying Ends in Suicide," CNN, July 31, 2013, http://www.cnn.com/video/data/2.0/video/world/2013/07/31/wedeman-italy-bullied-suicide.cnn.html. Carolina's uncle, Sebastian Bartolo, created a video tribute to Carolina that was posted on YouTube.[27]

Contractual terms may be the basis to educate, prevent, and intervene in cyberbullying in social media, or they may be the basis for parents, students, educational institutions, employees, social media websites and apps, and law enforcement to take action, or they may be the basis for legal action(s).

Court Decisions Involving Parents and Educational Institutions

In addition to statutory, regulatory, and contract legal sources that address cyberbullying in social media, court decisions also create a source of law for punishments and remedies. Parents can bring legal actions on behalf of their deceased children. Sometimes the legal action is filed against the educational institution based on civil rights issues.

Civil Rights Cases

Parent/Student Victims versus Educational Institutions In *Long v. Murray County School District* (2013),[28] Tyler Long, a student in the Murray County School District, was subjected to many instances of teasing and bullying during his high school years. The instances were reported to school officials, and school officials responded to those reports. Tyler had been diagnosed with Asperger's syndrome and had an IEP that addressed social needs and bullying. When Tyler was a junior, he committed suicide in his home.[29]

The parents claimed that the school district was deliberately indifferent under § 504 and the ADA. Three of their experts testified that the school district had failed to use diligence in recognizing and responding to the bullying, that the school district failed to prevent harassment by failing to meet generally accepted standards for schools and administrators, and that a psychological autopsy analysis concluded that bullying caused the suicide.[30]

The school district's policies prohibited all verbal and physical harassment, but there was no specific mention of disability-based harassment. The school district used the STEP discipline process (a progressive discipline system teachers use to address minor classroom concerns with the student and the student's parents), "Teachers as Advisors" program, and character education provided in ninth grade. However, no assemblies addressing the school district's anti-taunting, anti-bullying, or anti-harassment policies occurred, and there was no specific charge from the school leadership on anti-bullying processes. The school district had an online complaint form, but no confidential dropbox.[31]

The U.S. District Court for the Northern District of Georgia found that Tyler was subjected to severe and pervasive bullying throughout his high school years, but the court ruled that the school district responded effectively every time bullying was reported. Therefore, the court ruled that school administrators had not demonstrated deliberate indifference. Consequently, the court granted the school district's summary judgment motion to dismiss the case.[32]

The parents appealed the district court's decision challenging the propriety of the summary judgment on constitutional, ADA, and § 504 claims. Both parties had agreed that the deliberate indifference standard[33] in *Davis v. Monroe*[34] applied to the parent's § 504 and ADA claims, but they disagreed over the scope of its enforcement. The U.S. departments of Justice and Education filed briefs in support of the parents,[35] in which they argued that the question of deliberate indifference should be decided by a jury, and that a jury could find the school district was deliberately indifferent because of the school's ineffective remediation. In addition, they argued that deliberate indifference exists when the school district is ineffective in preventing sustained disability discrimination, and that the determination of deliberate indifference should include the use of known prevention strategies by the school district. The substance of the U.S. departments of Justice and Education's challenges followed the OCR's 2010 Dear Colleague Letter–Harassment and Bullying (see *supra* student chapter), OCR's 2000 Dear Colleague Letter–Prohibited Disability Harassment, and OCR's Revised Sexual Harassment Guidance: Harassment of Students by School Employees, Other Students, of Third Parties, Title IX,[36] which expanded the scope of the *Davis* standard.[37]

The National School Boards Association, Alabama Association of School Boards, Georgia School Boards Association, and Georgia School Superintendents Association filed a brief in support of the school district asking the court not to expand the *Davis* standard, not to conflate the *Davis* standard with the

OCR enforcement standards, not to expand the *Davis* actual notice requirement by triggering school responsibilities upon any report of peer "bullying," to recognize that schools are best placed to develop safe learning environment strategies, to recognize that a one-size-fits-all strategy is ill suited for the realities of school environments, and to uphold the precedent of strong deference to educational judgments of local school officials.[38]

The Eleventh Circuit Court of Appeals agreed with the district court's application of the facts, law, reasoning, and conclusions of law.[39] The court ruled that the school district was not liable for student-on-student harassment under either anti-discrimination disability statute, and that the school district was not deliberately indifferent to peer harassment of a disabled student. Here, the significance of the court's ruling is that failure to remediate the cyberbullying is not a per se indicator of deliberate indifferences.[40] The court stated that "deliberate indifference is an exacting standard; school administrators will only be deemed deliberately indifferent if their response to the harassment or lack thereof is clearly unreasonable in light of the known circumstances."[41] The court also stated that, with hindsight, the "defendants [school district] should have done more to address disability harassment, [but] Plaintiffs [have] fail[ed] to meet the high bar of deliberate indifference and [have failed to] demonstrate that Defendants' response was clearly unreasonable."[42]

In a second civil rights case, Jon Carmichael, a thirteen-year-old boy, took his own life after being bullying, harassed, and called names by his peers and what his parents claim was lack of action taken by school officials. Jon's parents filed a civil rights suit against the Joshua Independent School District in March 2011, *Carmichael v. Joshua Independent School District* (2012).[43] In their initial complaint, they alleged that Jon was thrown into a trash can and a dumpster, had his head flushed in a toilet, and was stripped nude, tied up, and again placed in a trash can and the video was posted on YouTube. The parents also claimed that Jon began seeing a school counselor, who knew of the bullying but did not report or investigate it, and that a teacher knew he was a victim of bullying and that he was suicidal but failed to arrange for an investigation. The school district enacted several policies prohibiting bullying and delineating procedures for responding to incidents of bullying and harassment, but no reports were made to school officials, and Jon's parents were never notified.[44]

Further, the parents claimed that the video was removed from YouTube at the direction of a school district staff member but that the staff member did not report the incident.[45] In an interview with Jon's mother, she claimed, "The lawsuit alleges that Joshua Schools ignored their own policy and accuses administrators of hiding video evidence of the bullying and Jon's private journal."[46]

Section 1983 Fourteenth Amendment substantive due process and equal protection claims and Title IX claims were filed against the school district by the parents. On the substantive due process claim, the U.S. District Court for the

Northern District of Texas decided that, because the parents did not adequately plead that a *state official caused* Jon the bodily harm (the students are private actors), and even considering exceptions where the state may be held liable for private actor's actions through the "special relationship" and "state-created danger theory," the parents could not succeed because no special relationship existed, and the Fifth Circuit did not recognize the state-created danger theory.[47]

On the equal protection claim, the court found that in response to incidents of bullying and harassment by other students, the parents failed to plead an equal protection claim because the school district followed school district bullying and harassment policies and procedures, that the parents failed to allege the school district treated similarly situated other students differently from Jon, and that the parents did not plead sufficient facts to allege gender discrimination.

As to the Title IX claim of discrimination based on sex, the court held that the parents did not plead a Title IX claim that the school district discriminated against Jon because he was male and that the bullying was based on his sex (the bullying and harassment was generally due to the "perpetrators' sociopathic behavior regardless of his gender").

The court permitted the parents to plead their case again by filing a second amended complaint. The parents added information about the bullying.

> A day or so before Jon's death, he was once again placed into a trash can. This time the acts of the bullies—all members of the middle school football team—escalated beyond just their regular assaults of Jon and now into a degrading sexual assault. Before they placed him in the trash can, they stripped him nude and tied him up. Then they proceeded to parade a group of boys before him while calling him "fag," "queer," "homo," and "douche." A number of the students in the locker room observed this deplorable behavior. Jon was, of course, devastated by this assault that placed his emerging sense of manhood under direct public attack.[48]
>
> Even more shocking than the incident itself is the fact that Jon's fellow student, J.R., videotaped the attack and uploaded it to YouTube. Sometime later, a teacher who had learned of the incident and video directed J.R. to remove it from the website and destroy it. The teacher did not report the incident.[49]

However, the court again granted the school district's motion to dismiss for the same reasons the court rendered in its ruling on the initial complaint.

The decision was appealed to the Fifth Circuit Court of Appeals on October 26, 2012, but no action has been taken to date.[50]

Parent/Student Victims and Employee Victim In a third civil rights case, a parent, student, educational institution, and employee believe they were aggrieved. In *Cash v. Lee County School District* (2012),[51] a parent (stepfather) sued the school district and an employee (principal) for what he alleged was a violation of his rights by the school principal. The principal of a middle school called a student into his office and asked her whether she had posted a message on Facebook that encouraged her classmates to wear blue jeans with holes in them to school. The student admitted that she had, after which the principal informed her that she would be held accountable if her classmates did indeed wear jeans with holes in violation of the school dress code. After telling her stepfather about the potential disciplinary proceedings, they asked for and were granted a conference with the principal to discuss their concerns about the punishment—that it was improper for the principal to view his stepdaughter's Facebook profile and it was unfair to punish his stepdaughter for the independent actions of other students. During the meeting, tensions escalated, resulting in the principal asking the stepfather to leave his office. Not believing the issue had been resolved and wanting it resolved before departing, the stepfather called the principal a coward when the principal attempted to leave his office. The principal then had a staff member call the police.[52]

When the police arrived, the stepfather identified himself to the two officers and attempted to explain the situation. The principal notified the officers that he wanted the stepfather arrested for disturbing the peace. The officers determined that an arrest was unnecessary and allowed the stepfather to leave. The principal later signed an affidavit alleging that the stepfather had come onto school property and created a public disturbance, and reported that "Mr. Cash placed his finger in [the principal's] face[,] called him a few names and told him to meet him outside."[53]

A few days later, the chief of police telephoned the stepfather to advise him that a warrant for his arrest had been issued as a result of the incident. He agreed to voluntarily turn himself in and had a bondsman meet him at the police station, where he was booked and then transported by two police officers to the home of the municipal judge. The judge informed him of the charges against him, and informed him that he was barred from appearing at any of the county schools. The stepfather was then transferred back to the station, where he was immediately released on bond.[54]

Later, the stepfather was permitted to enter school property to pick up his stepdaughter from school, but the underlying charge remained pending, and the principal saw him on school property. He contacted the police requesting the stepfather's arrest. Instead, the stepfather's attorney and the school district's attorney negotiated an arrangement whereby he was not arrested or issued any citation.[55] Eventually, the stepfather pled *nolo contendere* (defendant does not admit to the charge, but does not dispute it either) of disturbing the peace and appealed the conviction to the County Court of Lee County, where the charge was dropped. This was not the end of the case.

The stepfather then filed a § 1983 action, alleging that the school district and principal had violated his First and Fourth Amendment rights.[56] The First Amendment retaliation claim was premised on the theory that the principal sought to have him arrested in retaliation for criticizing the principal's actions. In order to succeed on a retaliation claim brought by an ordinary citizen (the stepparent), as opposed to a public employee, the stepfather was required to show: (1) that he was engaged in constitutionally protected activity, (2) that the principal's actions caused the stepfather to suffer an injury that would chill a person of ordinary firmness from continuing to engage in that activity, and (3) that the defendant's actions were substantially motivated by the plaintiff's exercise of the constitutionally protected activity.[57]

First, the Sixth Circuit Court of Appeals considered whether parental speech criticizing school officials was protected by the First Amendment. "The school district argued that to be protected by the First Amendment the parents' speech must have dealt with matters of truly public concern as opposed to matters of personal interest."[58] However, the court stated that the public concern test is unique to retaliation claims brought by public employees and does not apply to private citizens such as parents.[59]

In addressing the facts of the case, the court was unable to discern any reason why the stepfather's speech would not fall within the general protections of the First Amendment based on obscenity, defamation, or fighting words. Although the principal asserted that Cash pointed his finger in the principal's face as he was leaving the office, that account was disputed by other sworn testimony. The court therefore determined that the stepfather had produced sufficient evidence for a violation of his First Amendment right action, thus surviving the summary judgment motion.

The stepfather additionally attempted to raise a § 1983 claim premised on the alleged violation of his Fourth Amendment rights. He contended that without probable cause he was seized and arrested. The school district claimed that he could not succeed on such a claim because no arrest or seizure occurred because the type of seizure here would not support a Fourth Amendment claim.

The school district contended that no law enforcement officer went to Cash's home and took him into custody. The chief of police called Cash, told him about the warrant, asked him to come to the station, and told him what the bond would be so that Cash could immediately arrange for bail. Cash rode to the judge's house with the chief and another officer without being restrained with handcuffs or other restraints, and then he was returned to the station where his bondman posted bond, after which he returned home.

A seizure occurs when, in view of all of the circumstances surrounding the incident, a reasonable person would have believed that he was not free to leave. The court found that Cash was seized for purposes of his Fourth Amendment protections. The school district's motion for summary judgment as to the Fourth Amendment claim was therefore denied.

Cash's § 1983 *respondeat superior* claim against the school district could only succeed for acts directly attributable to the school district "through some official action or imprimatur."[60] To establish municipal liability under § 1983, Cash was required to show the deprivation of a federally protected right caused by action taken "pursuant to an official municipal policy."[61] He was required to identify "(1) an official policy (or custom), of which (2) a policymaker can be charged with actual or constructive knowledge, and (3) a constitutional violation whose 'moving force' is that policy or custom."[62]

The existence of a policy can be shown through evidence of an actual policy, regulation, or decision that is officially adopted and promulgated by lawmakers or others with policymaking authority.[63] "[A] single decision by a policy maker may, under certain circumstances, constitute a policy for which a [school district] may be liable."[64] However, this "single incident exception" is extremely narrow and gives rise to school district liability only if the school district actor is a final policymaker.[65]

Here, Cash did not allege that there was an officially adopted policy ratifying the acts of the principal, but he did allege that the principal's single decision to allegedly file a false report with the police was a custom for which the school district was liable and that the principal had impliedly delegated certain authorities as the final authority at the middle school. As such, he acted in an unconstitutional manner, and his action can be attributed to the school district. The court found that Cash did not provide facts or policies that showed the principal was the final decisionmaker and the policymaker. The court granted the school district's motion for summary judgment, thereby dismissing the case as to this claim.

Where parents, on behalf of their deceased children, have protections under civil rights laws and First Amendment speech rights with respect to school officials, they also have Fourth Amendment rights from unreasonable searches and seizures. Next, we examine parents' privacy rights.

Social Media Privacy Case

One of the problems parents have with their children is being aware of what their children are doing in social media. Parents are advised to review and supervise their children's online communications to determine if they are cyberbullying, sexting, and/or involved in other undesirable, forbidden, or unlawful activities. At the same time, their children claim they have a right to their privacy and give their parents a difficult time when parents want to review their communications, or the children are knowledgeable enough to use ways to conceal or screen their social media activities and sabotage their parents' supervision.

In a privacy case, *State v. Poling* (2010),[66] Poling requested that the court suppress certain evidence from being used against him by the state of Ohio for an alleged violation of a civil protection from abuse order. The evidence he wanted suppressed were emails that a sixteen-year-old girl's mother provided to the sheriff. Poling was charged with violating a protection order that prohibited him from having contact with the sixteen-year-old (his underage girlfriend), her mother, and any other member of her family.

One evening, the girl was using the home computer that was shared by all members of her family. During her use of the computer, her mother asked her to walk her cousins, who lived down the block, home. She left her MySpace account open on the computer while she was away. During the time she was gone, her mother checked her MySpace activities, copied some messages into a file that her mother maintained on the computer, and later reviewed the messages. Her mother discovered that the messages were between her daughter and Poling. She took the messages to the sheriff, who filed charges against Poling.[67]

The issue facing the court in this case was whether the sixteen-year-old's mother violated state or federal law by accessing her daughter's MySpace account and whether the emails were admissible against Poling at trial.

The Stored Communications Act applies, which does not provide for the exclusion from evidence of material that has been unlawfully obtained. Even if the mother's access to her daughter's account was determined to be unlawful, it could be deemed lawful under the concept of implied consent or authorization based on the mother's parental authority.

In this case, the mother's conduct did not violate the Stored Communications Act because it appeared to the court "to be authorized, at least implicitly, given her status as parent and how she observed the emails on the family computer without the use of her daughter's password."[68] "In addition, case law under the Wiretap Act holds that a parent may vicariously consent for the child to the intentional interception of communications as long as the parent has the good faith basis that is objectively reasonable for believing that such consent is necessary for the welfare of the minor child."[69] Further, the court stated, "Similarly, it is reasonable and within the parent's authority for the parent to monitor her child's use of the computer in the home for the welfare of the child, particularly under the circumstances presented here. If so, then the conduct would have been 'authorized' and thus not in violation of the Stored Communications Act."[70]

The court also found that the mother's conduct did not fall within the scope of Ohio's wiretap statute or other statute(s). Therefore, under federal and state law, the emails were entered as evidence against Poling.

Conclusion

Strong partnerships among parents, home, school, and community are crucial. Social media, the Internet, and mobile devices are important for communications, education, entertainment, research, socializing, business, and electronic commerce, but they can be problematic, hurtful, and dangerous in the hands of some students, educators, and parents. By parents, the school, and the community learning more about the use of social media, the Internet, mobile devices, apps, and additional related information, they can work together to help prevent cyberbullying.

Conclusion

Whether the victim of cyberbullying experienced the agony of a long and lonely journey that was difficult to escape or a calamitous one-time traumatizing event, or any of the cyberbullying that can occur along the continuum between the two, they suffered embarrassment, humiliation, torment, and more. Their life was negatively altered; talents and potential accomplishment were minimalized; and they were emotionally, mentally, or otherwise harmed by intentional or unintentional actions of a human perpetrator. What are the educational and legal aspects of cyberbullying in social media, and what do you do?

From an educational perspective, some cyberbullies need counseling; others need psychological, psychiatric, or medical help. Some confrontations necessitate that employees of educational entities protect other students and secure a safe learning environment. Yet at other times educators need to discipline students and employees and report them to law enforcement. Schools must work to educate students, employees, and parents about cyberbullying, to prevent cyberbullying, and, if it does happen, to intervene. Beyond these are the legal perspectives that students, employees, and parents may need to face. Some victims need to acquire a legal remedy against the cyberbully, whether through criminal punishment or civil liability.

In addressing each incident of cyberbullying, one must look at the specific facts and circumstances of the occurrence, the laws of the jurisdiction, the kind of social media service involved, and the decisions made by state and federal courts.

Every state and the District of Columbia has defined cyberbullying in their school code statutes or regulations, or they have delegated defining cyberbullying to the school district or state administrative department of education and combined the definition with requirements to deal with the cyberbullying problem. Although these definitions and requirements vary (for example, regarding application to on- or off-campus discipline for cyberbullying), generally the laws all focus on an electronic act of bullying through the use of the Internet, interactive and digital technologies, cellular mobile telephone or other mobile electronic devices, or any electronic communications.

In addition to school laws that protect students and employees, some state legislatures have enacted civil and criminal statutes relevant to school districts and institutions of higher education that focus on cyberbullying. Likewise, Congress has enacted laws that are applicable to cyberbullying.

Social media is more than merely a social networking website, such as Facebook or Twitter. Social media is a general term that includes websites, apps, mobile technology, and other services through which information is electronically and widely shared, and then disseminated in real time. It uses an interactive, user-generated dynamic and constantly altered content dialogue that is created and exchanged between publishers and users. Other examples of social media include ooVoo, Snapchat, Pinterest, Instagram, and YouTube. Social media services vary, and new ones are launched frequently.

Courts have examined cyberbullying in social media through cases in which the educational entity's actions were challenged as violating the student's First Amendment protected speech rights; where employees alleged they were defamed; where students, employees, and parents claimed they were harassed in violation of their civil rights; where students and employees claimed their privacy rights were invaded; where educational entities claimed students violated the schools' policies; and where law enforcement claimed a parent breached an applicable contract.

As applied to students, the First Amendment challenge is a particularly confusing area. Some courts do not find the area clear, but at least one court claims otherwise. Generally, in these cases school officials are faced with disciplining students for their off-campus conduct, which is frequently the situation when a student engages in cyberbullying in social media. Numerous legal standards have evolved through the courts' decisions. For example, there is the "material and substantial disruption standard," the "forecast of substantial disruption standard," the "true threat standard," the "*Fraser* standard," the "*Hazelwood* standard," and the "*Morse* standard." Yet qualified immunity may be a defense against all of them, or it may not be.

As applied to students, employees, and parents, a civil rights challenge could be based on Title XI of the Education Amendments of 1972, which prohibits discrimination based on sex; Title VI of the Civil Rights Act of 1964, which prohibits discrimination on the basis of race, color, or national origin; Section 504 of the Rehabilitation Act of 1973; Title II of the Americans with Disabilities Act; and the Individuals with Disabilities in Education Act (IDEA 2004), which prohibits discrimination on the basis of disability, as well as substantive due process, equal protection, and other statutes and policies.

Furthermore, employees and students bring defamation actions when they believe something untrue was published about them and their reputations were harmed. Also, students and employees bring invasion-of-privacy claims when they believe that their privacy was violated. For example, the cyberbully posted a nude or seminude photo or video of the victim, or the cyberbully edited a photo or video to include private information about the victim, or the victim believes he was pressured into disclosing his social media password so that his private social media section could be accessed by an administrator. Other claims include allegations that an unreasonable search prohibited by the Fourth Amendment of the U.S. Constitution was conducted.

Students, employees, parents, and educational institutions have at times been successful in their First Amendment, civil rights, and other actions. But then again, students, employees, parents, and educational institutions have also lost challenges. Having read the case summaries in this book, school employees, parents, students, the public, and policymakers have guidance in how and why courts have made their decisions in cyberbullying in social media cases. Considering the facts and circumstances of each incident compared to the facts and circumstances of the decided cases in light of the law is important and essential. Courts require that the legal standards be met. Decisions are made on a case-by-case basis.

Cyberbullying in social media is a difficult and complicated area to penetrate. Despicable, hateful, and ruinous behavior that "really, really hurts" and robs individuals and society of healthy growth today, tomorrow, and in the future is unsafe and unproductive. Will you lend a hand to help students, employees, parents, and hundreds and thousands of lives that touch educational institutions not be affected by cyberbullying in social media?

For updates to the book, please access the authors' website at www.cyberbullyingandsocialmedia.com, and do not hesitate to contact them.

Merle Horowitz, EdD, merlehorowitz@gmail.com
Dorothy M. Bollinger, Esquire, dbollinger@bollingerlawfirm.com

APPENDIX A

Table of State Bullying and Cyberbullying Laws

	State	Citation	On/Off Campus	Cyberbullying
1	**Alabama**	Ala. Code §§ 16-28B-1 to 16-28B-9	Behavior that takes place in the school, on school property, on a school bus, or at a school-sponsored function.	Yes. Electronic act is included in the definition of harassment.
2	**Alaska**	Alaska Stat. Ann. §§ 14.33.200 to 14.33.250	Each school district must adopt a policy that prohibits the harassment, intimidation, or bullying of any student. The statute does not specifically address off campus incidents, and neither does the Alaska Department of Education's list of model issues for school districts to use as they create their bullying policy. Proposed amendments to the law include incidents on school premises, on transportation systems used by schools, or at school-sponsored events or school-sanctioned activities.	No. Bullying is defined (and includes written acts), but it does not refer to electronic or cyberbullying.
3	**Arizona**	Ariz. Rev. Stat. Ann. § 15-341	Prosecute and enforce policies and procedures . . . for violations on school grounds, on school property, on school buses, at school bus stops, at school events and activities, and through use of electronic technology or electronic communications on school computers, networks, forums, and mailing lists.	Yes.
4	**Arkansas**	Ark. Code Ann § 6-18-514 Ark. Code Ann § 5-71-217	Both. For electronic acts that result in substantial disruption, directed at students or school personnel, and maliciously intended to disrupt and has a high likelihood of succeeding for that purpose.	Yes. Electronic act is included in the definition of bullying. Criminal Code—A person commits the offense of cyberbullying if (1) he or she transmits, sends, or posts a communication by electronic means with the purpose to frighten, coerce, intimidate, threaten, abuse, harass, or alarm another person; and (2) the transmission was in furtherance of severe, repeated, or hostile behavior toward the other person. The offense of cyberbullying is a Class B misdemeanor.

(continued)

	State	Citation	On/Off Campus	Cyberbullying
5	**California**	Cal. Educ. Code §§ 32261, 48900, 48900.2 to 48900.4 Ann. Cal. Educ. Code §§ 234.1 to 234.5	A pupil shall not be suspended or expelled for any enumerated act, unless the act is related to school activity or school attendance occurring within a school under the jurisdiction of the superintendent of the school district or principal or occurring within any other school district. A pupil may be suspended or expelled for acts that are enumerated and related to school activity or attendance that occur at any time, including, but not limited to, any of the following: (1) while on school grounds; (2) while going to or coming from school; (3) during the lunch period whether on or off the campus; (4) during, or while going to or coming from, a school-sponsored activity. "School property" includes, but is not limited to, electronic files and databases. A pupil enrolled in grades four to twelve, inclusive, may be suspended from school or recommended for expulsion if the superintendent or the principal of the school in which the pupil is enrolled determines that the pupil has intentionally engaged in harassment, threats, or intimidation, directed against school district personnel or pupils, that is sufficiently severe or pervasive to have the actual and reasonably expected effect of materially disrupting classwork, creating substantial disorder, and invading the rights of either school personnel or pupils by creating an intimidating or hostile educational environment.	Yes. Bullying includes an electronic act. An electronic act includes the transmission of a communication, including, but not limited to, a message, text, sound, or image, or a post on a social network Internet website, by means of an electronic device, including, but not limited to, a telephone, wireless telephone, or other wireless communication device, computer, or pager. Includes creating a "burn page" or false profile.
6	**Colorado**	C. R. S. A. § 22-32-109.1; C. R. S. A. §§ 22-93-101 to 106 (School Districts). Separate sections are available for charter schools.	No statement about off-campus applicability. Reference is to behavior on school grounds, in a school vehicle, or at a school activity or sanctioned event that is detrimental to the welfare or safety of other students or of school personnel, including, but not limited to, incidents of bullying and other behavior that creates a threat of physical harm to the student or to other students.	Yes. Electronic act or gesture is included in the definition of bullying.

(continued)

	State	Citation	On/Off Campus	Cyberbullying
7	**Connecticut**	Conn. Gen. Stat. Ann. § 10-222d	Both. Off campus, if it creates a hostile environment at school for the student to whom the bullying was directed, infringes on the rights of the student at school, or substantially disrupts the educational process or orderly operation of the school. Each regional and local board must create a plan that includes prohibiting bullying (A) on school grounds, at a school-sponsored or school-related activity, function, or program whether on or off school grounds, at a school bus stop, on a school bus or other vehicle owned, leased, or used by a local or regional board of education, or through the use of an electronic device or an electronic mobile device owned, leased, or used by the local or regional board of education, and (B) outside of the school setting if such bullying (i) creates a hostile environment at school for the student against whom such bullying was directed, (ii) infringes on the rights of the student against whom such bullying was directed at school, or (iii) substantially disrupts the education process or the orderly operation of a school. Outside of the school setting means at a location, activity, or program that is not school related, or through the use of an electronic device or a mobile electronic device that is not owned, leased, or used by a local or regional board of education.	Yes. Electronic communications and cyberbullying are included in the definition of bullying. *Cyberbullying* means any act of bullying through the use of the Internet, interactive and digital technologies, cellular mobile telephone or other mobile electronic devices, or any electronic communications. *Electronic communication* means any transfer of signs, signals, writing, images, sounds, data, or intelligence of any nature transmitted in whole or in part by a wire, radio, electromagnetic, photoelectronic, or photo-optical system.
8	**Delaware**	Del. Code Ann. tit. 14 § 4112D	Each school district policy must include a statement that prohibits bullying on school property or at school functions or by use of data or computer software that is accessed through a computer, computer system, computer network, or other electronic technology of a school district or charter school from kindergarten through grade twelve. School property means any building, structure, athletic field, sports stadium, or real property that is owned, operated, leased, or rented by any public school district or charter school including, but not limited to, any kindergarten, elementary, secondary, or vocational-technical school or charter school, or any motor vehicle owned, operated, leased, rented, or subcontracted by any public school or charter school.	Yes. Electronic bullying is included in the definition of bullying.

(*continued*)

	State	Citation	On/Off Campus	Cyberbullying
9	**District of Columbia**	D.C. Code Mun. Regs. tit. 5 § B2599 See also DC ST 2-1535	Both. Bullying (including electronic communications) are Tier III offenses enforceable by school authorities: (a) when the student is on school grounds; (b) when the student is on or off school grounds participating in or attending any function or activity, including field trips, class trips, extracurricular activities, or athletic contests, that are sponsored by or are under the auspices of DCPS; (c) when the student is off school grounds and traveling on transportation provided by DCPS and the activity involves any conduct prohibited by this chapter; (d) when the student commits a prohibited offense that occurs during before-school or after-school programs; and (e) when a student has committed a prohibited offense off school grounds or outside regular school hours that results in a significant disruption to the school environment.	Yes. Bullying includes sending threatening and abusive emails, text messages, or other electronic communications.
10	**Florida**	Fla. Stat. Ann. § 1006.147	Both. Bullying is prohibited (a) during any education program or activity conducted by a public K–12 educational institution; (b) during any school-related or school-sponsored program or activity or on a school bus of a public K–12 educational institution; or (c) through the use of data or computer software that is accessed through a computer, computer system, or computer network of a public K–12 educational institution; or (d) through the use of data or computer software that is accessed at a non-school-related location, activity, function, or program or through the use of technology or an electronic device that is not owned, leased, or used by a school district or school, if the bullying substantially interferes with or limits the victim's ability to participate in or benefit from the services, activities, or opportunities offered by a school or substantially disrupts the education process or orderly operation of a school. This paragraph does not require a school or staff to monitor any non-school-related activity, function, or program. The physical location or time of access of a computer-related incident cannot be raised as a defense in any disciplinary action.	Yes. *Cyberbullying* means bullying through the use of technology or any electronic communication, which includes, but is not limited to, any transfer of signals, writing, images, sounds, data, or intelligence of any nature transmitted in whole or in part by a wire, radio, electromagnetic system, photoelectronic system, or photo-optical system, including, but not limited to, electronic mail, Internet communications, instant messages, or facsimile communications. Cyberbullying includes the creation of a web page or web log in which the creator assumes the identity of another person, or the knowing impersonation of another person as the author of posted content or messages, if the creation or impersonation creates any of the conditions enumerated in the definition of bullying. Cyberbullying also includes the distribution by electronic means of a communication to more than one person or the posting of material on an electronic medium that may be accessed by one or more persons, if the distribution or posting creates any of the conditions enumerated in the definition of bullying.

(*continued*)

	State	Citation	On/Off Campus	Cyberbullying
11	**Georgia**	Ga. Code Ann. §§ 20-2-751.4 & 20-2-751.5	Possibly both. Bullying includes an act which occurs on school property, on school vehicles, at designated school bus stops, or at school-related functions or activities, or by use of data or software that is accessed through a computer, computer system, computer network, or other electronic technology of a local school system. Each student code of conduct must contain provisions that address any off-campus behavior of a student that could result in the student being criminally charged with a felony and that makes the student's continued presence at school a potential danger to persons or property at the school or which disrupts the educational process.	Yes. Bullying includes an act by use of data or software accessed through a school computer, computer system, computer network, or other school electronic technology. Proposed amendments to the legislation would include a separate definition for cyberbullying.
12	**Hawaii**	Haw. Code R. §§ 8-19-2 & 8-19-6	Both. Cyberbullying can occur (1) on campus, or other department of education premises, on department of education transportation, or during a department of education sponsored activity or event on or off school property; (2) through a department of education data system without department of education authorized communication; or (3) through an off-campus computer network that is sufficiently severe, persistent, or pervasive that it creates an intimidating, threatening, or abusive educational environment for the other student or school personnel, or both.	Yes. Cyberbullying is defined and includes electronically transmitted acts.
13	**Idaho**	Idaho Code Ann. § 18-917A; §§ 33-205 & 33-512	Possibly both. Bullying is broadly addressed in the criminal code. The local school board has the duty to prescribe rules for bullying, harassment, and intimidation and may also issue discipline.	Yes. As defined in the criminal code, an act of harassment, intimidation, or bullying may be committed through the use of a land line, car phone, or wireless telephone or through the use of data or computer software that is accessed through a computer, computer system, or computer network.

(*continued*)

	State	Citation	On/Off Campus	Cyberbullying
14	**Illinois**	105 Ill. Comp. Stat. Ann. 5/27-23-7; 5/10–14; & 5/10-22.6	Possibly both. No student shall be subjected to bullying: (1) during any school-sponsored education program or activity; (2) while in school, on school property, on school buses or other school vehicles, at designated school bus stops waiting for the school bus, or at school-sponsored or school-sanctioned events or activities; or (3) through the transmission of information from a school computer, a school computer network, or other similar electronic school equipment. The local school board in consultation with the parent-teacher advisory committee and other community-based organizations must include provisions in the student discipline policy to address bullying.	Yes. Bullying includes communications made in writing or electronically, directed toward a student or students. Harassment through the telephone is a class B misdemeanor.
15	**Indiana**	Ind. Code Ann. §§ 20-26-5-33, 20-33-8-13.5, & 20-33-8-0.2	Possibly both. The rules apply (1) on school grounds immediately before or during school hours, immediately after school hours, or at any other time when the school is being used by a school group; (2) off school grounds at a school activity, function, or event; (3) traveling to or from school or a school activity, function, or event; or (4) using property or equipment provided by the school.	Yes. The school district's discipline policy must prohibit bullying through the use of data or computer software accessed through a computer, computer system, or computer network, of a school corporation. The definition of bullying includes verbal or written communications or images transmitted in any manner (including digitally or electronically). A school corporation may offer classes, instruction, or programs regarding the potential risks and consequences of creating and sharing sexually suggestive or explicit materials through cellular telephones, social networking websites, computer networks, and other digital media.
16	**Iowa**	Iowa Code Ann. § 280.28	Possibly both. Bullying is prohibited in schools, on school property, and at any school function, or school-sponsored activity regardless of its location. Bullying is defined to include acts that create an objectively hostile school environment and meet listed broad conditions.	Yes. Bullying is defined to include electronic bullying. *Electronic* means any communication involving the transmission of information by wire, radio, optical cable, electromagnetic, or other similar means. Electronic includes, but is not limited to, communication via electronic mail, Internet-based communications, pager service, cell phones, and electronic text messaging.

(*continued*)

	State	Citation	On/Off Campus	Cyberbullying
17	**Kansas**	Kan. Stat. Ann. § 72-8256	Possibly both. The school board must adopt a policy and a plan to prohibit bullying on or while using school property, in a school vehicle, or at a school-sponsored activity or event.	Yes. Bullying is defined to include electronic bullying and cyberbullying. *Cyberbullying* means bullying by use of any electronic communication device through means including, but not limited to, email, instant messaging, text messages, blogs, mobile phones, pagers, online games, and websites.
18	**Kentucky**	Ky. Rev. Stat. Ann. § 525.070 & § 525.080 (Look for 158.148 to possibly be amended.)	Possibly both. A person is guilty of harassment when, with intent to intimidate, harass, annoy, or alarm another person, he or she being enrolled as a student in a local school district, and while on school premises, on school-sponsored transportation, or at a school-sponsored event causes one or more listed damages.	Yes. Harassing communications include (a) communicating with a person, anonymously or otherwise, by telephone, telegraph, mail, or any other form of written communication in a manner that causes annoyance or alarm and serves no purpose of legitimate communication; (b) makes a telephone call, whether or not conversation ensues, with no purpose of legitimate communication; or (c) communicates, while enrolled as a student in a local school district, with or about another school student, anonymously or otherwise, by telephone, the Internet, telegraph, mail, or any other form of electronic or written communication in a manner that a reasonable person under the circumstances should know would cause the other student to suffer fear of physical harm, intimidation, humiliation, or embarrassment and that serves no purpose of legitimate communication. Harassing communications is a class B misdemeanor.
19	**Louisiana**	La. Rev. Stat. Ann. §§ 14:40.7, 17:81(W); 17:416.13; 17:416.17; 17:416.21; & § Ch. C. Art. 730	Both. In the education code, cyberbullying includes harassment, intimidation, or bullying of a student on school property by another student using a computer, mobile phone, or other interactive or digital technology or harassment, intimidation, or bullying of a student while off school property by another student using any such means when the action or actions are intended to have an effect on the student when the student is on school property. Grounds for applicability of the children's code to families includes a child found to have engaged in cyberbullying.	Yes. Bullying, defined in the education code, includes "audio visual forms of expression" and cyberbullying. Crimes Code—*Cyberbullying* is defined in the criminal code as the transmission of any electronic textual, visual, written, or oral communication with the malicious and willful intent to coerce, abuse, torment, or intimidate a person under the age of eighteen.

(*continued*)

	State	Citation	On/Off Campus	Cyberbullying
20	**Maine**	Me. Rev. Stat. tit. 20-A §§ 254; 1001; & 6554	Both. Bullying that: (1) takes place at school or on school grounds, at any school-sponsored or school-related activity or event or while students are being transported to or from school or school-sponsored activities or events; or (2) takes place elsewhere or through the use of technology, but only if the bullying also infringes on the rights of the student at school as set forth in the statute, such as (a) creating an intimidating or hostile educational environment for the student; or (b) interfering with the student's academic performance or ability to participate in or benefit from the services, activities, or privileges provided by a school.	Yes. Bullying includes electronic expressions and cyberbullying. *Cyberbullying* means bullying through the use of technology or any electronic communication, including, but not limited to, a transfer of signs, signals, writing, images, sounds, data, or intelligence of any nature transmitted by the use of any electronic device, including, but not limited to, a computer, telephone, cellular telephone, text messaging device, and personal digital assistant.
21	**Maryland**	Md. Code Ann., Education §§ 7-424 & 7-424.1	Both. Includes conduct occurring on school property, at a school activity or event, or on a school bus or substantially disrupting the orderly operation of the school.	Yes. Bullying and electronic communications are both included. *Electronic communications* is defined as a communication transmitted by means of an electronic device, including a telephone, cellular phone, computer, or pager.
22	**Massachusetts**	Mass. Gen. Laws Ann. ch. 71, § 37H & 37O; Mass. Gen. Laws Ann. ch. 71B, §3	Both. Bullying is prohibited: (i) on school grounds, property immediately adjacent to school grounds, at a school-sponsored or school-related activity, function, or program whether on or off school grounds, at a school bus stop, on a school bus or other vehicle owned, leased, or used by a school district or school, or through the use of technology or an electronic device owned, leased, or used by a school district or school and (ii) at a location, activity, function, or program that is not school related, or through the use of technology or an electronic device that is not owned, leased, or used by a school district or school if the bullying creates a hostile environment at school for the victim, infringes on the rights of the victim at school, or materially and substantially disrupts the education process or the orderly operation of a school. School grounds is defined to be property on which a school building or facility is located or property that is owned, leased, or used by a school district, charter school, nonpublic school, approved private day or residential school, or collaborative school for a school-sponsored activity, function, program, instruction, or training.	Yes. Bullying is defined to include electronic expression and cyberbullying. *Cyberbullying* is defined as bullying through the use of technology or any electronic communication, which includes, but is not limited to, any transfer of signs, signals, writing, images, sounds, data, or intelligence of any nature transmitted in whole or in part by a wire, radio, electromagnetic, photoelectronic, or photo-optical system, including, but not limited to, electronic mail, Internet communications, instant messages, or facsimile communications. Cyberbullying also includes (i) the creation of a web page or blog in which the creator assumes the identity of another person or (ii) the knowing impersonation of another person as the author of posted content or messages, if the creation or impersonation creates any of the conditions enumerated in clauses (i) to (v), inclusive, of the definition of bullying. Cyberbullying also includes the distribution by electronic means of a communication to more than one person or the posting of material on an electronic medium that may be accessed by one or more persons, if the distribution or posting creates any of the conditions enumerated in clauses (i) to (v), inclusive, of the definition of bullying.

(*continued*)

	State	Citation	On/Off Campus	Cyberbullying
23	**Michigan**	Mich. Comp. Laws. Ann. §§ 380.1310b, 380.1347a, & 388.1631a	Both. *At school* means in a classroom, elsewhere on school premises, on a school bus or other school-related vehicle, or at a school-sponsored activity or event, whether or not it is held on school premises. *At school* includes conduct using a telecommunications access device or telecommunications service provider that occurs off school premises if the telecommunications access device or the telecommunications service provider is owned by or under the control of the school district or public school academy.	Yes. Bullying includes electronic communications. Proposed amendments include definition of cyberbullying.
24	**Minnesota**	Minn. Stat. Ann. §§ 121A.0695 & 120B.232 Executive Order 12-01, Establishing the Governors Task Force on the Prevention of School Bullying, February 21, 2012 *Safe and Supportive Minnesota Schools: The Prevention of School Bullying Task Force Report*, August 1, 2012	Not stated. The statute states that each school board must adopt a written policy prohibiting intimidation and bullying of any student.	Yes. Bullying includes electronic and Internet use. The Board's policy must address intimidation and bullying in all forms, including, but not limited to, electronic forms and forms involving Internet use.
25	**Mississippi**	Miss. Code Ann. §§ 37-11-20, 37-11-67, & 37-11-69 (Education) Miss. Code Ann. § 97-45-33 (Crimes Code) MS Const. art.15, § classification pending (2010)	On school property, at any school-sponsored event, or on the school bus.	Yes. The definition of bullying includes electronic communication. Crimes Code (Online Impersonation)—Any person who knowingly and without consent impersonates another actual person through or on an Internet website or by other electronic means for purposes of harming, intimidating, threatening, or defrauding another person is guilty of a misdemeanor. Electronic means includes opening an email account or an account or profile on a social networking Internet website in another person's name.

(continued)

	State	Citation	On/Off Campus	Cyberbullying
26	**Missouri**	Mo. Rev. Stat. §§ 160.775 & 162.946 Mo. Rev. Stat. § 565.225 (2008) (But also see 2013 proposed Engrossed version.)	Neither on or off a school campus is stated. The school district is required to adopt an antibullying policy.	Bullying is defined to include cyberbullying, electronic, or written communications. A person commits the crime of stalking if he or she purposely, through his or her course of conduct, harasses or follows with the intent of harassing another person. The crime of stalking shall be a class A misdemeanor unless the person has previously pleaded guilty to or been found guilty of a violation of this section, or of any offense committed in violation of any county or municipal ordinance in any state, any state law, any federal law, or any military law that, if committed in this state, would be chargeable or indictable as a violation of any offense listed in this section, in which case stalking shall be a class D felony. The crime of aggravated stalking shall be a class D felony unless the person has previously pleaded guilty to or been found guilty of a violation of this section, or of any offense committed in violation of any county or municipal ordinance in any state, any state law, any federal law, or any military law that, if committed in this state, would be chargeable or indictable as a violation of any offense listed in this section, in which case aggravated stalking shall be a class C felony.
27	**Montana**	Mont. Admin. R. §§ 10.55.701 & 10.55.719 Mont. Code Ann. § 45-8-213 (held unconstitutional by *State v. Dugan*)	The school district is required to create a written policy that addresses bullying, harassment, and intimidation. The Montana Office of Public Instruction model policy and the Administrative Regulations state that bullying, harassment, intimidation, and hazing is strictly prohibited: (1) in a classroom or any other location on school premises; (2) during any school-sponsored program, activity, or function where the school is responsible for the student, including on a school bus or other school-related vehicle; or (3) through the use of electronic communication as defined in 45-8-213 (Crimes Code), regardless of when or where it occurs, that substantially disrupts the orderly operation of the school or any school-sponsored program, activity, or function where the school is responsible for the student.	Policy should deter persistent threatening, insulting, or demeaning gestures or physical conduct, including an intentional written, verbal, or electronic communication or threat. The Montana Office of Public Instruction has developed a model policy for local school districts to use that does include electronic communications.

(*continued*)

	State	Citation	On/Off Campus	Cyberbullying
28	**Nebraska**	Neb. Rev. Stat. Ann. §§ 79-2,137 & 79-267	No off campus. On school grounds, in a vehicle owned, leased, or contracted by a school being used for a school purpose by a school employee or his or her designee, or at school-sponsored activities or school-sponsored athletic events.	Bullying is defined to include electronic abuse.
29	**Nevada**	Nev. Rev. Stat. Ann. §§ 236.073; 385.3469; 385.34692; 388.122 to 125; 388.129; 388.132; 388.135 to 139; 388.1325; 388.1341 to 1344; 388.1351to 1353; 389.520; 392.915 Nev. Rev. Stat. Ann § 200.737	Bullying is prohibited on the premises of any public school, at an activity sponsored by a public school, or on any school bus.	Yes. Bullying, cyberbullying, and electronic communications are defined. If a minor uses an electronic communications device to possess, transmit, or distribute sexual images of a minor, (s)he is subject to a misdemeanor penalty for a second or a subsequent offense.
30	**New Hampshire**	N.H. Rev. Stat. Ann. §§ 193-F:1 through F:6	Both. Bullying occurs on, or is delivered to, school property or a school-sponsored activity or event on or off school property; or bullying can occur off school property or outside of a school-sponsored activity or event, if the conduct interferes with a pupil's educational opportunities or substantially disrupts the orderly operations of the school or school-sponsored activity or event. "School property" means all real property and all physical plant and equipment used for school purposes, including public or private school buses or vans.	Yes. Bullying is defined to include electronic communications. Cyberbullying is defined to include the same as bullying except that it is undertaken through the use of electronic devices. Electronic devices include, but are not limited to, telephones, cellular phones, computers, pagers, electronic mail, instant messaging, text messaging, and websites.
31	**New Jersey**	N.J. Stat. Ann. §§ 2A:4A-71.1; 2C:43-3.8; 18A:6-112; 18A:7E-3; 18A:12-33; 18A:17-46; 18A:26-8.2; 18A: 37-2; 18A:37-13 through 18A:37-32; 52:17B-71.8	Both. The school district board of education must adopt a policy and provide for appropriate responses to harassment, intimidation, and bullying that takes place on school property, at any school-sponsored function, on a school bus, or off school grounds in cases in which a school employee is made aware of such actions that substantially disrupts the educational process or interferes with the orderly operation of the school or the rights of other students at school. The responses to harassment, intimidation, or bullying that occurs off school grounds must be consistent with the board of education's code of student conduct and other provisions of the board's policy on harassment, intimidation, or bullying.	Yes. Bullying includes electronic communication. *Electronic communication* means a communication transmitted by means of an electronic device, including, but not limited to, a telephone, cellular phone, computer, or pager.

(*continued*)

	State	Citation	On/Off Campus	Cyberbullying
32	**New Mexico**	N.M. Stat. Ann. § 22-2-21; N.M. Code R § 6.12.7	The New Mexico Department of Education must establish bullying guidelines. School districts must develop and implement bullying prevention policies and a specific cyberbullying prevention policy. Regulations state that bullying is prohibited in the school, on school grounds, in school vehicles, at a designated bus stop, or at school activities or sanctioned events.	Yes. Cyberbullying is defined in the statute. The regulations define bullying to include electronic expression.
33	**New York**	N.Y. Educ. Law §§ 10 through 16; 801-a. 2801 & 2801-a. N.Y. Family Court §§ 308.1, 749 & 754. N.Y. Penal Law § 60.37. N.Y. Social Services Law § 458.1.	No student shall be subjected to harassment or bullying by employees or students on school property or at a school function; nor shall any student be subjected to discrimination based on a person's actual or perceived race, color, weight, national origin, ethnic group, religion, religious practice, disability, sexual orientation, gender, or sex by school employees or students on school property or at a school function. "School property" shall mean in or within any building, structure, athletic playing field, playground, parking lot, or land contained within the real property boundary line of a public elementary or secondary school, or in or on a school bus. "School function" shall mean a school-sponsored extracurricular event or activity.	*Harassment* and *bullying* shall mean the creation of a hostile environment by conduct or by threats, intimidation, or abuse, including cyberbullying, that (a) has or would have the effect of unreasonably and substantially interfering with a student's educational performance, opportunities or benefits, or mental, emotional, or physical well-being; or (b) reasonably cause or would reasonably be expected to cause a student to fear for his or her physical safety; or (c) reasonably cause or would reasonably be expected to cause physical injury or emotional harm to a student; or (d) occurs off school property and creates or would foreseeably create a risk of substantial disruption within the school environment, where it is foreseeable that the conduct, threats, intimidation, or abuse might reach school property. Acts of harassment and bullying include, but are not limited to, those acts based on a person's actual or perceived race, color, weight, national origin, ethnic group, religion, religious practice, disability, sexual orientation, gender, or sex. For the purposes of this definition, the term *threats, intimidation or abuse* include verbal and nonverbal actions. *Cyberbully*ing means harassment or bullying where such harassment or bullying occurs through any form of electronic communication.

(*continued*)

	State	Citation	On/Off Campus	Cyberbullying
34	**North Carolina**	N.C. Gen. Stat. Ann. §§ 115C-366.4, 407.15 through 407-18 (Education) N.C. Gen. Stat. Ann. §§ 14-458.1 & 14-458.2 (Criminal Code)	On campus. Bullying that takes place on school property, at any school-sponsored function, or on a school bus.	Yes. Education statutes—Bullying is defined to include electronic communication. Criminal Code—Cyberbullying includes the use of a computer or computer network with the intent to intimidate or torment a minor by (1) building a fake profile or website; or (2) posing as a minor in (a) an Internet chat room; (b) an electronic mail message; or (c) an instant message; or (3) following a minor online or into an Internet chat room; or (4) posting or encourage others to post on the Internet private, personal, or sexual information pertaining to a minor. Criminal cyberbullying is also defined to include such conduct against a minor's parents or guardian, and against school employees and independent contractors and their employees.
35	**North Dakota**	N.D. Cent. Code Ann. §§ 15.1-19-17 through 15.1-19-21. N.D. Cent. Code Ann. §12.117-07	Bullying must be in a public school, on school district premises, in a district-owned or district-leased school bus or school vehicle, or at any public school or school-district sanctioned or school-sponsored activity or event.	Yes. Bullying includes the use of technology or other electronic media. Harassment by telephone and electronic communication is a misdemeanor.
36	**Ohio**	Ohio Rev. Code Ann. §§ 3301.22, 3311.742, 3313.666, & 3319.073	Bullying of any student on school property, on a school bus, or at school-sponsored events is prohibited.	Yes. Bullying is defined to include an electronic act. An electronic act means an act committed through the use of a cellular telephone, computer, pager, personal communication device, or other electronic communication device.
37	**Oklahoma**	Okla. Stat. tit. 70 §§ 24-100.2 through 24-100.5	Both. Bullying is prohibited at school and by electronic communication, whether or not such communication originated at school or with school equipment, if the communication is specifically directed at students or school personnel and concerns harassment, intimidation, or bullying at school. *At school* means on school grounds, in school vehicles, at school-sponsored activities, or at school-sanctioned events.	Bullying is defined to include electronic communication. *Electronic communication* means the communication of any written, verbal, pictorial information, or video content by means of an electronic device, including, but not limited to, a telephone, a mobile or cellular telephone or other wireless telecommunication device, or a computer.

(*continued*)

	State	Citation	On/Off Campus	Cyberbullying
38	**Oregon**	Or. Rev. Stat. Ann. §§ 339.351 through 339.364	Bullying takes place on or immediately adjacent to school grounds, at any school-sponsored activity, on school-provided transportation, or at any official school bus stop.	Harassment, intimidation, or bullying is defined as any act that: (1) substantially interferes with a student's educational benefits, opportunities, or performance, (2) takes place on or immediately adjacent to school grounds, at any school-sponsored activity, or on school-provided transportation or at any official school bus stop; (3) has the effect of: (a) physically harming a student or damaging a student's property; (b) knowingly placing a student in reasonable fear of physical harm to the student or damage to the student's property; or (c) creating a hostile educational environment, including interfering with the psychological well-being of a student; (4) may be based on, but not be limited to, the protected class status of a person. *Cyberbullying* means the use of any electronic communication device to harass, intimidate, or bully.
39	**Pennsylvania**	24 Pa. Cons. Stat. § 13-1303.1-A	In their required policy, a school entity is not prohibited from defining bullying in such a way as to encompass acts that occur outside a school setting if those acts meet the following requirements: (1) are directed at another student or students; (2) are severe, persistent, or pervasive; and (3) have the effect of doing any of the following: (i) substantially interfering with a student's education; (ii) creating a threatening environment; or (iii) substantially disrupting the orderly operation of the school. School setting means in the school, on school grounds, in school vehicles, at a designated bus stop, or at any activity sponsored, supervised, or sanctioned by the school.	Bullying is defined to include electronic information.

(*continued*)

	State	Citation	On/Off Campus	Cyberbullying
40	**Rhode Island**	R.I. Gen. Laws Ann. §§ 16-21-24, 16-21-33, & 16-21-34	Possibly both. The statewide approach is the prohibition of bullying at school. *At school* means on school premises, at any school-sponsored activity or event whether or not it is held on school premises, on a school-transportation vehicle, at an official school bus stop, using property or equipment provided by the school, or creating a material and substantial disruption of the education process or the orderly operation of the school.	Yes. Bullying includes an electronic expression. *Cyberbullying* means bullying through the use of technology or any electronic communication, which includes, but is not limited to, any transfer of signs, signals, writing, images, sounds, data, texting, or intelligence of any nature transmitted in whole or in part by a wire, radio, electromagnetic, photoelectronic, or photo-optical system, including, but not limited to, electronic mail, Internet communications, instant messages, or facsimile communications. For purposes of this section, cyberbullying also includes: (1) the creation of a web page or blog in which the creator assumes the identity of another person; (2) the knowing impersonation of another person as the author of posted content or messages; or (3) the distribution by electronic means of a communication to more than one person or the posting of materials on an electronic medium that may be accessed by one or more persons, if the creation, impersonation, or distribution results in any of the conditions enumerated in the definition of bullying.
41	**South Carolina**	S.C. Code Ann. §59-63-110 through 150	*At school* means in a classroom, on school premises, on a school bus or other school-related vehicle, at an official school bus stop, at a school-sponsored activity or event whether or not it is held on school premises, or at another program or function where the school is responsible for the child.	Yes. Bullying is defined to include electronic communication.

(*continued*)

	State	Citation	On/Off Campus	Cyberbullying
42	**South Dakota**	S.D. Codified Laws §§ 13-32-14 through 13-32-19	Both, if the incident involves the use of computers or other electronic devices. Neither the physical location nor the time of day of any incident involving the use of computers or other electronic devices is a defense to any disciplinary action taken by a school district for conduct determined to meet the definition of bullying. The model policy of the statute limits the scope to the school property (within jurisdiction of the school board), school-owned or school-operated vehicles, and while students are attending or engaged in school-operated activities. Investigations are made where bullying is committed against a child while the child is aboard a school bus, at a school bus stop, or at a school-sponsored event.	Yes. Bullying includes any threatening use of data or computer software, incidents involving the use of computers or other electronic devices.
43	**Tennessee**	Tenn. Code Ann. §§ 49-6-813; 49-6-1014 through 49-6-1019 Tenn. Code Ann. §39-17-308	Both, if the bullying is specifically directed at student(s) and has the effect of creating a hostile environment or otherwise creating a substantial disruption to the educational environment or learning process. If the act takes place off school property or outside of a school-sponsored activity, it is directed specifically at a student or students and has the effect of creating a hostile educational environment or otherwise creating a substantial disruption to the education environment or learning process. If the act takes place on school grounds, at any school-sponsored activity, on school-provided equipment or transportation, or at any official school bus stop, the act has the effect of creating a hostile educational environment or otherwise creating a substantial disruption to the education environment or learning process.	Yes. Cyberbullying includes bullying with electronic devices. Electronic devices include, but are not limited to, telephones, cellular phones or other wireless telecommunication devices, personal digital assistants (PDAs), computers, electronic mail, instant messaging, text messaging, and websites. Threats by electronic communications (including email, text messages, or Internet service and others) are subject to the criminal code, and could result in up to thirty (30) hours of community service, without compensation, for charitable or governmental agencies as determined by the court, or a Class A misdemeanor through a Class E felony, depending on the violation.

(continued)

	State	Citation	On/Off Campus	Cyberbullying
44	**Texas**	Tex. Educ. Code Ann. §§ 21.451, 25.0342, 28.002, 37.001, 37.083, 37.0832, 37.217, 37.218, 161.325	Bullying must occur on school property, at a school-sponsored or school-related activity, or in a vehicle operated by the district.	Yes. Bullying is defined to include an expression through electronic means. *Cyberbullying* means the use of any electronic communication device to engage in bullying or intimidation.
45	**Utah**	Utah Code Ann. §§ 53A-11a-102 through 53A-11a-402	Possibly both. No school employee or student may engage in bullying or harassing a school employee or student: (a) on school property; (b) at a school-related or sponsored event; (c) on a school bus; (d) at a school bus stop; or (e) while the school employee or student is traveling to or from a location or event described above in sections (a) through (d). No school employee or student may engage in hazing or cyberbullying a school employee or student at any time or in any location.	Yes. Bullying includes cyberbullying. *Cyberbullying* means using the Internet, a cell phone, or another device to send or post text, video, or an image with the intent or knowledge, or with reckless disregard, that the text, video, or image will hurt, embarrass, or threaten an individual, regardless of whether the individual directed, consented to, or acquiesced in the conduct, or voluntarily accessed the electronic communication. Communication includes conveying a message electronically.
46	**Vermont**	Vt. Stat. Ann. tit. 16 §§11a (26) & (30) & (32); 16 § 165; 16 § 570; 16 § 570a through §570c; 16 § 1161a	Both. Bullying (i) occurs during the school day on school property, on a school bus, or at a school-sponsored activity, or before or after the school day on a school bus or at a school-sponsored activity; or (ii) does not occur during the school day on school property, on a school bus, or at a school-sponsored activity and can be shown to pose a clear and substantial interference with another student's right to access educational programs.	Bullying is defined to include acts conducted by electronic means. Each school district must prepare a plan for responding to student misbehavior, must include descriptions of behaviors on and off school grounds that constitute harassment, bullying, and hazing.
47	**Virginia**	Va. Code Ann. §§ 8.01-220.1:2; 9.1-104, 22.1-208.01; 22.1-276.01; 22.1-279.6; & 22.1-291.4. (Education Code) Va. Code Ann. § 18.2-152.7:1 (Criminal Code)	Both. Bullying (i) occurs during the school day on school property, on a school bus, or at a school-sponsored activity, or before or after the school day on a school bus or at a school-sponsored activity; or (ii) does not occur during the school day on school property, on a school bus, or at a school-sponsored activity and can be shown to pose a clear and substantial interference with another student's right to access educational programs.	Yes. Bullying includes cyberbullying. Harassment by computer is included in the criminal code.

(*continued*)

	State	Citation	On/Off Campus	Cyberbullying
48	**Washington**	Wash. Rev. Code §§ 28A.300.285; 28A.300.2851; 28A.300.475; and 28A.600.480	No off campus. The superintendent of public instruction in consultation with numerous other representatives, including, among others, the Washington state school directors, must develop a model policy prohibiting acts of harassment, intimidation, or bullying that are conducted via electronic means by a student while on school grounds and during the school day, as well as other items.	Yes. Bullying is defined to include an electronic act. *Electronic* or *electronic means* "means any communication where there is the transmission of information by wire, radio, optical cable, electromagnetic, or other similar means."
		Wash. Rev. Code §§ 7.92.020; 9.61.260; and 9A.46.060 (Criminal Code)	Cyberstalking is included as a crime in the legal definition of *harassment*.	A person may be guilty of cyberstalking by electronic communications if they meet the statutory requirements. Electronic communications involves "the transmission by wire, radio, optical cable, electromagnetic, or other similar means," and it includes "electronic mail, Internet-based communications, pager service, and electronic text messaging."
49	**West Virginia**	W.Va. Code Ann. §§18-2C-1 through 2C-5; & 18A-5-1c	No off campus. Each County Board of Education is required to create a policy that prohibits harassment, intimidation, or bullying of any student on school property, a school bus, at a school bus stop, or at school-sponsored events.	Yes. Bullying is defined to include electronic acts. An electronic act, communication, transmission, or threat includes, but is not limited to, one that is administered via telephone, wireless phone, computer, pager, or any electronic or wireless device whatsoever, and includes, but is not limited to, transmission of any image or voice, email, or text message using any such device.

(*continued*)

	State	Citation	On/Off Campus	Cyberbullying
50	**Wisconsin**	Wis. Stat. Ann. §§ 118.019; 118.02(9t); 118.46 (Schools) Wis. Stat. Ann. § 947.0125 (Criminal Code)	The State Department is required to create a model policy that includes items mandated in the statute, among them is the requirement to identify the school-related events at which the policy applies; the property owned, leased, or used by the school district on which the policy applies; and the vehicles used for pupil transportation on which the policy applies. Schools must adopt a policy prohibiting bullying by pupils, but they are not required to adopt the model policy.	The State Department is required to create a model policy that includes items mandated in the statute; among them is a requirement to create the definition of bullying. The State Department's model policy includes indirect bullying that is defined as spreading cruel rumors, intimidation through gestures, social exclusion, and sending insulting messages or pictures by mobile phone or using the Internet—also known as cyberbullying. Criminal Code—Unlawful Use of Computerized Communication Systems. Class B Misdemeanor 1) With intent to frighten, intimidate, threaten, abuse, or harass another person, a person sends a message to the person on an electronic mail or other computerized communication system and in that message threatens to inflict injury or physical harm to any person or the property of any person, or in that message uses any obscene, lewd, or profane language or suggests any lewd or lascivious act, or intentionally prevents or attempts to prevent the disclosure of his or her own identity. 2) With intent to frighten, intimidate, threaten, abuse, or harass another person, sends a message on an electronic mail or other computerized communication system with the reasonable expectation that the person will receive the message and in that message threatens to inflict injury or physical harm to any person or the property of any person, or with the reasonable expectation that the person will receive the message and in that message uses any obscene, lewd, or profane language or suggests any lewd or lascivious act, or while intentionally preventing or attempting to prevent the disclosure of his or her identity and with intent to frighten, intimidate, threaten, or abuse another person, sends a message on an electronic mail or other computerized communication system with the reasonable expectation that the person will receive the message. Class B forfeitures are also available for various violations, such as computerized communication violations.

(*continued*)

	State	Citation	On/Off Campus	Cyberbullying
51	**Wyoming**	Wyo. Stat. Ann. §§ 21-4-311 through 315	No off campus. Bullying is prohibited that is initiated, occurring, or received at school. School includes a classroom or other location on school premises, a school bus or other school-related vehicle, a school bus stop, an activity or event sponsored by a school, whether or not it is held on school premises, and any other program or function where the school is responsible for the child.	Yes. Bullying includes electronic communication in its definition.

APPENDIX B

Cyberbullying in Social Media Cases

CYBERBULLYING IN SOCIAL MEDIA: STUDENTS

Cyberbullying and Social Media Defined

Doe v. Jindal et al., 853 F. Supp. 2d 596 (M.D. La. 2012).
Doe v. Prosecutor, Marion County, Indiana, No. 1:12-cv-00062-TWP-MJD (S.D. Ind. June 22, 2012).
Doe v. State of Nebraska et al., Nos. 8:09CV456, 4:10CV3266, and 4:10CV3005 (D.Neb. October 17, 2012).

Cyberbullying in Social Media: It Really, Really Hurts

Gelinas v. Boisselle, No. 10-30192-KPN (D.Mass. October 17, 2011).

Cyberbullying in Social Media: Statutes and Cases

U.S. v. Cassidy, 814 F. Supp. 2d 574 (D.Md. 2011).
U.S. v. Sayer, Criminal Nos. 2:11-CR-113-DBH and 2:11-CR-47-DBH (D.Me. 2012).
United States v. Walker, 665 F.3d 212 (1st Cir. 2011).

Examination of Adjudicated State and Federal Cyberbullying in Social Media Cases

A.B. v. State (Indiana), 863 N.E. 2d 1212 (Ind. App. 2007); 885 N.E. 2d 1223 (Ind. 2008) (vacated).
Barnes v. Zaccari, 757 F. Supp. 2d 1313 (N.D. Ga. 2010); 669 F.3d 1295 (11th Cir. 2012).
Barnett v. Tipton County Board of Education, 601 F. Supp. 2d 980 (W.D. Tenn. 2006).

Bell v. Itawamba County School Board, 859 F. Supp. 2d 834 (N.D. Miss. 2012).
Bethel School District No. 403 v. Fraser, 478 U.S. 675 (1986).
Burns v. Gagnon, 727 S.E. 2d 634 (Va. 2012).
Davis v. Monroe County Board of Education, 526 U.S. 629 (1999).
D.C. v. R.R., 106 Cal. Rptr. 3d 399 (March 15, 2010, *as modified* April 8, 2010).
DeShaney v. Winnebago County Department of Social Services, 489 U.S. 189 (1989).
D.J.M. v. Hannibal Public School District, 647 F.3d 754 (8th Cir. 2011).
Doe v. Pulaski County Special School District, 306 F.3d 616 (8th Cir. 2002) (*en banc*).
Doninger v. Niehoff, 514 F. Supp. 2d 199 (D. Conn. 2007); 527 F.3d 41 (2nd Cir. 2008); 594 F. Supp. 2d 211 (D. Conn. 2009), NO. 3:07CV1129 MRK (D. Conn. March 19, 2009) (*unreported*); NO. 3:07CV1129 MRK (D. Conn. May 14, 2009) (*unreported*); 642 F.3d 334 (2nd Cir. 2011); 132 S.Ct. 499 (*mem*) (U.S. 2011) (*cert. denied*).
D.R. v. Middle Bucks Area Vocational Technical School, 972 F.2d 1364 (3rd Cir. 1992).
Evans v. Bayer, 684 F. Supp. 2d 1365 (S.D. Fla. 2010).
Fennell et al. v. Marion Independent School District, CV. No. SA: 12-CV-00941-DAE (W.D. Tex. January 28, 2013); C.V. No.: 5:12-CV-0941-DAE, Plaintiff's Second Amended Complaint (W.D. Tex. March 14, 2013).
Finkel v. Daubert, 29 Misc. 3d 325 (N.Y. Sup. Ct. 2010).
Fitzgerald v. Barnstable School Committee, 555 U.S. 246 (2009).
G.D.S. v. Northport-East Northport Union Free School District, 727 S.E. 2d 634 (E.D.N.Y. 2012).
Gebser v. Lago Vista Independent School District, 524 U.S. 274 (1998).
Gertz v. Robert Welch, Inc., 94 S.Ct. 2997 (1974).
Hazelwood School District v. Kuhlmeier, 484 U.S. 260 (1988).
In Re I.M.L., 61 P.3d 1038 (Utah 2002).
J.C. v. Beverly Hills Unified School District, No. 08-03824 (C.D. Cal. November 16, 2009); 711 F. Supp. 2d 1094 (2010).
Jones v. Reynolds, 438 F.3d 685 (6th Cir. 2006).
J.S. v. Bethlehem Area School District, No. 1998-CE-7696 (Pa. Northampton Co. July 23, 1999); 757 A.2d 412 (Pa. Commw. Ct. 2000) *reargument denied* September 7, 2000; 717 A.2d 1290 (Pa. 2001) (*appeal granted*); 794 A.2d 936 (Pa. Commw. Ct. 2002), *reargument denied* April 11, 2002; 807 A.2d 847 (Pa. 2002); 818 A.2d 506 (2003) (*allocatur denied*).
J.S. v. Blue Mountain School District, No. 307CV585 (M.D. Pa. 2007); No. 307CV585 (M.D. Pa. September 11, 2008); 593 F.3d 286 (3rd Cir. 2010); 650 F.3d 915 (3rd Cir. 2011); 132 S.Ct. 1097 (*mem*) (U.S. 2012) (*cert. denied*).
Kowalski v. Berkeley County Schools, 652 F.3d 271 (4th Cir. 2011); 132 S.Ct. 1095 (*mem*) (U.S. 2012) (*cert. denied*).

Layshock v. Hermitage School District, 412 F. Supp. 2d 502 (W.D. Pa. 2006); No. 2-06-CV-116 (W.D. Pa. April 7, 2006); 496 F. Supp. 2d 587 (W.D. Pa. 2007); 593 F.3d 249 (3rd Cir. 2010); 650 F.3d 205 (3rd 2011); 132 S.Ct. 1097 (*mem*) (U.S. 2012) (*cert. denied*).

Logan v. Sycamore Community School Board, 780 F. Supp. 2d 594 (S.D. Ohio 2011); No. 1:09-cv-00885 (S.D. Ohio June 5, 2012).

Long v. Murray County School District, Civil Action File No. 4:10-CV-00015-HLM (May 21, 2012); No. 12-13248 (11th Cir. June 18, 2013).

Lovell v. Poway Unified School District, 90 F.3d 367 (9th Cir. 1996).

Miller v. Clinton County, 541 F.3d 464 (2nd Cir. 2008).

Monell v. Department of Social Services, 436 U.S. 658 (1978).

Monroe v. Pape, 365 U.S. 167 (1961).

Morrow v. Balaski, No. 10-292 (W.D. Pa. March 16, 2011); 685 F.3d 1126 (3rd Cir. 2012); 719 F.3d 160 (3rd Cir. 2013); (*cert. denied*) No. 13-302 (U.S. December 16, 2013).

Morse v. Frederick, 551 U.S. 393 (2007).

New Jersey v. T.L.O., 469 U.S. 325 (1985).

New York Times v. Sullivan, 84 S.Ct. 710 (1964).

Requa v. Kent School District No. 415, 492 F. Supp. 2d 1272 (W.D. Wash. 2007).

Rosario v. Clark County School District, No. 2:13-CV-362 JCM (PAL) (July 3, 2013).

R.S. v. Minnewaska Area School District No. 2149, Civ. No. 12-588 (MJD/LIB) (D. Minn. September 6, 2012).

Shively v. Green Local School District, No. 5:11CV2398 (N.D. Ohio February 28, 2013) (*unreported*).

S.J.W. v. Lee's Summit R-7 School District, 696 F.3d 771 (8th Cir. 2012).

State of New Jersey v. Dharun Ravi, New Jersey Judiciary, Superior Court–Appellate Division, Criminal Case Information Statement, Middlesex Ind. No. 11-04-00596-I (*filed* June 4, 2012); Dharun Ravi, Indictment, File No. 10002681, Second Grand Jury, March 2011 Stated Session, July Term 2010.

Tafuto v. New Jersey Institute of Technology, 800 N.W. 2d 811 (Minn. App. 2011); 816 N.W. 2d (2012).

Tatro v. University of Minnesota, 800 N.W. 2d 811 (Minn. App. 2011); 816 N.W. 2d 509 (Minn. 2012).

Tinker v. Des Moines Independent Community School District, 393 U.S. 503 (1969).

T.K. and S.K. v. New York City Department of Education, 779 F. Supp. 2d 289 (E.D.N.Y. 2011).

T.V. ex rel. B.V. v. Smith-Green Community School Corporation, 267 F.R.D. 234 (N.D. Ind. 2010); 807 F. Supp. 2d 767 (N.D. Ind. 2011).

Tyrrell v. Seaford Union Free School District, 792 F. Supp. 2d 601 (E.D.N.Y. 2011).

Vernonia School District 47J v. Acton, 515 U.S. 646 (1995).
Vidovic v. Mentor City School District, No. 1:10 CV 1833 (N.D. Ohio January 31, 2013).
Vogel v. Felice, 26 Cal.Rptr. 3d 350 (Cal. App. March 24, 2005).
Watts v. U.S., 394 U.S. 705 (1969).
Wisniewski v. Board of Education of Weedsport Central School District, No. 5:02CV1403 (N.D.N.Y. June 20, 2006); 494 F.3d 34 (2nd Cir. 2007); 128 S.Ct. 1741 (*mem*) (U.S. 2008) (*cert. denied*).
Wyatt v. Fletcher, No. 11-41359 (5th Cir. May 31, 2013).
Zimmerman v. Board of Trustees of Ball State University, No. 1:12-cv-01475-JMS-DML (S.D. Ind. April 15, 2013).

Examination of Cyberbullying in Social Media Cases Filed, But Not Adjudicated

Boston (Alex) (Cobbs County, GA)—Dorie Turner and Greg Bluestein, "Victims of Cyberbullying Fight Back in Lawsuits," *Online Athens* (April 26, 2012), http://onlineathens.com/breaking-news/2012-04-26/victims-cyberbullying-fight-back-lawsuits; see also http://www.huffingtonpost.com/2012/04/26/school-cyberbullying-vict_n_1457918.html.
Jason Medley (Houston, GA)—http://www.huffingtonpost.com/2012/04/26/school-cyberbullying vict_n_1457918.html.
S.M., et al. v. Griffith Public Schools, No 2:12-cv-00160-JD-APR (N.D.Ind. Hammond Division); Legal Clips, National School Board Association's Council of School Attorneys, *The Source*, quoting Michelle L. Quinn, "Indiana District and ACLU Settle Lawsuit over Students Expelled for Making Facebook Threats," *Post-Tribune*, March 18, 2013.

CYBERBULLYING IN SOCIAL MEDIA: EMPLOYEES

Barnes v. Zaccari, 669 F.3d 1295 (11th Cir. 2012).
Barnett v. Tipton County Board of Education, 601 F. Supp. 2d 980 (W.D. Tenn. 2006).
Bell v. Itawamba County School Board, 859 F. Supp. 2d 834 (N.D. Miss. 2012).
Connick v. Myers, 103 S.Ct. 1694 (1983).
Doninger v. Niehoff, 527 F.3d 41 (2d Cir. 2008); 642 F.3d 334 (2nd Cir. 2011).
Evans v. Bayer, 684 F. Supp. 2d 1365 (S.D. Fla. 2010).
In the Matter of the Tenure Hearing of Jennifer O'Brien, 2013 WL 132508 (N.J. A.D.) (January 11, 2013) (*opinion*).
J.S. v. Bethlehem Area School District, No. 1998-CE-7696 (Pa. Northampton Co. July 23, 1999); 757 A.2d 412 (Pa. Commw. Ct. 2000) *reargument denied* September 7, 2000; 717 A.2d 1290 (Pa. 2001) (*appeal granted*); 794

A.2d 936 (Pa. Commw. Ct. 2002), *reargument denied* April 11, 2002; 807 A.2d 847 (Pa. 2002); 818 A.2d 506 (2003) (*allocatur denied*).

J.S. v. Blue Mountain School District, 650 F.3d 915 (3rd Cir. 2011); No. 08-4138 (3rd Cir. 2011).

Layshock v. Hermitage School District, 412 F. Supp. 2d 502 (W.D. Pa. 2006); No. 2-06-CV-116 (W.D. Pa. April 7, 2006); 496 F. Supp. 2d 587 (W.D. Pa. 2007); 593 F.3d 249 (3rd Cir. 2010); 650 F.3d 205 (3rd 2011); 132 S.Ct. 1097 (*mem*) (U.S. 2012) (*cert. denied*).

Munroe v. Central Bucks School District, No. 2:12-cv-03546-CMR (E.D. Pa.); No. 2:12-cv-03546-CMR, Amended Complaint (E.D. Pa.); No. 2:12-cv -03546-CMR, Answer with Affirmative Defenses to Plaintiff's Amended Complaint (E.D. Pa.).

Requa v. Kent School District No. 415, 492 F. Supp. 2d 1272 (W.D. Wash. 2007).

Rubino v. City of New York, No. 107292/11 (Supreme Court, New York County, N.Y.) (February 1, 2012) (*Unreported Disposition*).

Schroeder v. Hamilton School District, 282 F.3d 946 (7th Cir. 2002).

Wisniewski v. Board of Education of Weedsport Central School District, 494 F.3d 34 (2nd Cir. 2007).

CYBERBULLYING IN SOCIAL MEDIA: PARENTS

Brown v. Bryan County, 219 F.3d 450 (5th Cir. 2000).

Burge v. St. Tammany Parish, 336 F.3d 363 (5th Cir. 2003).

Carmichael v. Joshua Independent School District, 3:11-CV-622-D, First Complaint 2012 BL 1023 (N.D. Tex. Jan 4, 2012); Second Amended Complaint 2012 B.L. 247442 (N.D. Tex. September 26, 2012).

Carmichael et al. v. Ronnie Galbraith et al., Docket No. 12-11074 (5th Cir. October 26, 2013).

Cash v. Lee County School District, No. 1:11-CV-00154-SA-DAS (N.D. Mississippi December 28, 2012).

Davis v. Monroe County Board of Education, 526 U.S. 629 (1999).

Long v. Murray County School District, No. 4:10-cv-00015-HLM (N.D. Ga. 2012) (unpublished); No. 12-13248 (11th Cir. 2013) (unpublished).

Monell v. Department of Social Services, 436 U.S. 658 (1978).

Pickering v. Board of Education, 88 S. Ct. 1724 (1968).

Piotrowski v. City of Houston, 237 F.3d 567 (5th Cir. 2001).

State v. Poling, 938 N.E. 2d 1118 (Hocking Co. Municipal Court, Logan, OH 2010).

U.S. v. Drew, 2:08-cr-00582-UA (May 15, 2008); 259 F.R.D. 449 (C.D. Cal. 2009).

Woodard v. Andrus, 419 F.3d 348 (5th Cir. 2005).

APPENDIX C

References

Agatston, P. W., Kowalski, R., & Limber, S. (2007). Students' perspectives on cyberbullying. *Journal of Adolescent Health*, 41 (6), S59–60.

Ali, R. (2010). Dear colleague letter: Harassment and bullying. *United States Department of Education, Office of Civil Rights.* October 26, 2010.

Barnes, N. G., & Lescault, A. M. (2011). Social media adoption soars as higher-ed experiments and reevaluates its use of new communication tools. Retrieved December 12, 2012, from http://sncr.org/sites/default/files/higherEd.pdf.

BBC News Education & Family. (2012). Cyberbullying may force out young teachers, says union. Retrieved November 19, 2012, from http://www.bbc.com/news/education-20339484.

Bocij, P. (2004). *Cyberstalking: Harassment in the Internet age and how to protect your family.* Westport, CT: Praeger Publishers.

Boyd, D. M. (2008). Taken out of context: American teen sociality in networked publics. Dissertation Abstract, University of California, Berkeley.

Brown, J. (2011). Pew Internet report outlines teen SNS usage, cyberbullying activity. Retrieved July 13, 2012, from http://www.cybercrimereview.com/2011/11/pew-internet-report-outlines-teen-sns.html.

Buck, S. (2012). 12 things students should never do on social media. Retrieved December 22, 2012, from http://mashable.com/2012/09/04/students-social-media-warnings/.

Bureau of Justice Statistics. (2013). Cyber/bullying statistics. Retrieved October 20, 2013, from http://www.statisticbrain.com/cyber-bullying-statistics/.

Careless, J. (2012). Social media: It does have a place in the classroom. Retrieved February 16, 2012, from http://www.techlearning.com/features/0039/social-media-it-does-have-a-place-in-the-classroom/52186.

Carr, N. (2006). Parents today require new forms of outreach. Retrieved March 21, 2008, from http://www.eschoolnews.com/2006/12/18/parents-today-require-new-forms-of-outreach/.

Carr, N. (2004). Parents expect email accessibility. Retrieved March 21, 2008, from http://www.eschoolnews.com/2004/03/01/parents-expect-email-accessibility/.

Carter, S. (2002). The impact of parent/family involvement on student outcomes: An annotated bibliography of research from the past decade. *Consortium for Appropriate Dispute Resolution in Special Education.* Retrieved April 16, 2014, from http://www.directionservice.org/cadre/pdf/the%20impact%20of%20parent%20family%20involvement.pdf.

Chew, K. (2011). Cyberbullying of teachers on the rise. Retrieved August 15, 2011, from http://www.care2.com/causes/cyberbullying-of-teachers-on-the-rise.html.

Conn, K. (2004). *Bullying and harassment: A legal guide for educators.* Alexandria, VA: Association of Supervision and Curriculum Development.

Cotton, K., & Wikelund, K. R. (1989). Parent involvement in education. *Northwest Regional Educational Laboratory School Improvement Research Series, Close Up #6.* Retrieved March 8, 2008, from http://www.nwrel.org.

Culhane, J. (2013). A public health approach to school bullying: Prevention, populations, and one definition of success. Presented February 23, 2013, at Temple University Law School's Conference on Bullying: Redefining Boundaries, Responsibility and Harm.

Cyber Bully Alert. (2012). Cyber bully data, statistics and facts. Retrieved July 28, 2012, from http://www.cyberbullying.us.

Davis, M. R. (2011). State cyberbullying laws range from guidance to mandate. *Education Week.* Retrieved April 16, 2014, from http://www.edweek.org/dd/articles/2011/02/09/02cyberbullying-laws.h04.html.

Dispute resolution in special education. Retrieved March 8, 2008, from http://www.directionservice.org.

Englander, E. (2012). Low risk associated with most teenage sexting: A study of 617 18 year-olds. *Massachusetts Aggression Reduction Center.* Bridgewater, MA. Retrieved April 14, 2014, from https://webhost.bridgew.edu/marc/SEXTING%20AND%20COERCION%20report.pdf.

eSchool News. (2011). For educators, painful lessons in social media use. Retrieved October 14, 2011, from http://www.eschoolnews.com/2011/08/25/for-educators-painful-lessons-in-social-media-use/.

Etheridge, P. (2012). Young people and social media: Docs examine pitfalls. Retrieved November 28, 2012, from http://www.cnn.com/2012/11/23/health/youth-social-media/.

Evans, J. R. (2011). Parents who cyberbully teachers should be punished. Retrieved August 16, 2011, from http://thestir.cafemom.com/big_kid/124593/parents_who_cyberbully_teachers_should.

Garling, C. (2011). Study: 26% of teachers cite cyberbullying by parents. Retrieved August 16, 2011, from http://www.digitaltrends.com/web/study-26-percent-of-teachers-cite-cyberbullying-by-parents/#!EnRX2.

Gielen, G. (2010). E-communication 4 schools 2 parents. Retrieved December 25, 2012, from http://ecom4s2p.mixxt.com/networks/content/.

Gilkerson, L. (2012). Bullying statistics: Fast facts about cyberbullying. Retrieved July 28, 2012, from http://www.covenanteyes.com/2012/01/17/bullying-statistics-fast-facts-about-cyberbullying/.

Glanz, J. (2006). *School community leadership.* Thousand Oaks, CA: Corwin Press.

Hammer, L. (2013). Be aware of your teen's online habits. *Women's Health Source.* Main Line Health.

Hardy, D. (2011). Central Bucks East teacher struggles with celebrity after blog uproar. *Philadelphia Inquirer*, February 18, 2011.

Hardy, D. (2010). Ex-teacher learns the hard way: Watch what you put online. *Philadelphia Inquirer*, June 9, 2010.

Hellmich, N. (2013). Lessons learned from latest cyberbullying tragedy. *USA Today*. Retrieved October 20, 2013, http://www.usatoday.com/story/news/nation/2013/10/15/cyberbullying-parents-internet-guide/2988651/.

Helms, A. D. (2012). N.C. may be first state to charge students with cyber crimes. *Charlotte Observer*. Retrieved December 3, 2012, from http://www.charlotteobserver.com/2012/12/01/3700359/nc-may-be-first-state-to-charge.html#.U06ykeZdXok.

Hinduja, S., & Patchin, J. W. (2011). High-tech cruelty. *Educational Leadership*, 68 (5), 48–52.

Hinduja, S., & Patchin, J. W. (2009). *Bullying beyond the schoolyard.* Thousand Oaks, CA: Corwin Press.

Hinduja, S., & Patchin, J. W. (2006). Cyberbullying fact sheet. Retrieved February 26, 2008, from http://www.cyberbullying.us/cyberbullying_fact_sheet.pdf.

Hitchcock, J. (2008). Online harassment/cyberstalking statistics. Retrieved March 21, 2008, from http://www.haltabuse.org/resources/stats/.

Horowitz, M. (2010). Administrative Council Workshop, Marple Newtown School District. Presentation by author.

Horowitz, M. (2009). Educator experiences with and reactions to uncomfortable and distracting e-mails. Doctoral Dissertation, University of Pennsylvania.

Huffington Post. (2012). Michigan student arrested for threatening teacher online. Retrieved April 16, 2014, from http://www.huffingtonpost.com/2012/12/21/michigan-student-arrested_n_2346959.html.

I Keep Safe. (2012). Your digital footprint. Retrieved December 23, 2012, from http://www.ikeepsafe.org/digital-citizenship-2/your-digital-footprint/.

International Society for Technology in Education. (2007). National education technology standards for teachers. Washington, DC: International Society for Technology in Education.

Joinson, A. M. (1998). Causes and implications of disinhibited behavior on the Internet. In J. Gackenbach (Ed.), *Psychology and the Internet: Interpersonal and transpersonal implications*, 43–60. New York: Academic Press.

Kaufman, G. (2011). Cyberbullying, sexting widespread, MTV/AP survey reveals. Retrieved December 19, 2012, from http://www.mtv.com/news/articles/1671547/cyberbullying-sexting-mtv-ap-survey.jhtml.

Kean, T. H., & Sawhill, I. V. (2008). Sex and tech: Results from a survey of teens and young adults. The National Campaign to Prevent Teen and Unplanned Pregnancy, Washington, DC.

Keller, B. (2008). Schools seek to channel parent involvement. *Education Week*, 27 (31), 1 and 17.

Knorr, C. (2012). When texting turns to torment. Retrieved December 19, 2012, from http://www.commonsensemedia.org/blog/when-texting-turns-to-torment.

Lenhart, A. (2012). Teens, smartphones & texting. Pew Research Center's Internet & American Life Project. Pew Research Center, Washington, DC.

Lenhart, A. (2010). Cyberbullying 2010: What the research tells us. Pew Research Center's Internet & American Life Project. Pew Research Center, Washington, DC.

Libman, A. (2008). Is e-mail a teacher's friend or foe? Retrieved September 4, 2008, from http://www.edweek.org/ew/articles/2008/08/27/01libman.h28.html.

Liss, J. (2012). Social media use rises among university faculty. *Cavalier Daily*. Retrieved December 22, 2012, from http://www.cavalierdaily.com/article/2012/10/social-media-use-rises-among-university-faculty.

Listfield, E. (2011). Generation wired. *The Philadelphia Inquirer, Parade Magazine*, October 7, 2011.

Logsdon, A. (2007). Why parents file IDEA complaints, lawsuits. Retrieved March 29, 2008, from http://learningdisabilities.about.com/od/disability laws/tp/Reasons-for-Complaints.htm.

Los Angeles Daily News. (2012). Editorial: There's a right way for teachers and students to use social media together. Retrieved January 2, 2012, from http://www.dailynews.com/20111229/editorial-theres-a-right-way-for-teachers-and-students-to-use-social-media-together.

Marple Newtown School District. (2012). Social media policy. Retrieved December 22, 2012, from http://www.mnsd.net/docs/POLMARP816.pdf.

Marzano, R. J. (2003). *What works in schools: Translating research into action.* Alexandria, VA: Association for Supervision & Curriculum Development.

Massachusetts Session Laws: Chapter 92 of the Acts of 2010. (2010). Retrieved December 19, 2012, from https://malegislature.gov/Laws/SessionLaws/Acts/2010/Chapter92.

Mishna, F., Cook, C., Gadalla, T., Daciuk, J., & Solomon, S. (2010). Cyberbullying behavior among middle school and high school students. *American Journal of Orthopsychiatry*, 80 (3), 362–74.

Mulholland, H. (2012). Teachers report widespread cyberbullying by pupils and parents. Retrieved April 6, 2012, from http://www.guardian.co.uk.

Murray, C. (2013). 25 eye-opening statistics about cyberbullying. *EdTech*. Retrieved October 20, 2013, from http://www.edtechmagazine.com/k12/article/2012/07/cyberbully-takedown-infographic.

Murray, D. (2011). Online gradebooks help parents communicate, but teacher says sometimes students need a little space. Retrieved December 23, 2012, from http://www.mlive.com/education/index.ssf/2011/11/online_gradebooks_help_parents.html.

National Campaign to Prevent Teen & Unplanned Pregnancy. (2008). Sex and tech: Results from a survey of teens and young adults. Retrieved April 16, 2014, from http://thenationalcampaign.org/sites/default/files/resource-primary-download/sex_and_tech_summary.pdf.

National Center for Missing and Exploited Children. (2012). What is sexting? Retrieved July 13, 2012, from http://esd113.org/cms/lib3/WA01001093/Centricity/Domain/22/policystatementonsexting-ncmec.pdf.

National School Boards Association. (2006). Funding and integration still biggest challenges for education technology. Alexandria, VA: National School Boards Association.

O'Keeffe, G. S., & Clarke-Pearson, K. (2011). Clinical report—The impact of social media on children, adolescents, and families. *Pediatrics*, 127 (4), 800–804.

Ogilvie, E. (2000). The Internet and cyberstalking. Australian Institute of Criminology. Retrieved August 12, 2008, from http://www.aic.gov.au/media_library/conferences/stalking/ogilvie2.pdf.

Pennsylvania Department of Education. (2010). Field notices: Notification of teaching certificate actions. Email from Pennsylvania Department of Education, November 30, 2010.

Pennsylvania Department of Education. (2010). Field notices: Notification of teaching certificate actions. Email from Pennsylvania Department of Education, May 3, 2010.

Pennsylvania State Education Association. (2012). Safe social media for educators. Retrieved July 3, 2012, from https://psea.org/socialmedia/.

Pennsylvania State Education Association. (2012). Social networking tips and information. Retrieved July 3, 2012, from http://www.psea.org/general.aspx?mid=953&id=4030.

Pennsylvania State Education Association Workshop. (2011). Workshop for Marple Newtown School District. Presentation by PSEA.

Pew Internet Research Study. (2007). Retrieved October 27, 2012, from http://www.pewinternet.org.

Pew Research Center Study. (2009). Retrieved October 27, 2012, from http://www.pewinternet.org.

Pileiro, F. (2012). Three simple C's of social media success for educators. Retrieved February 16, 2012, from http://www.techlearning.com/Default.aspx?tabid=67&EntryId=3414.

Poe, K. (2012). North Carolina to outlaw student cyberbullying of teachers. *Charlotte Observer*. Retrieved October 27, 2012, from http://www.newsobserver.com/2012/10/23/2430928/north-carolina-to-outlaw-student.html.

Public Agenda. (2003). America's principals and superintendents—railing against a torrent of local, state and federal mandates. Retrieved March 29, 2008, from http://www.publicagenda.org/press-releases/americas-principals-and-superintendents-railing-against-torrent-local-state-and-federal-mandates.

Rice, E., Rhoades, H., Winetrobe, H., Sanchez, M., Montoya, J., Plant, A., & Kordic, T. (2012). Sexually explicit cell phone messaging associated with sexual risk among adolescents. *Pediatrics*, 130 (4), 667–74.

Rogers, F. (2011). How Craigslist got a school administrator axed. Retrieved May 19, 2011, from http://www.law360.com/articles/245658/how-craigslist-got-a-school-administrator-axed.

Sacco, D., Argudin, R., Maguire, J., Tallon, K., & Cyberlaw Clinic. (2010). Sexting: Youth practices and legal implications. Retrieved June 22, 2010, from https://cyber.law.harvard.edu/publications/2010/Sexting_Youth_Practices_Legal_Implications.

Salamon, Maureen. (2012). "Sexting" may go hand-in-hand with unprotected sex among teens. HealthDay.com. Retrieved October 6, 2012, from http://consumer.healthday.com/health-technology-information-18/misc-computer-health-news-150/sexting-may-go-hand-in-hand-with-unprotected-sex-among-teens-668666.html.

School Superintendent's Insider. (2010). Do bachelorette party photos expose tenured teacher to dismissal?

Shah, Nirvi. (2012). GAO report questions whether bullying laws protect all students. Retrieved June 11, 2012, from http://blogs.edweek.org/edweek/campaign-k-12/2012/06/gao_report_questions_whether_b.html.

Shariff, S., & Gouin, R. (2005). Cyber-dilemmas: Gendered hierarchies, free expression and cyber-safety in schools. Department of Integrated Studies in Education, McGill University, Montreal, Quebec, Canada.

Sostek, A. (2011). Texting, "friending" a morass for educators. *Pittsburgh Post Gazette*. Retrieved January 16, 2011, from http://www.post-gazette.com/news/education/2011/01/16/Texting-friending-a-morass-for-educators/stories/201101160296.

Sponcil, M., & Gitimu, P. (2012). Use of social media by college students: Relationship to communication and self-concept. Retrieved December 22, 2012, from http://www.aabri.com/manuscripts/121214.pdf.

Sticca, F., Ruggieri, S., Alsaker, F., & Perren, S. (2013). Longitudinal risk factors for cyberbullying in adolescence. *Journal of Community & Applied Social Psychology*, 23 (1).

Strauss, V. (2006). Putting parents in their place: Outside class. Retrieved March 8, 2008, from http://www.washingtonpost.com/wp-dyn/content/article/2006/03/20/AR2006032001167.html.

Suler, J. R. (2003). E-mail communication and relationships. Retrieved March 2, 2008, from http://truecenterpublishing.com/psycyber/emailrel.html.

Taylor, R. (2012). Cyber-bullying laws now also protect teachers. *School Law Bulletin*, 39 (23).

University of Louisville Dean of Students. (2012). Social media guidelines. Retrieved December 22, 2012, from https://louisville.edu/dos/students/studentpoliciesandprocedures/social-media-guidelines.

Willard, N. (2006). *Cyberbullying and cyberthreats: Responding to the challenge of online social aggression, threats, and distress.* Eugene, OR: Center for Safe and Responsible Internet Use.

Williams, J-J. (2008). Hovering parents bully teachers. *Baltimore Sun*. Retrieved March 6, 2008, from http://www.baltimoresun.com.

Williams, R. (2010). Teachers suffer cyberbullying by pupils and parents. *The Guardian*. Retrieved March 30, 2010, from http://www.theguardian.com/education/2010/mar/30/teachers-bullied-online.

Zieger, L. B., & Tan, J. (2012). Improving parent involvement in secondary schools through communication technology. *Journal of Literacy and Technology*, 13 (1), 30–54.

Zucker, A. (2008). *Transforming schools with technology.* Cambridge, MA: Harvard University Press.

APPENDIX D

Centers and Resources

A Thin Line: http://www.athinline.org
- Provides information that empowers individuals to draw their own line between digital use and digital abuse

Berkman Center for Internet and Society: http://cyber.law.harvard.edu
- The Berkman Center at Harvard University works to address the legal and policy implications of cyberspace

Bullying No Way! (Australia): http://www.bullyingnoway.gov.au
- Provides evidence-informed information and advice on bullying, harassment, and violence for teachers, parents, and students

Bullying Statistics: http://bullyingstatistics.org
- Helps educate the public on bullying issues
- Offers information for teens, families, schools, and communities

Common Sense Media: http://www.commonsensemedia.org
- Provides resources to improve the lives of children and families
- Studies the effects that media and technology have on young users

Connect Safely: http://www.connectsafely.org
- Provides tips and advice for everyone engaged in and interested in the impact of the social web

Crimes Against Children Research Center: http://www.unh.edu/ccrc
- Provides high-quality research and statistics to combat crimes against children

Cyberbullying Research Center: http://cyberbullying.us/
- Provides up-to-date information about the nature, extent, causes, and consequences of cyberbullying among adolescents
- Includes resources to help prevent and respond to cyberbullying incidents

Cybersmart (Australian Communications Media Authority): http://www.cyber smart.gov.au
- Provides activities and practical advice to help young kids, teens, and parents safely enjoy the online world

CyberSmart!: http://www.cybersmart.org
- Fosters twenty-first-century skills to increase student engagement
- Prepares students to achieve in today's digital society

CyberWise: http://www.cyberwise.org

- Helps parents, educators, and students learn to use new media to invigorate education

Define the Line: http://www.definetheline.ca

- Provides research about clarifying the blurred lines between cyberbullying and socially responsible digital citizenship

Digital Media and Learning Central: http://dmlcentral.net

- Supports and disseminates current information about digital media and learning

Embrace Civility in the Digital Age: http://embracingdigitalyouth.org

- Promotes approaches that will best ensure young people become "cyber-savvy"
- Addresses youth in a positive and restorative manner

iKeepSafe: http://www.ikeepsafe.org

- Includes safety, security, and ethics tools and resources for helping families and educators teach children to use the Internet safely and wisely

International Association for K–12 Online Learning: http://www.inacol.org

- Advocates for activities and policies that remove barriers and support effective online education
- Facilitates, conducts, and disseminates research
- Identifies promising practices
- Develops national K–12 online learning quality standards

Internet Safety Project: http://www.internetsafetyproject.org

- Promotes Internet safety education for children and youth

National Crime Prevention Council: http://www.ncpc.org/cyberbullying

- Addresses the causes of crime and violence and reduces the opportunities for crime to occur
- Provides resources about bullying and cyberbullying

NetFamilyNews: http://www.netfamilynews.org

- Provides a public service for parents, educators, and everyone interested in young people's use of technology
- Provides resources for families about social media and media literacy

OnGuardOnline: http://www.onguardonline.org

- Provides individuals with information about protecting kids online

Pennsylvania Attorney General: http://www.attorneygeneral.gov/kidsparents.aspx

- Provides tools for kids, parents, and schools from the office of the Pennsylvania Attorney General

Pew Research Center: http://www.pewinternet.org

- Researches and publishes reports on issues about teens and technology, including cyberbullying, video games, mobile phones, sexting, social media, and social networks

Safe Communications, Inc.: http://www.safecom.net

- Provides open and secure family communications that are in step with advances in social media

SafeKids: http://www.safekids.com

- Provides parents with practical, proven resources to protect kids from the dangers of using the Internet

StopBullying: http://www.stopbullying.gov

- Provides resources from the federal government on bullying and cyber-bullying

StopCyberbullying: http://stopcyberbullying.org/

- Teaches about cyberbullying and provides options for getting help
- Provides information about cyberbullying prevention programs

Wired Safety: http://www.wiredsafety.org

- Provides information and resources about cyberbullying for students

Yahoo! Safely: http://www.safely.yahoo.com

- Helps individuals make smart and safer choices online

APPENDIX E

Questions and Ideas for Staff Development

EDUCATION

1. What are the different forms of cyberbullying? Provide examples of each one.
2. What are some of the ramifications of sexting for today's adolescents?
3. What is Facebook Depression, and how does it affect adolescents?
4. How can email communication be either a friend or a foe for educators?
5. How can social media be detrimental for today's tech-savvy students?
6. What are some of the continuum of actions and consequences for electronic harassment by parents?
7. Have your school district or educational institution's policies been updated to reflect the changes in state laws regarding cyberbullying and social media?

LAW

1. Make a video about cyberbullying in social media to use to inform students about examples of what constitutes cyberbullying and what legal consequences could be used to punish them. Then make a video for employees, and another video for parents.
2. Create a one-page handout to share with students that warns them of some legal consequences for cyberbullying in social media, and list contact information for reporting cyberbullying in social media at the federal, state, local, and school district level.
3. Consider the "deliberate indifference" standard that the school district must meet to defend its actions following a report of cyberbullying from a student-victim and her parent, and then prepare a checklist of what an employee and school district must do to succeed in a civil rights case.
4. Assume that the parent(s) have sued the school district and you (as an employee) for violating their child's Fourth Amendment rights to be free from an unreasonable search in a cyberbullying social media incident. What must you not do to violate the student's rights? What must you do to protect his or her rights?

5. Assume the school district has been notified of a cyberbullying incident that occurred on Facebook, and that the school district accessed the student's alleged cyberbullying by reviewing the Facebook page of the student who reported the incident. What makes this acceptable, and when would the access be considered a violation of the cyberbully's rights? Now, assume that instead of the cyberbullying occurring on Facebook it occurred through the Instagram app. Is there any difference in your answer? If not, why not? If so, why?
6. A school district has a policy that does not forbid employees and students from "friending" each other on social media sites and through apps, but it holds both employees and students responsible for their unlawful and inappropriate behaviors that violate federal, state, and local laws, school policies, regulations, rules, procedures, guidelines, and website or app contract terms. Assume Student Carl and Teacher Ann decide to "friend" each other in a social media website and exchange information, photos, and videos. Student Carl takes a video that Teacher Ann sent to him and "edits" it with his software at home to portray her sexually involved with him and reposts it on his (Student Carl's) social media site. Teacher Ann sees the video on Student Carl's Facebook page and complains to the school district principal, who suspends Student Carl. Student Carl and his parents sue the school district for violating his First Amendment free speech rights. What laws would Student Carl and his parents rely on to support their case? What laws would the school district rely on to support their case? Who do you think would win the case? Why?

Notes

CHAPTER ONE

1. *T.K. and S.K. v. New York City Department of Education*, 779 F. Supp. 2d 289 (E.D.N.Y. 2011).

2. S. Hinduja & J. W. Patchin, "High-Tech Cruelty," *Educational Leadership*, 68 (5) (2011).

3. S. Shariff & R. Gouin, "Cyber-Dilemmas: Gendered Hierarchies, Free Expression and Cyber Safety in Schools," Department of Integrated Studies in Education, McGill University, Montreal, Quebec, Canada, 2005.

4. The State Department's model policy includes indirect bullying, which is defined as spreading cruel rumors, intimidation through gestures, social exclusion, and sending insulting messages or pictures by mobile phone or using the Internet—also known as cyberbullying.

5. Montana has 419 school districts. Available at http://opi.mt.gov/PDF/Measurement/EdFacts2012-13.pdf. The Montana Office of Public Instruction has developed a model policy for school districts to use. The model policy does include electronic communications in the definition of bullying. Available at http://www.opi.mt.gov/pdf/Bullying/ModelBully_FreePolicy.pdf. Additional Montana bullying information is available at http://opi.mt.gov/Programs/TitlePrgms/SafeSchools/bully.html.

6. Appendix A, "Table of State Bullying and Cyberbullying Laws."

7. Montana and Wisconsin may also address cyberbullying; however, policies are not available.

8. Conn. Gen. Stat. Ann. § 10-222d.

9. California (social network Internet website), Kansas (blogs), Massachusetts (blogs, web pages), Mississippi (social networking), and Rhode Island (blogs). *See* appendix A, "Table of State Bullying and Cyberbullying Laws," for the statutory language.

10. Appendix A, "Table of State Bullying and Cyberbullying Laws." Alaska does not address the issue in a statute.

11. *School setting* is defined as "in the school, on school grounds, in school vehicles, at a designated bus stop or at any activity sponsored, supervised or sanctioned by the school." 24 Pa. Cons. Stat. § 13-1303.1-A.

12. 24 Pa. Cons. Stat. § 13-1303.1-A.

13. Appendix A, "Table of State Bullying and Cyberbullying Laws."

14. Minnesota, Missouri, and Montana permit local school districts to address the issue.

15. Ala. Code §§ 16-28B-1 to 16-28B-9.

16. Idaho Code Ann. § 18-917A.

17. Ky. Rev. Stat. Ann. § 158.148.

18. Ky. Rev. Stat. Ann. § 525.070 (*see also* Ky. Rev. Stat. Ann. 158.148 for definition of cyberbullying).

19. Fla. Stat. Ann. § 1006.147.

20. The location of the statutory sections for all of the states that have bullying statutes, whether the state provides for on- or off-campus bullying, or both, and whether the state provides for cyberbullying, is located in appendix A.

21. Appendix A, "Table of State Bullying and Cyberbullying Laws."

22. Cal. Educ. Code §§ 99120 to § 99122.

23. La. Rev. Stat. Ann. § 14:91.5 (§ 91.5).

24. *Id.* For a first conviction, the Act punishes those who commit the crime of unlawful use or access of social media with a fine not more than ten thousand dollars and imprisonment with hard labor for not more than ten years without benefit of parole, probation, or suspension of sentence. For those committing a second or subsequent conviction, the person is fined not more than $20,000 and imprisoned with hard labor for not less than five years or more than twenty years without benefit of parole, probation, or suspension of sentence. La. Rev. Stat. Ann. § 14:91.5(D).

25. La. Rev. Stat. Ann. 14:91.5(A)(1).

26. La. Rev. Stat. Ann. 14:91.5(c)(1)(3)(4). The Act does not specifically define social media other than it is to include chat rooms, peer-to-peer networks, and social networking.

27. *Doe v. Jindal et al.*, 853 F. Supp. 2d 596 (M.D. La. 2012).

28. *Id.*

29. *Id.*

30. *Id.*

31. *Doe v. Jindal*, 853 F. Supp. 2d at 596.

32. Ind. Code Ann. § 35-42-4-12.

33. *Id.*

34. *Doe v. Prosecutor, Marion County, Indiana*, No. 1:12-cv-00062-TWP-MJD (S.D. Ind. June 22, 2012).

35. It is a defense to prosecution that a person did not know the website or program allowed minors under eighteen years of age to use it, and that once the person discovered the website or program was used by various minors, the person immediately ceased to access the website or program. Ind. Code § 35-42-4-12.

36. *Doe v. Prosecutor, Marion County, Indiana*, No. 1:12-cv-00062-TWP-MJD (S.D. Ind. June 22, 2012).

37. *Id.* Alternatives included the ability to congregate with others; attend civic meetings; call in to radio shows; write letters to newspapers and magazines; post on message boards; comment on online stories that do not require a Facebook (or some other prohibited) account; email friends, family, associates, politicians, and other adults; publish a blog; and use social networking sites that do not allow minors (e.g., LinkedIn and a number of other sites that allow only adults).

38. *Id.*

39. Neb. Rev. Stat. Ann. § 28-322.05.

40. Neb. Rev. Stat. Ann. § 28-322.05 (1). The first offense is a Class I misdemeanor; any second or subsequent conviction is a Class IIIA felony. Neb. Rev. Stat. Ann. § 28-322.05 (2).

41. Neb. Rev. Stat. Ann. § 29-4001.01 (3)(10) and (13).

42. *Doe v. State of Nebraska et al.*, Nos. 8:09CV456, 4:10CV3266, 4:10CV3005 (D. Neb. October 17, 2012).

43. Neb. Rev. Stat. Ann. § 28-322.05 (1) and Neb. Rev. Stat. Ann. § 29-4001.01 (3) (10) and (13).

44. *Doe v. State of Nebraska et al.*, Nos. 8:09CV456, 4:10CV3266, 4:10CV3005 (D. Neb. October 17, 2012).

45. *Id.*

46. Devjani Mishra, "Web 2.0.10: Untangling the Risks of Electronic Social Media and Adapting Your Workplace Policies to Meet Them," 1830 *PLI/Corp* 47 (September 2010).

47. This summary is based on a newspaper article written by James Queally after the writer interviewed Nafeesa Onque, her mother, and the police. Because the case is in New Jersey Family Court where the case is not open to the public, the legal documents are not available. The article was published by the *Star-Ledger*. James Queally, "Newark Teen's Online Identity Stolen and Used to Destroy Her Reputation," *Star-Ledger (N.J.)*, February 13, 2011, available at http://www.nj.com/news/index.ssf/2011/02/someone_had_stolen_a_newark_te.html.

48. This summary is based on the reported facts on Ryan Halligan's Wikipedia web page. Available at http://en.wikipedia.org/wiki/Suicide_of_Ryan_Halligan.

49. Susan Donaldson James, "Jamey Rodemeyer Suicide: Police Consider Criminal Bullying Charges," *ABC News*, September 22, 2011. Available at http://abcnews.go.com/Health/jamey-rodemeyer-suicide-ny-police-open-criminal-investigation/story?id=14580832.

50. *Id.*

51. N.Y. Educ. Law § 11(7) (McKinney).

52. *Gelinas v. Boisselle*, No. 10-30192-KPN (D.Mass. October 17, 2011). Gelinas filed a First Amendment action against the chairman of the South Hadley School Committee. Apparently, the chairman prevented him from criticizing the school administration for its alleged failure to properly monitor and control school bullying, particularly matters related to the suicide of Phoebe Prince. He also alleged a Fourth Amendment action against two on-duty police officers for seizing him and escorting him out of the committee meeting. The court granted the two police officers motion for summary judgment but permitted the case to proceed against the chairman. E. J. Fleming, *Tread Softly: Bullying and the Death of Phoebe Prince* (eBook 2012). *See* S.T.A.R.: School Technology Action Report, eSchool Media, published by Houghton Mifflin Harcourt in 2012, available at http://www.eschoolnews.com/2012/06/05/tackling-school-bullying/.

53. Fred Contrada, "Phoebe Prince Bullying Case Over; In Court, Tears and a Portrait of a Mother's Loss," MassLive.com, available at http://www.masslive.com/news/index.ssf/2011/05/phoebe_prince_bullying_cases_o.html.

54. "Amanda Todd's Story: Struggling, Bullying, Suicide, Self Harm," YouTube, available at http://www.youtube.com/watch?v=ej7afkypUsc.

55. *Rutgers Today*, "The Tyler Clementi Center at Rutgers University," available at http://news.rutgers.edu/medrel/fact-sheets/2013/the-tyler-clementi-c-20130204.

56. H.B. 1261 (2009).

57. Cal. Penal Code § 653.2.

58. 18 P.S. § 6312(f) & § 6321.

59. 18 P.S. § 6321(a)(1) & (2).

60. 18 P.S. § 6321 (b).

61. 18 P.S. § 6321 (c)(1) & (2).

62. 18 P.S. §§ 6312 and 18 P.S. § 6321 (a), (b), (c).

63. 18 P.S. § 6321(e) & (f); 42 Pa. C.S. § 1520 Criminal Rules of Civil Procedure; Pa. R.C.P. 320 (relating to expungement upon successful completion of an ARD program).

64. For example, in their harassment legislation, Alabama, Arizona, Connecticut, Hawaii, Illinois, New Hampshire, and New York included prohibitions against harassing electronic, computer, or email communications; and in their antistalking laws Alaska, Florida, Oklahoma, Wyoming, and California incorporated electronically communicated statements as conduct constituting stalking. In addition, Texas enacted the Stalking by Electronic Communications Act of 2001, and Missouri revised its state harassment statutes to include stalking and harassment by telephone and electronic communications (as well as cyberbullying).

65. Computer Fraud and Abuse Act, 18 U.S.C. § 1030.

66. Electronic Communications Privacy Act, 18 U.S.C. §§ 2510–2522.

67. 18 U.S.C. § 2261A.

68. *U.S. v. Sayer*, Criminal Nos. 2:11-CR-113-DBH and 2:11-CR-47-DBH (D.Me. 2012); *U.S. v. Cassidy*, 814 F. Supp. 2d 574 (D.Md. 2011); *U.S. v. Walker*, 665 F.3d 212 (1st Cir. 2011).

69. 18 U.S.C. § 2261A.

70. *U.S. v. Cassidy*, 814 F. Supp. 2d 574 (D.Md. 2011) (the restriction placed on speech by an interstate stalking statute, criminalizing anyone for intentionally causing substantial emotional distress to another person using an interactive computer service, was greater than was essential to the furtherance of government's interest in preventing the use of the Internet and other interactive computer services to inflict emotional distress on others, and thus the provision, as applied to the defendant charged under the statute for using an Internet blog and a real-time information network to engage in conduct that caused substantial emotional distress to an easily identifiable public figure, was determined to be unconstitutional as applied).

71. U.S. Federal Anti-Cyberstalking Law, 47 U.S.C § 223. *See* Sentencing Guideline 2A6.1 for 47 U.S.C. § 223(a)(C)(D) & (E), and Sentence Guideline 2G3.2 for 47 U.S.C. § 223(b)(A).

72. Cases and developments are used based on their applicability and significance. Not every case in existence is included.

73. U.S. Const. amend. I.

74. *Tinker v. Des Moines Independent Community School District*, 393 U.S. 503 (1969).

75. *Bethel School District No. 403 v. Fraser*, 478 U.S. 675 (1986).

76. *Hazelwood School District v. Kuhlmeier*, 484 U.S. 260 (1988).

77. *Layshock v. Hermitage School District*, 412 F. Supp. 2d 502 (W.D. Pa. 2006); No. 2-06-CV-116 (W.D. Pa. April 7, 2006); 496 F. Supp. 2d 587 (W.D. Pa. 2007); 593 F.3d 249 (3rd Cir. 2010); 650 F.3d 205 (3rd 2011); 132 S.Ct. 1097 (*mem*) (U.S. 2012) (*cert. denied*).

78. *J.S. v. Blue Mountain School District*, No. 307CV585 (M.D. Pa. 2007); No. 307CV585 (M.D. Pa. September 11, 2008); 593 F.3d 286 (3rd Cir. 2010); 650 F.3d 915 (3rd Cir. 2011); 132 S.Ct. 1097 (*mem*) (U.S. 2012) (*cert. denied*).

79. *Kowalski v. Berkeley County Schools*, 652 F.3d 271 (4th Cir. 2011); 132 S.Ct. 1095 (*mem*) (U.S. 2012) (*cert. denied*).

80. *Tinker*, 393 U.S. at 503.

81. *Id.*

82. *Id.*

83. *Id.*

84. *Kowalski*, 652 F.3d at 271; 132 S.Ct. at 1095.

85. *Kowalski*, 652 F.3d at 271.

86. *Kowalski*, 652 F.3d at 271; 132 S.Ct. at 1095.

87. *Id.*

88. *J.C. v. Beverly Hills United School District*, No. 08-03824 (C.D. Cal. November 16, 2009); 711 F. Supp. 2d 1094 (2010).

89. *J.C. v. Beverly Hills Unified School District*, 711 F. Supp. 2d at 1094.

90. *Id.*

91. *Id.*

92. *S.J.W. v. Lee's Summit R-7 School District*, 696 F.3d 771 (8th Cir. 2012).

93. *Id.*

94. *Id. See Rosario v. Clark County School District*, No. 2:13-CV-362 JCM (PAL) (July 3, 2013).

95. *S.J.W*, 696 F.3d at 771.

96. *Id.*

97. *Id.*

98. Donald Bradley, "Brothers and School District Settle Free Speech Case," *Kansas City Star*, February 20, 2013.

99. *Requa v. Kent School District No. 415*, 492 F. Supp. 2d 1272 (W.D. Wash. 2007).

100. *Id.*

101. *Id.*

102. *J.S. v. Bethlehem Area School District*, No. 1998-CE-7696 (Pa. Northampton Co. July 23, 1999); 757 A.2d 412 (Pa. Commw. Ct. 2000) *reargument denied* September 7, 2000; 717 A.2d 1290 (Pa. 2001) (*appeal granted*); 794 A.2d 936 (Pa. Commw. Ct. 2002), *reargument denied* April 11, 2002; 807 A.2d 847 (Pa. 2002); 818 A.2d 506 (2003) (*allocatur denied*).

103. *Id.* (J.S. violated the school district's acceptable use policy).

104. *Id.*

105. *Id.*

106. *Id.*

107. *Id.*

108. *J.S. v. Bethlehem Area School District*, 807 A.2d at 847, quoting *Fraser*, 478 U.S. at 675.

109. *J.S. v. Bethlehem Area School District*, 807 A.2d at 847.
110. *Evans v. Bayer*, 684 F. Supp. 2d 1365 (S.D. Fla. 2010).
111. *Id.*
112. *Id.*
113. *Layshock*, 650 F.3d at 205.
114. *Id.*
115. *Id.*
116. *Id.*, quoting *Fraser*, 478 U.S. at 675.
117. *Barnett v. Tipton County Board of Education*, 601 F. Supp. 2d 980 (W.D. Tenn. 2006).
118. *Id.*
119. *Id.*
120. *Tinker*, 393 U.S. at 503.
121. *Id.*
122. *J.S. v. Blue Mountain School District*, 650 F.3d at 915, quoting *Doninger v. Niehoff*, 527 F.3d 41 (2nd Cir. 2008).
123. *J.S. v. Blue Mountain School District*, 650 F.3d at 915, quoting *LaVine v. Blaine School District*, 257 F.3d 981 (9th Cir. 2001).
124. *Tinker*, 393 U.S. at 503.
125. *Watts v. U.S.*, 394 U.S. 705 (1969).
126. *D.J.M. v. Hannibal Public School District*, 647 F.3d 754 (8th Cir. 2011).
127. *Id.*
128. *Id.*
129. *J.S. v. Blue Mountain School District*, 650 F.3d at 915.
130. *J.S. v. Blue Mountain School District*, 650 F.3d at 915, quoting *Tinker*, 393 U.S. at 503.
131. *Wisniewski v. Board of Education of Weedsport Central School District*, 494 F.3d 34 (2nd Cir. 2007).
132. *Id.*
133. *Id.*
134. *Doninger v. Niehoff*, 527 F.3d 41 (2d Cir. 2008); 642 F.3d 334 (2nd Cir. 2011).
135. *Doninger*, 527 F.3d at 41.
136. *Id.*, quoting *Wisniewski*, 494 F.3d at 34.
137. *Doninger*, 527 F.3d at 41; 642 F.3d at 334.
138. *Id.*
139. *Bell v. Itawamba County School Board*, 859 F. Supp. 2d 834 (N.D. Miss. 2012).
140. *Id.*, the court followed the Fifth Circuit Court's precedent in *Porter v. Ascension Parish School District*, 393 F.3d 608 (5th Cir. 2004), where the *Porter* Court appeared to add an interpretation of the *Tinker* language referring to "in class or out of it" to mean that off-campus conduct causing material and substantial disruption at school can be regulated at school where the speech is intended to reach the school.
141. *Watts*, 394 U.S. at 705.
142. *Id.*
143. *Doe v. Pulaski County Special School District*, 306 F.3d 616 (8th Cir. 2002) (*en banc*); *Lovell v. Poway Unified School District*, 90 F.3d 367 (9th Cir. 1996).
144. *Doe v. Pulaski County Special School District*, 306 F.3d at 616.

145. *D.J.M.*, 647 F.3d at 754. *See* "Forecast of Substantial Disruption Standard" section.
146. *Fraser*, 478 U.S. at 675.
147. *Id.*
148. *Id.*
149. *Id.*
150. *T.V. ex rel. B.V. v. Smith-Green Community School Corporation*, 267 F.R.D. 234 (N.D. Ind. 2010); 807 F. Supp. 2d 767 (N.D. Ind. 2011), quoting *Eberhardt v. O'Malley*, 17 F.3d 1023 (7th Cir. 1994).
151. *Id.*
152. *T.V. ex rel. B.V.*, 267 F.R.D. at 234; 807 F. Supp. 2d at 767.
153. *Id.*
154. *Hazelwood School District*, 484 U.S. at 260.
155. *Id.*
156. *Id.*
157. *Id.*
158. *Morse v. Frederick*, 551 U.S. 393 (2007).
159. *Id.*
160. *Id.*
161. *Id.*
162. *Id.*
163. *Id.*
164. *Tatro v. University of Minnesota*, 800 N.W. 2d 811 (Minn. App. 2011); 816 N.W. 2d 509 (Minn. 2012).
165. *Id.*
166. *Id.*
167. *Tatro*, 816 N.W. 2d at 509, quoting *Tinker*, 393 U.S. at 503; *Morse*, 551 U.S. at 393; and *Fraser*, 478 U.S. at 675.
168. *Tatro*, 800 N.W. 2d at 811; 816 N.W. 2d at 509.
169. *Barnes v. Zaccari*, 669 F.3d 1295 (11th Cir. 2012).
170. *Id.*
171. *Id.*
172. *Id.*
173. *Id.*
174. *Id.*
175. *Id.*
176. *T.V. ex rel. B.V.*, 267 F.R.D. at 234; 807 F. Supp. 2d at 767.
177. *Morse*, 551 U.S. at 393.
178. *J.S. v. Blue Mountain School District*, 650 F.3d at 915.
179. *A.B. v. State (Indiana)*, 885 N.E. 2d 1223 (Ind. 2008) (a speech and criminal action was brought against a student). In *A.B. v. State of Indiana*, a student created a MySpace page containing derogatory content aimed at an assistant principal. A third student (the plaintiff in this action) posted obscene and threatening content on the page. The plaintiff further created a MySpace group dedicated to disparaging the assistant principal. In response, the state filed a delinquency petition, alleging that if these acts were committed by an adult, they would constitute identity deception and harassment, both felonies under the state criminal code. The state later dropped the identity deception

charge. On appeal from a judgment against the student, the appellate court reviewed the nature of the student's postings and concluded that were the state to succeed on their allegations of harassment, it would constitute an impermissible abridgment of the student's freedom of speech under state and federal constitutions. Therefore, the court vacated the lower court's guilty verdict.

180. 42 Pa. C.S.A. § 8343.

181. 42 Pa. C.S.A. § 8343.

182. *Vogel v. Felice*, 127 Cal. App. 4th 1006; 26 Cal. Rptr. 3d 350 (Cal. App. 2005).

183. *New York Times v. Sullivan*, 84 S.Ct. 710 (1964); and *Gertz v. Robert Welch, Inc.*, 94 S.Ct. 2997 (1974).

184. *Finkel v. Daubert*, 29 Misc. 3d 325 (N.Y. Sup. Ct. 2010).

185. N.Y. Educ. Law § 11(7).

186. *D.C. v. R.R.*, 106 Cal. Rptr. 3d 399 (March 15, 2010, *as modified* April 8, 2010).

187. U.S.C.A. Const. amend. I; West's Ann. C.C.P. § 425.16.

188. *D.C. v. R.R.*, 106 Cal. Rptr. 3d at 399.

189. *Id.*

190. *Id.*

191. *Id.*

192. *Id.*

193. *In Re I.M.L.*, 61 P.3d 1038 (Utah 2002).

194. *Id.*

195. 20 U.S.C. § 1681 et seq. "No person in the United States shall, on the basis of sex, be excluded from participation in, be denied the benefits of, or be subject to discrimination under any education program or activity receiving Federal financial assistance."

196. 42 U.S.C. § 2000d et seq. "No person in the United States shall, on the ground of race, color, or national origin, be excluded from participation in, be denied the benefits of, or be subject to discrimination under any program or activity receiving Federal financial assistance."

197. 29 U.S.C. § 794(a). "No otherwise qualified individual with a disability in the United States, as defined in section 705(20) of this title, shall, solely by reason of her or his disability, be excluded from the participation in, be denied the benefits of, or be subjected to discrimination under any program or activity receiving Federal financial assistance or under any program or activity conducted by any Executive agency or by the United States Postal Service."

198. 42 U.S.C. § 12131 et seq. "Subject to the provisions of this subchapter, no qualified individual with a disability shall, by reason of such disability, be excluded from participation in or be denied the benefits of the services, programs, or activities of a public entity, or be subjected to discrimination by any such entity."

199. 20 U.S.C. § 1412. "A state is eligible for assistance under this subchapter for a fiscal year if the State submits a plan that provides assurances to the Secretary that the State has in effect policies and procedures to ensure that the State meets each of the following conditions . . . (a) free appropriate public education is available to all children with disabilities residing in the State between the ages of 3 and 21."

200. 42 U.S.C. § 1983. *See Monroe v. Pape*, 365 U.S. 167 (1961) and *Monell v. Department of Social Services*, 436 U.S. 658 (1978), in which the U.S. Supreme Court began accepting an expansive definition of rights, privileges, or immunities and held

that the Act does cover the actions of state and municipal officials, even if they had no authority under state statute to act as they did in violating someone's federal rights. Allegations of deprivation of students' substantive due process rights or due process rights are brought under the Fourteenth Amendment of the U.S. Constitution.

201. *Vidovic v. Mentor City School District*, No. 1:10 CV 1833 (N.D. Ohio January 31, 2013).

202. *Logan v. Sycamore Community School Board*, 780 F. Supp. 2d 594 (S.D. Ohio 2011), No.1:09-cv-00885 (S.D. Ohio June 5, 2012), quoting *Russo v. City of Cincinnati*, 953 F.2d 1036 (6th Cir. 1992) and *West v. Atkins*, 487 U.S. 42 (1988).

203. *Shively v. Green Local School District Board of Education et al.*, No. 5:11CV2398 (N.D. Ohio February 28, 2013) (*unreported*).

204. *Gebser v. Lago Vista Independent School District*, 524 U.S. 274 (1998).

205. *Tafuto v. New Jersey Institute of Technology*, No. 10-cv-4521 (PGS) (D. N.J. July 26, 2011); No. 10-cv-4521 (PGS) (D. N.J. April 13, 2012).

206. *Id.*

207. *Id.*

208. 20 U.S.C. § 1681.

209. *Tafuto*, Civil Action No. 10-cv-4521 (PGS) (D. N.J. 2011).

210. *Id.*

211. *Id.*

212. *Id.*

213. *Id.*

214. *Logan v. Sycamore Community School Board*, 780 F. Supp. 2d at 594; No. 1:09-cv-00885 (S.D. Ohio June 5, 2012).

215. *Id.*

216. *Id.*

217. *Id.*

218. *Id.*

219. *Id.*

220. *Id.*

221. *Id.*

222. *Id.*

223. *Id.*

224. *Tyrrell v. Seaford Union Free School District*, 792 F. Supp. 2d 601 (2011).

225. *Id.*

226. *Id. See Wyatt v. Fletcher*, No. 11-41359 (5th Cir. May 31, 2013). Coaches met with student softball player about her relationship with an older woman and threatened to tell her mother that she was in a sexual relationship with her (they believed the student was causing dissension on the team and that the older woman was potentially dangerous and an underage user of drugs and alcohol). The coaches met with the mother, who inferred her daughter's sexual orientation from the coaches' comments. The student filed a complaint, claiming, among other actions, that the school district violated her constitutional right to the privacy of her sexual orientation, including the right that it not be disclosed to her parent. The court found that no such right was established. The court ruled that the disclosure of the student's sexual orientation to the mother did not violate clearly established constitutional rights.

227. *Tyrrell*, 792 F. Supp. 2d at 601.

228. Children's Internet Protection Act, 47 U.S.C. § 254 (5)(B)(iii).

229. *Tyrrell*, 792 F. Supp. 2d at 601. Children's Internet Protection Act, 47 U.S.C. § 254 (5)(B)(iii).

230. *Tyrrell*, 792 F. Supp. 2d at 601.

231. *Tyrrell*, 792 F. Supp. 2d at 601. The student's mother reported the incident to the police, who investigated the incident.

232. *Tyrrell*, 792 F. Supp. 2d at 601.

233. *Davis v. Monroe County Board of Education*, 526 U.S. 629 (1999). Davis brought an action against the defendant school district, alleging her fifth-grade daughter was the victim of sexual harassment by another student in her class. Davis claimed monetary and injunctive relief under Title IX of the Education Amendments of 1972. 20 U.S.C.S. § 1681.

234. *Fitzgerald v. Barnstable School Committee*, 555 U.S. 246 (2009); *Gebser v. Lago Vista Independent School District*, 524 U.S. 274 (1998).

235. *Davis*, 526 U.S. at 629.

236. *Fennell et al. v. Marion Independent School District*, CV. No. SA: 12-CV-00941-DAE (W.D. Tex. January 28, 2013).

237. *Id.*

238. Plaintiff's Second Amended Complaint, *Kyana Fennell v. Marion Independent School District*, Civil Action No.: 5:12-CV-0941-DAE (W.D. Tex. March 14, 2013).

239. *Long v. Murray County School District*, No. 12-13248 (11th Cir. June 18, 2013). A student with disabilities committed suicide at home and the school district was not liable for peer harassment because it was not deliberately indifferent when the school district responded to reports of harassment and bullying. *Long v. Murray County School District*, Civil Action File No. 4:10-CV-00015-HLM (May 21, 2012). Sonja H. Trainor, "District Liability for Peer Bullying and Harassment: Federal Initiatives, Plaintiffs' Complaints, and Current Legal Standards," NSBA's Council of School Attorneys Conference Publication (April 19–21, 2012).

240. Kings County Indictment, "11, 12-Year-Old Girls Charged for Cyberstalking Classmate," available at http://barthel.tumblr.com/post/4977862111/11-12-year-old-girls-charged-for-cyberstalking.

241. Wash. Rev. Code § 9(A).52.110.

242. Wash. Rev. Code § 9.61.260. *See* Wash. Rev. Code §§ 7.92.020 and 9A.46.060 (Criminal Code).

243. "11, 12-Year-Old Girls Charged for Cyberstalking Classmate."

244. U.S. Const. amend. XIV § 1.

245. *Shively v. Green Local School District Board of Education et al.*, No. 5:11CV2398 (N.D. Ohio 2013). *See DeShaney v. Winnebago County Department of Social Services*, 489 U.S. 189 (1989); *Morrow v. Balaski*, No. 11-2000 (3rd Cir. June 14, 2013).

246. *Burns v. Gagnon*, 727 S.E. 2d 634 (Va. 2012). *See DeShaney*, 489 U.S. at 189; *Vernonia School District 47J v. Acton*, 515 U.S. 646 (1995); *D.R. v. Middle Bucks Area Vocational Technical School*, 972 F.2d 1364 (3rd Cir. 1992); *Morrow v. Balaski*, No. 11-2000 (3rd Cir. June 14, 2013) (court declined to hold school districts alleged failure to enforce administrative policy).

247. *Shively*, No. 5:11CV2398 (N.D. Ohio February 28, 2013), quoting *Jones v. Reynolds*, 438 F.3d 685 (6th Cir. 2006) (*additional citations omitted*). *See DeShaney v. Winnebago County Department of Social Services*, 489 U.S. 189 (1989); *Morrow v. Balaski*, No. 11-2000 (3rd Cir. 2013).

248. *Shively*, No. 5:11CV2398 (N.D. Ohio February 28, 2013).

249. *G.D.S. v. Northport-East Northport Union Free School District*, 727 S.E. 2d 634 (E.D.N.Y. 2012), quoting *Miller v. Clinton County*, 541 F.3d 464 (2nd Cir. 2008).

250. *Shively*, No. 5:11CV2398 (N.D. Ohio February 28, 2013).

251. *G.D.S.*, 727 S.E. 2d at 634.

252. *Shively*, No. 5:11CV2398 (N.D. Ohio February 28, 2013).

253. The complete portrayal of the attacks are not included in this case summary due to their offensive nature.

254. *Shively*, No. 5:11CV2398 (N.D. Ohio February 28, 2013).

255. *Id.*

256. *Id.*

257. *Id.*

258. *Id.*

259. *Id.* (Parents agreed that if any of the substantive due process and equal protection actions fail on the merits in this court, then no Monell claim can survive.)

260. *Shively*, No. 5:11CV2398 (N.D. Ohio February 28, 2013).

261. *G.D.S.*, 727 S.E. 2d at 634.

262. *Id.*

263. *Id.*

264. *Id.*

265. *Id.*

266. *Id.*

267. *Id.*

268. *Zimmerman v. Board of Trustees of Ball State University*, No. 1:12-cv-01475-JMS-DML (S.D. Ind. April 15, 2013).

269. *Id.*

270. *Id.*

271. *Id.*

272. *Id.*

273. *Id.*

274. Indiana Code § 21-39-2-3.

275. *Zimmerman*, No. 1:12-cv-01475-JMS-DML (S.D. Ind. April 15, 2013).

276. *Catfishing* refers to "the phenomenon of internet predators that fabricate online identities and entire social circles to trick people into emotional/romantic relationships (over a long period of time)." Available at http://urbandictionary.com, quoted in *Zimmerman*, No. 1:12-cv-01475-JMS-DML (S.D. Ind. April 15, 2013) (*see also* the 2010 movie *Catfish* and Heidi Stevens, "Manti Te'o Hoax: Where Did the 'Catfish' Come From?" *Chicago Tribune*, January 17, 2013).

277. *Zimmerman*, No. 1:12-cv-01475-JMS-DML (S.D. Ind. April 15, 2013).

278. *Id.*

279. *Id.*

280. The court stated that by reading the students' later pleadings they appear to have abandoned these claims.

281. *Zimmerman*, No. 1:12-cv-01475-JMS-DML (S.D. Ind. 2013), relying on *U.S. v. Alvarez*, 132 S.Ct. 2537 (2012).

282. *Zimmerman*, No. 1:12-cv-01475-JMS-DML (S.D. Ind. April 15, 2013).

283. *Zimmerman*, No. 1:12-cv-01475-JMS-DML (S.D. Ind. April 15, 2013).

284. Letter from Russlyn Ali, Assistant Secretary for Civil Rights, U.S. Department of Education, Office for Civil Rights, to Dear Colleague (October 26, 2010) (pertaining to harassment and bullying), available at http://www2.ed.gov/about/offices/list/ocr/letters/colleague-201010.html. *See also* Sonja H. Trainor, "School District Liability for Peer Bullying and Harassment: Federal Initiatives, Plaintiffs' Complaints, and Current Legal Standards," National School Boards Association, Counsel of School Attorneys, School Law Seminar, Boston, MA, April 19–21, 2012.

285. Letter from Russlyn Ali, Assistant Secretary for Civil Rights, U.S. Department of Education, Office for Civil Rights, to Dear Colleague (October 26, 2010).

286. Letter from Francisco Negrón, General Counsel, National School Boards Association, to Charlie Rose, General Counsel, U.S. Department of Education (December 7, 2010) (letter on file at NSBA).

287. *Davis*, 526 U.S. at 629.

288. Letter from Francisco Negrón, General Counsel, National School Boards Association, to Charles Rose, General Counsel, U.S. Department of Education (December 7, 2010).

289. Letter from Russlyn Ali, Assistant Secretary for Civil Rights, U.S. Department of Education, Office for Civil Rights, to Francisco Negrón, General Counsel, National School Boards Association (March 25, 2011). *See Gebser v. Lago Vista Independent School District*, 524 U.S. 274 (1998).

290. Letter from Eugene Volokh, Professor of Law, University of California, Los Angeles School of Law to U.S. Commission on Civil Rights (May 13, 2011), available at http://www.eusccr.com/27.%20Eugene%20Volokh,%20UCLA%20School%20of%20Law.pdf.

291. *T.K. and S.K.*, 779 F. Supp. 2d at 289.

292. *Long*, No. 12-13248 (11th Cir. June 18, 2013).

293. Ron Wenkart, J.D. General Counsel, Orange County Department of Education, Costa Mesa, California, "The OCR-Created 'Right' to a Free Appropriate Public Education Under Section 504; Time for a Challenge," *Inquiry and Analysis*, NSBA's COSA, January 2013.

294. Letter from Michael K. Yudin, Acting Assistant Secretary for the Office of Special Education and Rehabilitative Services, Department of Education, to Dear Colleague (August 20, 2013) (addressing disability harassment and peer-to-peer bullying), available at http://www.fcps.edu/dss/ips/ssaw/violenceprevention/bullyinginfo/USEDBullyingDisabilityLetter.pdf.

295. One who intentionally intrudes, physically or otherwise, upon the solitude or seclusion of another or his private affairs or concerns, is subject to the other for intrusion of his privacy, if the intrusion would be highly offensive to the reasonable person. Restatement (Second) of Torts § 652B.

296. One who gives publicity to a matter concerning the private life of another is subject to liability to the other for invasion of his privacy, if the matter publicized is a kind that (a) would be highly offensive to a reasonable person, and (b) is not of legitimate concern to the public. Restatement (Second) of Torts § 652D.

297. One who gives publicity to a matter concerning another that places the other before the public in a false light is subject to liability to the other for invasion of privacy, if (a) the false light in which the other was placed would be highly offensive to a reasonable person, and (b) the actor had knowledge of or acted in reckless disregard as to the falsity of the publicized matter and the false light in which the other would be placed. Restatement (Second) of Torts § 652E.

298. One who appropriates to his own use or benefit the name or likeness of another is subject to the other for invasion of privacy. Restatement (Second) of Torts § 652C.

299. *State of New Jersey v. Dharun Ravi*, New Jersey Judiciary, Superior Court–Appellate Division, Criminal Case Information Statement, Middlesex Ind. No. 11-04-00596-I (*filed* June 4, 2012).

300. J. Schwartz, "Bullying, Suicide, Punishment," *New York Times*, October 2, 2010, available at http://www.nytimes.com/2010/10/03/weekinreview/03schwartz.html; K. Zernike, "After Gay Son's Suicide, Mother Finds Blame in Herself and in Her Church," *New York Times*, August 24, 2012, available at http://www.nytimes.com/2012/08/25/nyregion/after-tyler-clementis-suicide-his-parents-make-painful-changes-in-the-search-for-why.html.

301. Dharun Ravi, Indictment, File No. 10002681, second Grand Jury, March 2011 Stated Session, July Term 2010.

302. *State of New Jersey v. Dharun Ravi*, New Jersey Judiciary, Superior Court–Appellate Division, Criminal Case Information Statement, Middlesex Ind. No. 11-04-00596-I (*filed* June 4, 2012).

303. *Id.*

304. *Id. State of New Jersey v. Dharun Ravi*, New Jersey Judiciary, Superior Court–Appellate Division, Criminal Case Information Statement, Middlesex Ind. No. 11-04-00596-I (*filed* June 4, 2012); Dharun Ravi, Indictment, File No. 10002681, Second Grand Jury, March 2011 Stated Session, July Term 2010.

305. "Dharun Ravi, Ex-Student Convicted in Rutgers Spycam Case, Released from Jail," *CBS New York*, June 19, 2012, available at http://newyork.cbslocal.com/2012/06/19/dharun-ravi-former-student-convicted-in-rutgers-webcam-spy-case-expected-to-be-released-from-jail/.

306. *R.S. v. Minnewaska Area School District No. 2149*, Civ. No. 12-588 (MJD/LIB) (D. Minn. September 6, 2012).

307. *Id.*

308. *Id.*

309. *Id.*

310. *Id.*

311. *Id.*

312. *Id.*

313. *Id.*

314. *Id.*

315. *Id.*

316. *Id.*

317. *Id.*

318. *Id. See also* Student Press Law Center report pertaining to a middle school student and her mother's letter to Everett School District (March 15, 2013) asserting that the middle school student was forced by her vice principal to log into her Facebook account so that he could view other students' posts in an investigation in which another student was bullied. According to the letter, the vice principal copied a photo from the account and said, "If you keep this a secret, I will to[o]," and that he would close out of her Facebook account that was on his computer screen. Reportedly, the investigated student was called to the vice principal's office and disciplined (suspended from school allegedly for using a cell phone during school hours but not cyberbullying), and while there saw the middle school student's open Facebook screen. The middle school student began to be called a "snitch" and "tattletale" and faced threatening emails, harassment, and hostility from her peers when they discovered her involvement. Before the incident she was an honor student with many friends. Student Press Law Center, "Washington Eighth-Grader's Facebook Illegally Searched by Administrator, ACLU Contends," March 19, 2013, available at http://www.splc.org/news/newsflash.asp?id=2548. The school spokesman declined to discuss the discipline but said that the vice principal was investigating what he understood to be cyberbullying done via a cell phone on school grounds during the school day. Legal Clips, "Second Circuit Rules That Extended School Year Services Must Satisfy LRE Requirements," March 28, 2014, available at http://legalclips.nsba.org. The letter claimed that the middle school student was not being investigated for cyberbullying but was being used to investigate another student, and this was a violation of the Fourth Amendment that prohibits unreasonable searches and seizures. Further, reference was made to *New Jersey v. T.L.O.*, 469 U.S. 325 (1985), in which the U.S. Supreme Court recognized "students['] legitimate expectation of privacy, observing that 'students may carry on their persons or in their purses or wallets such non-disruptive yet highly personal items as photographs, letters, and diaries'" and established the school district search inquiry observed by schools today (Student Press Law Center). The letter demanded that the school district take various steps to lessen the impact on the middle school student's harm from the alleged illegal search or further action would be taken (*see* March 15, 2013, letter).

319. *R.S.*, No. 12-588 (MJD/LIB) (D. Minn. September 6, 2012).

320. *Id.*

321. Dorie Turner and Greg Bluestein, "Victims of Cyberbullying Fight Back in Lawsuits," *Online Athens*, April 26, 2012, available at http://www.foxnews.com/us/2012/04/26/victims-cyberbullying-fight-back-in-lawsuits/; *see also* Turner and Bluestein, "School Cyberbullying Victims Fight Back in Lawsuits," Huffington Post, April 26, 2012, available at http://www.huffingtonpost.com/2012/04/26/school-cyber bullying-vict_n_1457918.html.

322. *Id.*

323. Turner and Bluestein, "School Cyberbullying Victims Fight Back in Lawsuits."

324. Turner and Bluestein, "School Cyberbullying Victims Fight Back in Lawsuits."

325. *S.M., et al. v. Griffith Public Schools*, No 2:12-cv-00160-JD-APR (N.D. Ind. Hammond Division).

326. *Id.*; Legal Clips, NSBA's COSA, quoting Michelle L. Quinn, "Indiana District and ACLU Settle Lawsuit over Students Expelled for Making Facebook Threats," *Post-Tribune*, March 18, 2013.

CHAPTER TWO

1. Arkansas, California, Colorado, Florida, Hawaii, Mississippi, North Carolina, Oklahoma, and Utah.
2. Ark. Code Ann § 6-18-514.
3. Cal. Educ. Code §§ 48900.4.
4. 2013 California Assembly Bill No. 256, California 2013 to 2014 Regular Session (bill proposed to amend Cal. Educ. Code §§ 48900 and 48900.4). This bill would provide that conduct constituting bullying by means of an electronic act, even if the conduct originated from an off-campus location, is considered conduct related to a school activity or school attendance and a student may be suspended or expelled for this conduct.
5. C.R.S.A. § 22-32-109.1.
6. Fla. Stat. Ann. § 1006.147.
7. Fla. Stat. Ann. § 1006.147. ("Cyberbullying means bullying through the use of technology or any electronic communication, which includes, but is not limited to, any transfer of signs, signals, writing, images, sounds, data, or intelligence of any nature transmitted in whole or in part by a wire, radio, electromagnetic system, photo electronic system, or photo optical system, including, but not limited to, electronic mail, Internet communications, instant messages, or facsimile communications. Cyberbullying includes the creation of a webpage or weblog in which the creator assumes the identity of another person, or the knowing impersonation of another person as the author of posted content or messages, if the creation or impersonation creates any of the conditions enumerated in the definition of bullying. Cyberbullying also includes the distribution by electronic means of a communication to more than one person or the posting of material on an electronic medium that may be accessed by one or more persons, if the distribution or posting creates any of the conditions enumerated in the definition of bullying.")
8. Fla. Stat. Ann. § 1006.147.
9. Fla. Stat. Ann 784.048. ("Cyberstalk means to engage in a course of conduct to communicate, or to cause to be communicated, words, images, or language by or through the use of electronic mail or electronic communication, directed at a specific person, causing substantial emotional distress to that person and serving no legitimate purpose.")
10. Fla. Stat. Ann. § 784.048.
11. Haw. Code R. §§ 8-19-2 & 8-19-6.
12. Miss. Code Ann. § & 37-11-67 & 37-11-69 (Education).
13. *Id.*
14. Miss. Code Ann. § 97-45-33 (Crimes Code).
15. N.C. Gen. Stat. Ann. § 115C-407.15 (Education).
16. N.C. Gen. Stat. Ann. § 115C-366.4 and § 115C-407.15 (Education).
17. N.C. Gen. Stat. Ann. §14-458.2 (Criminal Code).
18. *Id.*

19. Jessica Hatcher, "Will New Cyber Law Challenge Free Speech?" available at http://www.technicianonline.com/article_ebbec46a-6b63-11e2-839b-0019bb30f31a.html.

20. Helen Yoshida, "States Move to Protect Teachers from Cyberbullying," available at http://neatoday.org/2013/07/24/states-move-to-protect-teachers-from-cyberbullying/.

21. Okla. Stat. tit. 70 §§ 24-100.2 through 24-100.5.

22. Utah Code Ann. § 53A-11a-102 and § 53A-11a-201.

23. Utah Code Ann. § 53A-11a-102, § 53A-11a-201, § 53A-11a-202, and § 53A-11a-301.

24. *Requa v. Kent School District No. 415*, 492 F. Supp. 2d 1272 (W.D. Wash. 2007).

25. *J.S. v. Bethlehem Area School District*, No. 1998-CE-7696 (Pa. Northampton Co. July 23, 1999); 757 A.2d 412 (Pa. Commw. Ct. 2000) *reargument denied* September 7, 2000; 717 A.2d 1290 (Pa. 2001) (*appeal granted*); 794 A.2d 936 (Pa. Commw. Ct. 2002), *reargument denied* April 11, 2002; 807 A.2d 847 (Pa. 2002); *allocatur denied* 818 A.2d 506 (2003).

26. *Wisniewski v. Board of Education of Weedsport Central School District*, 494 F.3d 34 (2nd Cir. 2007).

27. *Doninger v. Niehoff*, 527 F.3d 41 (2d Cir. 2008); 642 F.3d 334 (2nd Cir. 2011).

28. *Barnett v. Tipton County Board of Education*, 601 F. Supp. 2d 980 (W.D. Tenn. 2006).

29. *Bell v. Itawamba County School Board*, 859 F. Supp. 2d 834 (N.D. Miss. 2012).

30. *Evans v. Bayer*, 684 F. Supp. 2d 1365 (S.D. Fla. 2010).

31. *Barnes v. Zaccari*, 669 F.3d 1295 (11th Cir. 2012).

32. *Layshock v. Hermitage School District*, 412 F. Supp. 2d 502 (W.D. Pa. 2006); No. 2-06-CV-116 (W.D. Pa. April 7, 2006); 496 F. Supp. 2d 587 (W.D. Pa. 2007); 593 F.3d 249 (3rd Cir. 2010); 650 F.3d 205 (3rd Cir. 2011); 132 S.Ct. 1097 (*mem*) (U.S. January 17, 2012) (*cert. denied*).

33. *J.S. v. Blue Mountain School District*, 650 F.3d 915 (3rd Cir. 2011).

34. *J.S. v. Blue Mountain School District*, No. 08-4138 (3rd Cir. 2011).

35. *Wisniewski v. Board of Education of Weedsport Central School District*, 494 F.3d 34 (2nd Cir. 2007); *J.S. v. Bethlehem Area School District*, No. 1998-CE-7696 (Pa. Northampton Co. July 23, 1999); 757 A.2d 412 (Pa. Commw. Ct. 2000) *reargument denied* September 7, 2000; 717 A.2d 1290 (Pa. 2001) (*appeal granted*); 794 A.2d 936 (Pa. Commw. Ct. 2002), *reargument denied* April 11, 2002; 807 A.2d 847 (Pa. 2002); (*allocatur denied*) 818 A.2d 506 (Pa. 2003); *Schroeder v. Hamilton School District*, 282 F.3d 946 (7th Cir. 2002).

36. *Pittsburgh Post Gazette*, "West Mifflin Area Sues over Disparaging E-mails," October 30, 2012, available at www.post-gazette.com/pg/10303/10303/1099344-298.stm.

37. *Rubino v. City of New York*, No. 107292/11 (Supreme Court, New York County, N.Y.) (February 1, 2012) (*Unreported Disposition*).

38. *Id.*

39. *Id.*

40. *Id.*

41. *Id.*

42. *Id.*

43. *Id.*

44. *Id.*
45. *Id.*
46. *Id.*
47. *Id.*
48. *Id.*
49. *Id.*
50. *Id.*
51. *Rubino v. City of New York*, No. 9813 107292/11 (Supreme Court, Appellate Division, First Department May 7, 2013).
52. *Id.*
53. *In the Matter of the Tenure Hearing of Jennifer O'Brien*, 2013 WL 132508 (N.J. A.D.) (January 11, 2013) (*Unpublished Opinion*).
54. *Id.*
55. *Id.*
56. *Id.*
57. *Id.*
58. *Id.*
59. *Munroe v. Central Bucks School District*, No. 2:12-cv-03546-CMR (E.D. Pa. *filed* June 20, 2012).
60. Andrea Canning and Olivia Katrandjian, "Teacher Defends Insulting Blog Posts about Her Students: 'I Hear the Trash Company Is Hiring,'" *Good Morning America*, February 16, 2011, available at http://abcnews.go.com/US/pennsylvania-teacher-wrote-insulting-blog-posts-students-suspended/story?id=12929001.
61. Amended Complaint, *Munroe v. Central Bucks School District*, No. 2:12-cv-03546-CMR (E.D. Pa. *filed* March 15, 2013).
62. Answer with Affirmative Defenses to Plaintiff's Amended Complaint, *Munroe v. Central Bucks School District*, No. 2:12-cv-03546-CMR (E.D. Pa. *filed* April 4, 2013).

CHAPTER THREE

1. Prepared by Merle Horowitz and Dorothy M. Bollinger.
2. Merle Horowitz, "Educator Experiences with and Reactions to Uncomfortable and Distracting E-mails," doctoral dissertation, University of Pennsylvania, Philadelphia (2009).
3. Numerous civil actions are available to the school district depending upon the facts and circumstances, including without limitation stalking, various kinds of harassment or discrimination, defamation, invasion of privacy, speech, and other electronic transmission causes of actions.
4. For example, Florida's Jeffrey Johnston Stand Up for All Students Act (Fla. Stat. Ann. §1006.147). *See* Idaho's criminal code, which provides that "any student who commits or conspires to commit, an act of harassment, intimidation or bullying shall be guilty of a misdemeanor" (Idaho Code Ann., 18-917A); Kentucky's code, which requires that the discipline code prohibit harassment, intimidation, bullying, or cyberbullying against students and defines the terms (KRS 158.148) and also expands the crime of harassment to include harassment, intimidation, bullying, or cyberbullying as defined in KRS

158.148 by students on school property and at school-sponsored events (KRS 525.070). At the end of this book, *see* appendix A, "Table of State Bullying and Cyberbullying Laws," for additional state statutory language for Arkansas, Illinois, Louisiana, Mississippi, Missouri, Montana, Nevada, North Carolina, North Dakota, Tennessee, Virginia, and Wisconsin.

5. Arelis R. Hernández, "Funeral Today for Cyberbullying Victim Rebecca Ann Sedwick," *Orlando Sentinel*, September 16, 2012, available at www.orlandosentinel.com/news/local/breakingnews/os-rebecca-sedwick-cyberbullying-funeral-20130916,0,1909346.story; Tamara Lush, "Rebecca Ann Sedwick Bullied for Months Before Suicide, Sheriff Said," September 13, 2013, www.huffingtonpost.com/2013/09/13/rebecca-ann-sedwick_n_3922738.html?utm_hp_ref+miami&ir=Miami; http://www.wjla.com/articles/2013/09/rebecca-ann-sedwick-authorities-consider-charges-in-bullying-case--94015.html.

6. Lush, "Rebecca Ann Sedwick," and http://www.wjla.com/articles/2013/09/rebecca-ann-sedwick-authorities-consider-charges-in-bullying-case--94015.html.

7. Fla. Stat. Ann § 784.048; § 784.0485; § 784.0487; § 790.233; and § 815.03.

8. Jeffrey Johnston Stand Up for All Students Act, Fla. Stat. Ann. § 1006.147.

9. Tracy Conner, "Charges Dropped Against Girls in Florida Cyber-Bullying Suicide Case," *U.S. News on NBC News* (November 20, 2013), available at http://usnews.nbcnews.com/_news/2013/11/20/21551488-charges-dropped-against-girls-in-florida-cyber-bullying-suicide-case?lite.

10. *Id.*

11. *See* Horowitz study, chapter III, "Employees," and chapter IV, "Parents," Continuum Chart.

12. Patricia J. Whitten and Jennifer Smith, "Placing Limits on Parental Communications," *Inquiry & Analysis*, National School Board Association Counsel of School Attorneys (November 2008).

13. *Id.*

14. *Id.*

15. *Id.*

16. Cases interpreting both "clickwrap agreement" and "browsewrap agreement" terms of service are plentiful. Examples include *Wachter Management Co. v. Dexter*, 144 P.3d 747 (Kan. 2006); *Hubbert v. Dell Corp.*, 835 N.E.2d 113 (Ill. Ct. App. 2005); and *Specht v. Netscape Communications Corporation*, 2002 WL 31166784 (2d Cir.).

17. *U.S. v. Drew*, 259 F.R.D. 449 (2009).

18. *U.S. v. Drew*, 259 F.R.D. 449 (C.D. Cal. August 28, 2009) (*see* Reporter's Transcripts of Hearings on September 4 and October 3, 2008).

19. 18 U.S.C. § 1030(c)(2)(B)(ii).

20. 18 U.S.C. § 371.

21. 18 U.S.C. § 1030(a)(2)(C) and § 1030(c)(2)(B)(ii).

22. *U.S. v. Drew*, 2:08-cr-00582-UA (May 15, 2008).

23. *Drew*, 259 F.R.D. at 449.

24. Ben Wedeman, "Online Bullying Ends in Suicide," CNN, July 31, 2013, available at http://www.cnn.com/video/data/2.0/video/world/2013/07/31/wedeman-italy-bullied-suicide.cnn.html; Ben Wedeman, "Facebook May Face Prosecution over Bullied Teenager's Suicide in Italy," *CNN*, July 31, 2013, www.cnn.com/2013/07/31/world/europe/Italy-facebook-suicide/index.html; and "Carolina Picchio's Suicide & Facebook Bullying:

5 Fast Facts You Need to Know," Heavy.com, http://www.heavy.com/news/2013/05/carolina-picchio-suicide-facebook-bully-lawsuit/.

25. Wedeman, "Online Bullying Ends in Suicide"; Wedeman, "Facebook May Face Prosecution."

26. "Carolina Picchio's Suicide & Facebook Bullying," www.heavy.com/news/2013/05/carolina-picchio-suicide-facebook-bully-lawsuit.

27. Sebastian Bartolo's YouTube video tribute to Carolina Picchio is available at http://www.youtube.com/watch?v=hjmUnmMEauA.

28. *Long v. Murray County School District*, No. 4:10-cv-00015-HLM (N.D. Ga. 2012) (*unpublished*); *Long v. Murray County School District*, No. 12-13248 (11th Cir. 2013) (*unpublished*).

29. *Long*, No. 4:10-cv-00015-HLM (N.D. Ga. 2012).

30. *Id.*

31. *Id.*

32. *Id.*

33. The *Davis* "deliberate indifference standard" requires plaintiffs such as the Longs to show: (1) the plaintiff is an individual with a disability, (2) he or she was harassed based on that disability, (3) the harassment was sufficiently severe or pervasive that it altered the condition of his or her education and created an abusive educational environment, (4) the defendant knew about the harassment, and (5) the defendant was deliberately indifferent to the harassment. *See Long*, No. 12-13248 (11th Cir. 2013).

34. *Davis*, 526 U.S. at 629.

35. The Council of Parent Attorneys and Advocates (COPAA) also filed a brief in support of the parents. *See* http://www.copaa.org/news/news.asp?id=105805&hhSearchTerms=%22Long%22, accessed October 19, 2013.

36. Russlynn Ali, assistant for civil rights, Dear Colleague Letter–Harassment and Bullying, U.S. Department of Education, Office for Civil Rights (October 26, 2010). Norma V. Cantu, assistant secretary of civil rights, and Judith E. Heumann, assistant secretary, Office of Special Education and Rehabilitative Services, Dear Colleague Letter–Prohibited Disability Harassment, U.S. Department of Education, Office for Civil Rights (July 25, 2000). Revised Sexual Harassment Guidance: Harassment of Students by School Employees, Other Students, of Third Parties, Title IX, U.S. Department of Education, Office for Special Education (January 2001).

37. Brief for the United States as Amicus Curiae Supporting Plaintiffs-Appellants and Urging Reversal in Part, *Long*, No. 12-13248 (11th Cir. *filed* September 28, 2012).

38. Brief of Amici Curiae National School Boards Association, Alabama Association of Schools Boards, Georgia School Boards Association, and Georgia School Superintendents Association in Support of Defendants-Appellees and Urging Affirmance, *Long*, No. 12-13248 (11th Cir. *filed* November 28, 2012).

39. *Long*, No. 4:10-cv-00015-HLM (N.D. Ga. 2012); and *Long*, No. 12-13248 (11th Cir. 2013).

40. *Long*, No. 12-13248 (11th Cir. 2013).

41. *Id.*

42. *Long*, No. 4:10-cv-00015-HLM (N.D. Ga. 2012); and *Long*, No. 12-13248 (11th Cir. 2013).

43. *Carmichael v. Joshua Independent School District*, 3:11-CV-622-D (N.D. Tex. *filed* March 28, 2011). First Complaint, 2012 BL 1023 (N.D. Tex. *decided* January 4, 2012). Second Amended Complaint, 2012 B.L. 247442 (N.D. Tex. *decided* September 26, 2012).

44. First Complaint, *Carmichael v. Joshua Independent School District*, 2012 BL 1023 (N.D. Tex. *decided* January 4, 2012).

45. *Carmichael v. Joshua Independent School District*, 3:11-CV-622-D (N.D. Tex. *filed* March 28, 2011). First Complaint, 2012 BL 1023 (N.D. Tex. *decided* January 4, 2012). Second Amended Complaint, 2012 B.L. 247442 (N.D. Tex. *decided* September 26, 2012). Natalie DiBlasio, "More Bullying Cases Have Parents Turning to Courts," *USA Today*, available at http://usatoday30.usatoday.com/news/education/story/2011-09-11/bullying-lawsuits-parents-self-defense-courts/50363256/1.

46. Casey Norton, "Parents of Suicide Victim Sue Joshua ISD," WFAA8 ABC Dallas-Fort Worth, April 1, 2011, available at http://www.wfaa.com/news/local/Joshua-bullying-119065109.html; DiBlasio, "More Bullying Cases Have Parents Turning to Courts."

47. *Carmichael et al. v. Ronnie Galbraith et al.*, Docket No. 12-11074 (5th Cir. 2012).

48. Second Amended Complaint ¶ 61, *Carmichael v. Galbraith*, 2012 B.L. 247442 (N.D. Tex. *decided* September 26, 2012).

49. Second Amended Complaint ¶ 62, *Carmichael v. Galbraith*, 2012 B.L. 247442 (N.D. Tex. *decided* September 26, 2012).

50. *Carmichael v. Galbraith*, Docket No. 12-11074 (5th Cir. 2012).

51. *Cash v. Lee County School District*, No. 1:11-CV-00154-SA-DAS (N.D. Mississippi December 28, 2012).

52. *Id.*

53. *Id.*

54. *Id.*

55. *Id.*

56. *Id.*

57. *Id.*

58. *Id.*

59. *Pickering v. Board of Education*, 88 S.Ct. 1734 (1968) and *Connick v. Myers*, 103 S.Ct. 1694 (1983).

60. *Piotrowski v. City of Houston*, 237 F.3d 567 (5th Cir. 2001).

61. *Monell v. Department of Social Services*, 436 U.S. 658 (1978).

62. *Piotrowski*, 237 F.3d at 567.

63. *Burge v. St. Tammany Parish*, 336 F.3d 363 (5th Cir. 2003).

64. *Brown v. Bryan County*, 219 F.3d 450 (5th Cir. 2000).

65. *Woodard v. Andrus*, 419 F.3d 348 (5th Cir. 2005).

66. *State v. Poling*, 938 N.E. 2d 1118 (Hocking Co. Municipal Court, Logan, OH 2010).

67. *Id.*

68. *Id.*

69. *Poling*, 938 N.E. 2d at 1118, citing *Pollock v. Pollock*, 154 F.3d 601 (6th Cir. 1998).

70. *Poling*, 938 N.E. 2d at 1118.

About the Authors

Merle Horowitz, EdD, has been the superintendent of the Marple Newtown School District in Delaware County, Pennsylvania, since 2005.

Merle received her bachelor's degree from Syracuse University and her master's degree, principal certification, Superintendent's Letter of Eligibility, and doctorate in educational leadership at the University of Pennsylvania.

Merle has spent the past twenty years studying and implementing programs for bully prevention. This research led Merle to her dissertation on the topic of the online harassment of educators.

Merle is the 2012–2014 president of the Pennsylvania Association of School Administrator's Women's Caucus; she also serves on the Board of Governors of the Pennsylvania Association of School Administrators, and on the Board of the 21st Century Cyber Charter School.

Dorothy M. Bollinger is an attorney whose law practice focuses on Internet, computer, information, technology, and copyright legal issues. Among those she represents are numerous school districts, intermediate units, career and technology centers, and other educational institutions.

Prior to founding The Bollinger Law Firm, LLC, Dotti was a member of the Corporate and Intellectual Property Departments, and the Media, Defamation, and Privacy Law and Education Law Practice Groups at the law firm of Fox Rothschild LLP. She leveraged her education and work experiences with software and computers into her legal practice.

Before entering the legal field, Dotti was a superintendent of schools and an administrator and teacher in schools, colleges, and universities. While attending law school, she worked full time in Temple University Counsel's Office.

Dotti is a past chair of the Philadelphia Bar Association's Business Law Section's Cyberspace and e-Commerce Committee and the Pennsylvania representative to the International Technology Law Association (iTechLaw). She serves as an adjunct professor at Temple University's Beasley School of Law, where she teaches "Cyberprivacy in the Networked World" and "Cyberlaw and Policy: Practical Applications in Organizational Settings."

See http://www.bollingerlawfirm.com/attorneyprofile.html for additional information.